Your PREGNANCY

Every Woman's Guide

Also by Glade B. Curtis, M.D.

Your Pregnancy Week by Week

Your Pregnancy After 30

Your Pregnancy Questions & Answers

Your PREGNANCY

Every Woman's Guide

Glade B. Curtis, M.D., OB/GYN

FISHER
BOOKS™

Library of Congress Cataloging-in-Publication Data
Curtis, Glade B.
      Your Pregnancy / Glade B. Curtis.
        p. cm.
      Includes index.
      ISBN 1-55561-154-0
        1. Pregnancy—Miscellanea. 2. Childbirth—Miscellanea.
      I. Title.
      RG525.C918 1999   99-12270
      618.2'4—dc21   CIP

Fisher Books is a member of the Perseus Books Group.

Find us on the World Wide Web at http://www.perseusbooks.com

Fisher Books are available at special discounts for bulk purchases in the U.S. by corporations, institutions, and other organizations. For more information, please contact the Special Markets Department at the Perseus Books Group, 11 Cambridge Center, Cambridge, MA 02142, or call (617)252-5200.

  8 9 10—RRD/HSB 03

Contents

About This Book

Dr. Glade Curtis may be the most beloved obstetrician in the world. Hundreds of thousands of his pregnancy books are in print in many editions, in the United States, Canada, Europe and Asia. Dr. Curtis's success is based squarely on his commitment to providing the most up-to-date information about pregnancy. Drawing on his experience as a practicing obstetrician, Dr. Curtis has met that commitment in this completely revised edition of *Your Pregnancy*.

The easy-to-use format combined with Dr. Curtis's friendly style helps women stay informed throughout their pregnancies, from preparation for pregnancy to giving birth and feeding the new baby. It's just as easy to dip into this book for a speedy answer to one pressing question as it is to spend an evening reading about all of the exciting changes going on in your body, and how you can best prepare for the birth of your baby. Dr. Curtis has identified the most common questions about pregnancy he hears from his patients, and they are highlighted in this book. Boxes, charts and checklists make it easy to find the information you want, when you want it. Illustrations supply additional insight about tests, the baby's development and special situations, such as Cesarean delivery.

Having a baby is an exciting event in your life, but it can sometimes be bewildering, too. *Your Pregnancy* is a warm and reassuring resource you will turn to again and again, one that can provide answers to most of your big and little questions about having a baby. Let *Your Pregnancy* provide the kind of information that will help you enjoy this special time to the fullest!

Acknowledgments

My appreciation and thanks to an understanding wife and family for the time taken from them to work on these projects and at the profession of OB/GYN, with its unique demands.

I would like to recognize the unique relationship I have established with Judi Schuler over almost 20 years of collaboration. Her attention to detail, accuracy and motivational skills remain a large part of our success.

I appreciate the support of Bill and Howard Fisher and others at Fisher Books over the years. I am continually reminded by their dedication that things of value and meaning often take time to develop. These things of value are the result of effort and teamwork.

Glade B. Curtis, M.D., OB/GYN

About the Author

Glade B. Curtis, M.D., is board-certified by the American College of Obstetricians and Gynecologists. He is in private practice in obstetrics, gynecology and infertility in Sandy, Utah.

One of Dr. Curtis's goals as a doctor is to provide patients with many types of information about gynecological and obstetrical conditions they may have, problems they may encounter and procedures they may undergo. In pursuit of that goal, he has written several books especially for pregnant women, including *Your Pregnancy Week by Week* and *Your Pregnancy After 30.*

Dr. Curtis is a graduate of the University of Utah and the University of Rochester School of Medicine and Dentistry, Rochester, New York. He was an intern, resident and chief resident in Obstetrics and Gynecology at the University of Rochester Strong Memorial Hospital. He lives in Sandy. He and his wife have five children and one grandchild.

To the Readers
of This Book

I have tried to include all the questions posed to me (and other physicians I know) dealing with every aspect of pregnancy and childbirth. If you have any questions I haven't covered, which might be of interest to other pregnant women, I would appreciate your sending them to me in care of Fisher Books. If possible, I will address your question in subsequent editions of this book.

Pregnancy is a special time in a woman's life—and an enjoyable one. By being informed and working with your healthcare provider, you can provide your baby with the best possible start in life.

Before Pregnancy

Part **1**

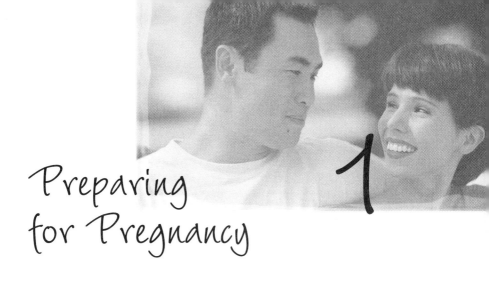

Preparing for Pregnancy

In my practice, I often see women who are surprised to discover they are pregnant. They tell me they weren't really planning a pregnancy, or they weren't ready to have a baby yet. Most of them have healthy pregnancies and give birth to healthy babies. However, planning your pregnancy *before* you get pregnant helps ensure that your baby gets the best start in life that you can possibly give him or her. For that reason, many physicians and other healthcare workers are now considering pregnancy a 12-month term.

The actual length of a pregnancy (growth from a fertilized egg into a normal-size baby) is 9 months. But now we know the few months before you get pregnant can be as important as the 9 months in which the fetus develops inside of you.

With good preparation on your part, you can give your baby the best start toward a healthy life. The months that you plan for your pregnancy give you time to prepare your body and make any necessary lifestyle changes. You can eat nutritiously, cut out alcohol and tobacco use, begin an exercise program, get your weight under control and talk to your doctor about any other medical concerns you have.

What should I do to prepare for pregnancy?
You can do many things to prepare for pregnancy.
* Exercise regularly.
* Find out if medications you take regularly can be decreased or discontinued. Ask your physician if they are safe to take during pregnancy.
* Get your weight under control. Pregnancy is not the time to lose weight.
* If you need X-rays or medical tests, get them done before trying to get pregnant.
* It's a good time to control or to eliminate tobacco, alcohol or drug use.
* Decide who will deliver your baby.
* Check on your insurance coverage for pregnancy.

Paying attention to these details before you get pregnant makes your pregnancy safer and more enjoyable.

When to See Your Doctor

If possible, see your doctor *before* you get pregnant. A visit before pregnancy clears up questions about medications you are taking. You can have a Pap smear and any other tests your healthcare provider decides are necessary. With your healthcare provider, you can evaluate your current weight and set a target weight gain for your pregnancy. You will know you're in good health before getting pregnant; if you're not, you can make plans to get into the best shape you can before you get pregnant.

Your doctor may order a range of tests, including:

•Pap smear
•Rh-factor test
•blood typing
•rubella titers
•mammogram, if you are 35 or older

If you know you have other specific or chronic medical problems, such as diabetes, have these checked. If you have been exposed to hepatitis or AIDS, tests should be done for these.

My last two pregnancies ended in miscarriages. Should I talk with my doctor before I get pregnant, or can I wait until my first visit when I am pregnant?
The history of previous pregnancies can be important in the success of your next pregnancy. It's true that in many situations nothing can be done to avoid problems. The safest thing to do is talk with your doctor before you try to conceive. Tell your doctor what has happened in the past. Find out if you can do anything now or if there are risks you may have to deal with.

Costs of Having a Baby

It costs a lot to have a baby. Costs vary from one part of the country to another, depending on how long you stay in the hospital and whether you or your baby have complications. Prices in 1999 range from $4,500 to $15,000 for a delivery. Total cost depends on how long you and your baby are in the hospital, if you have an epidural and if you deliver vaginally or by Cesarean section.

To find out exactly how much it will cost in your area, check with the hospital and your insurance company, if you have insurance. Someone in your doctor's office can usually help you with this. Don't be embarrassed or afraid to ask about it. Most offices have a person who works with insurance companies all the time and knows about things you haven't thought about. They realize how important this is.

The Canadian healthcare system is very different from the healthcare system in the United States. Canadians pay a healthcare premium on a monthly basis, and cost varies depending on the province you live in. The doctor who delivers your baby is paid by the government.

What Insurance Covers

Coverage can vary quite a lot from company to company, so there is no simple answer to this question. You can find out what your insurance company covers by asking the following questions.

- What type of coverage do I have?
- Are there maternity benefits? What are they?
- Do maternity benefits cover Cesarean deliveries?
- What kind of coverage is there for a high-risk pregnancy?
- Do I have to pay a deductible? If so, what is it?
- How do I submit claims?
- Is there a cap (limit) on total coverage?
- What percentage of my costs are covered?
- Does my coverage restrict the kind of hospital accommodations I may choose, such as a birthing center or a birthing room?
- What procedures must I follow before entering the hospital?
- Does my policy cover a nurse-midwife?
- Does coverage include medications?
- What tests during pregnancy are covered under the policy?
- What tests during labor and delivery are covered under the policy?
- What types of anesthesia are covered during labor and delivery?
- How long can I stay in the hospital?
- Does payment go directly to my healthcare provider or to me?
- What conditions or services are *not* covered?
- What kind of coverage is there for the baby after it is born?
- How long can the baby stay in the hospital?
- Is there an additional cost to add the baby to the policy?
- How do I add the baby to the policy?
- Can we collect a percentage of a fee from my husband's policy and the rest from mine?

Changes during Pregnancy

Your body goes through incredible changes during pregnancy! Your breasts enlarge, and the number of milk ducts to produce breast milk increases. Your organs are crowded by your enlarging uterus, which may cause more-frequent urination, heartburn or indigestion. Your legs, feet and hands may swell. Your hair and skin often undergo changes. Compare the illustration on this page with that on page 132 to see what changes a woman's body may undergo during a pregnancy.

How Pregnancy Occurs

During your menstrual cycle, your body prepares for the possibility of pregnancy. An egg is released from one of your ovaries, and changes take place in the lining of your uterus to provide an environment for the development of a fertilized egg. If fertilization does not take place, the enriched lining is discarded through the menstrual flow.

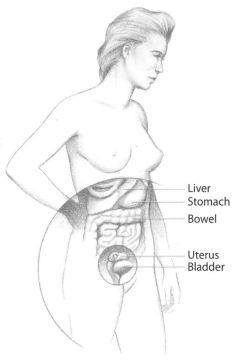

Liver
Stomach
Bowel

Uterus
Bladder

Fertilization is believed to occur in the middle part of the Fallopian tube, not inside the uterus. Sperm travel through the uterine cavity and out into the tube to meet the egg that comes from the ovary. See the illustration on page 8.

This illustration shows a nonpregnant uterus and various organs in a woman's body. Pregnancy will cause many changes! Compare this illustration with the one of a pregnant woman's body on page 132.

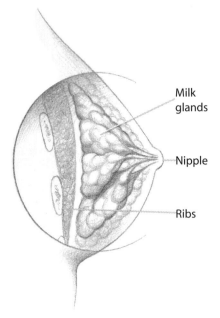

Milk
glands

Nipple

Ribs

After fertilization, the fertilized egg begins to divide and to grow. Within 3 to 7 days, it travels down the Fallopian tube into the uterus and attaches to the wall of the uterus. The developing baby is now called an *embryo*. (After 8 weeks it is called a *fetus*.)

By about day 12, the amniotic sac begins to form around the developing embryo. The sac contains fluid in which the baby can move around easily. Amniotic fluid also cushions the fetus against injury and regulates temperature.

Your breasts go through many changes during pregnancy. Compare this illustration of a breast in a nonpregnant woman with the illustration of a pregnant woman's breast on page 148.

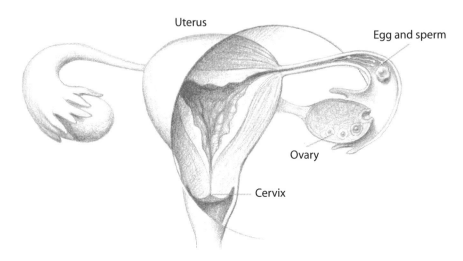

Uterus

Egg and sperm

Ovary

Cervix

Scientists believe the egg is fertilized by the sperm in the Fallopian tube.

Your Current Contraception Methods

Most doctors recommend staying off **the Pill** for two or three normal menstrual cycles before trying to get pregnant. Use some other form of contraception, such as the barrier method (condom), until you want to get pregnant.

The best and easiest time to remove an **intrauterine device (IUD)** is during your period. Wait for a couple of normal cycles after your IUD is removed before trying to conceive. Use a barrier contraceptive during the waiting time.

If you use the **Norplant® implant** for birth control, wait at least two or three menstrual cycles after it is removed before trying to get pregnant.

The **Depo-provera® injection** works for 3 months. I'd advise you to have at least two normal periods before you attempt a pregnancy.

Nutrition before Pregnancy

Many of my patients who are considering pregnancy tell me they love hamburgers, French fries and other junk foods, and they hate to give them up. They wonder if their eating habits will affect their pregnancy. The answer is yes. Avoid junk food. Eat fresh, nutritious foods, including lots of fruits and vegetables. Prepare them simply, with little added fat.

Start Eating Well Now

It is best for you and your baby if you develop good eating habits *before* you get pregnant. Eat nutritiously for all 12 months of pregnancy.

By the time many women know they're pregnant, they are 7 or 8 weeks into the pregnancy—or more! These early weeks of pregnancy are important in the development of your baby. That's why it's important to be prepared and to start eating right *before* you are pregnant.

About Weight

Pregnancy is not the time to start a new diet or to try to lose weight. Dieting can cause temporary deficiencies in vitamins and minerals that are important to your developing baby. Ask your healthcare provider about a good eating plan before getting pregnant, and make necessary changes before pregnancy.

Exercise before Pregnancy

Exercise is good for you, whether or not you are pregnant. It's an important part of a healthy pregnancy, too. Develop a good exercise program before getting pregnant to help you feel better, control weight and increase stamina. Exercise can also help make labor and delivery easier.

To find and maintain a good exercise program, choose exercise you enjoy and can do in any type of weather. A great deal of information on various types of exercise programs is available from your local hospital, your healthcare provider and health clubs. The American College of Obstetricians and Gynecologists (ACOG) has tapes available on exercise during and after pregnancy. Ask your healthcare provider for ordering information.

If you love to exercise, that's great! But don't overdo it while you are pregnant. General guidelines for exercise before and during pregnancy include those listed below.

- Before starting a new program, consult your doctor about past medical problems and past pregnancy complications.
- Start exercising before you get pregnant.
- Exercise on a regular basis.
- Start gradually, and increase as you build strength.
- Wear comfortable clothing.
- Avoid contact sports or risky exercise, such as water-skiing or horseback riding.

- Allow plenty of time for warming up and cooling down.
- Check your pulse every 10 to 15 minutes during exercise.
- Don't let your pulse exceed 140 beats a minute.
- Once you're pregnant, be careful when changing positions.
- After the fourth month of pregnancy, don't lie flat on your back when exercising. This decreases blood flow to your baby.
- Stop exercising and consult your doctor if you have any bleeding, loss of fluid from the vagina, shortness of breath, dizziness, abdominal pain or other serious problems.

Your Prepregnancy Health

If you are in good health before and during your pregnancy, you'll do a lot to ensure the good health of your baby. But in many cases, you can have a successful pregnancy even if you have a chronic health problem. Many women with health problems have successful pregnancies and healthy babies.

It is very important for you to discuss your particular situation with your doctor before becoming pregnant. Follow his or her instructions carefully. Below are short discussions about some common health problems a pregnant woman may have.

Diabetes

A lot of progress has been made regarding diabetes and the pregnant woman. However, diabetes can have serious effects during pregnancy. Risks to you and your baby can be decreased with good control of blood sugar during pregnancy. Discuss your concerns with your physician before you try to conceive.

The longer your diabetes is under control before you become pregnant, the better—but most doctors recommend having your condition under control *at least* 2 or 3 months before pregnancy begins. This helps lower the risk of miscarriage or of fetal development being affected.

Most problems for diabetic women occur during the first trimester—the first 13 weeks of pregnancy. However, problems can occur throughout pregnancy, which is why it's important to have your diabetes under good control before you conceive. A woman's insulin requirement often increases in the last 13 weeks of pregnancy.

I've heard depression and stress can keep me from getting pregnant. Is this true?
It may be true. A recent study showed that emotions may play a part in a woman's ability to conceive. Nearly half the women in the study who were unable to get pregnant did get pregnant when they learned to reduce and to manage their stress.

Heart Problems

Some heart problems may be serious during pregnancy and require special care. Other heart problems may affect your health so adversely that your physician will advise against pregnancy. This serious question must be discussed with your heart specialist and your obstetrician *before* you get pregnant.

Anemia

If you have been anemic in the past, your doctor can easily check you for anemia now. When you're pregnant, great demands are made on your body's iron supplies for the baby. Many women start taking vitamins or iron before getting pregnant. Because you have had a problem in the past, discuss this with your doctor before pregnancy.

I've heard there's a new drug now used for sickle-cell anemia, which I have. Can I use it while I try to get pregnant?
You are probably referring to hydroxyurea, which has proved to be the first effective treatment of sickle-cell anemia. It helps reduce the excruciating pain of some sickle-cell attacks, but its use carries some risk and it cannot be given to all sickle-cell sufferers. We do not know the long-term effects of the drug, so women contemplating pregnancy are advised not to use it.

Thyroid Condition

If you take medication for a thyroid condition, don't make any changes without first consulting your physician. Medication for thyroid problems is very important during pregnancy.

My friend had surgery for breast cancer a few months ago, and now she's talking about getting pregnant. Is that dangerous?
This problem affects individuals differently. Decisions your friend makes depend on the seriousness of her cancer and the type of treatment she received. It is important for your friend to talk to her doctor if she is thinking about getting pregnant and she is being treated for cancer. It is easier and safer for the woman to make decisions about treatments or medications *before* becoming pregnant than after.

X-rays and Other Tests

If you have a condition, such as a back problem, that requires X-rays, CT-scans or MRI tests, complete them while you are still using contraception, before you consider conceiving. A good time to schedule these tests is right after the end of your period, so you know you're not pregnant.

Vaccinations

If you have recently received a vaccination, discuss the matter with your doctor before you try to become pregnant. Some vaccinations are safe during pregnancy. Others, such as the vaccination against rubella, are not. Most physicians believe it's wise to continue contraception for at least 3 months after receiving any type of vaccination.

Medications

If you commonly take medications for various problems, it's best to be cautious with your use of these substances while you are preparing for pregnancy and while you are trying to conceive. Follow the guidelines below for safe use.

- Ask your doctor if the medications you are taking are safe to use during pregnancy.
- Take all prescription medications as prescribed.
- Don't use old medications for current problems.
- Be careful with over-the-counter medications. Many contain caffeine, alcohol and other additives.
- Never use anyone else's medication for your medical problem.
- Notify your doctor immediately if you are using medication and believe you might be pregnant.

I often take vitamins and herbs. Can I continue to take them while I prepare for pregnancy?

It isn't a good idea to self-medicate with anything while preparing for pregnancy or during your pregnancy. In excessive amounts, certain vitamins, such as vitamin A, can increase the risk of birth defects. The key to vitamin, mineral and herb use and good nutrition during pregnancy is balance. A multivitamin is the only supplementation most women need while they are trying to conceive.

I read somewhere that caffeine can make a woman infertile. Is that true?

Studies have shown drinking 8 cups of coffee a day (1600mg of caffeine) is associated with a decrease in a woman's ability to get pregnant. Some researchers have found an association between excessive caffeine consumption and miscarriage.

Chronic Illnesses

Lupus

The autoimmune disease lupus can sometimes affect the kidneys. Any situation that results in loss of kidney function can be serious during pregnancy. Be sure your physician knows about this situation if it applies to you before you get pregnant. You will need to make a plan to follow during your pregnancy.

Epilepsy

In the past, women who had epilepsy may have been advised not to try to have a baby. Every woman with epilepsy has a special set of health circumstances. If you have epilepsy, your full medical history must be taken into account when this decision is made. Some seizure medications are safe to take during pregnancy, and I know women with epilepsy who have had successful pregnancies.

One such medication, phenobarbital, has long been given during pregnancy, and it was generally regarded as safe to use. However, its use is now being questioned. Discuss its use or the use of other medications with your physician, but do not discontinue or decrease the medication on your own!

Should I Consider Genetic Counseling?

The answer is based on many factors, including your age, your past health, your partner's health and your family medical history. Genetic counseling is something to discuss with your doctor.

Genetic counseling is not necessary for every woman. If there is a family history of problems, it is probably advisable to seek counseling. Other situations in which genetic counseling should be considered include:

• a woman will be over 35 when she delivers

• when either you or your partner has a birth defect

• if you have delivered a baby with a birth defect

• if you have had three or more miscarriages in a row

• if you and your partner are related

Genetic counseling won't give you an exact answer, but a counselor can discuss possibilities or probabilities regarding a planned pregnancy and your baby. Ask your own doctor for advice.

Pregnancy for Older Couples

There are several advantages to being older when you have your first baby or add to your family. You are more mature and probably have more patience. Your financial situation may be better than when you were younger.

On the other hand, problems you have with chronic illnesses, such as high blood pressure or diabetes, can worsen and affect both you and your baby. There are also increased risks for the baby. For a thorough discussion of pregnancy in the older woman, read my book *Your Pregnancy After 30.*

Many of my patients who are over 35 ask me about the possible problems they might have during pregnancy. Risks are varied and include:

• a slightly increased risk of a baby with Down syndrome

• a higher risk of Cesarean section

• problems with diabetes or high blood pressure

• a harder, longer labor

If you have other chronic medical problems, such as thyroid disease, or take medications regularly, discuss your concerns with your doctor before getting pregnant.

Father's Age

Researchers believe that the father's age can also affect the pregnancy and the baby. It has been shown that chromosomal abnormalities occur more often in babies born to women over 35 and men over 40. Men over age 55 are twice as likely as younger men to father a child with Down syndrome.

I don't mean to imply you shouldn't get pregnant when you're older, but a pregnancy may be a little more difficult for you. This is an individual situation that you and your partner should discuss with your doctor.

More Tests

If you haven't had a mammogram, have one prior to becoming pregnant if you are over 35.

The older you are when you become pregnant, the more sense it may make to have additional tests during your pregnancy. Tests to consider include ultrasound, amniocentesis, chorionic villus sampling, alpha-fetoprotein and diabetes testing. If you haven't had a mammogram, have one prior to becoming pregnant if you are over 35.

Sexually Transmitted Diseases

Sexually transmitted diseases (STDs) can damage your uterus or Fallopian tubes, making it more difficult to get pregnant. If you get an STD while you're pregnant, it could affect your pregnancy. Having your partner use condoms is a good way to protect yourself against STDs, especially if you have more than one sexual partner.

STDs include gonorrhea, chlamydia, genital herpes, genital warts (condyloma), syphilis and HIV (the virus that causes AIDS). Use a condom before trying to get pregnant if you have a problem with infections or are exposed to infections frequently, even if you use other forms of birth control. If you get an infection, get it cleared up before you try to get pregnant. Specific STDs and their treatment are discussed in chapter 11.

Substance Use

As we learn more about pregnancy, it is clear that the substances in cigarettes, alcohol and street drugs can all adversely affect a fetus. Stop using these substances completely well *before* you become pregnant—and definitely *after* you become pregnant. Your partner's use of these substances can also affect conception in some cases.

Cigarette Smoking

There's no doubt that smoking affects pregnancy and development of the fetus. Low birthweight and slow growth-rate problems occur in babies born to mothers who smoke. For your health and the health of your baby, stop smoking *before* you consider pregnancy.

Alcohol Consumption

My patients often ask if it's OK for them to drink alcoholic beverages "occasionally" during pregnancy, as long as they do not "abuse" alcohol by drinking a lot. In the past, we believed a little alcohol was OK during pregnancy, but now we know differently.

Most healthcare providers believe *it's best not to drink any alcohol during pregnancy.* Every time you take a drink, your baby does too! Stop using alcohol from the time you are *preparing* to conceive until *after* your baby is born.

My friend just found out she is 8 weeks pregnant. She uses cocaine once or twice a week but says she'll stop now she's pregnant. Is this bad for the baby?

Any kind of substance abuse or drug abuse is usually harmful during pregnancy. Get these problems under control before stopping birth control or trying to conceive. A healthcare provider can help a woman find assistance. (Doctors who deal with these problems are called *addictionologists*.) It is extremely important to *stop* using cocaine before conceiving. Research has shown that cocaine damage to the baby can occur as early as 3 days after conception!

Marijuana

Marijuana can be a dangerous drug during pregnancy. While some people think its side effects (to them) are mild, it truly can harm a developing baby. Marijuana crosses the placenta and enters the baby's system. A fetus exposed to marijuana before birth can have attention deficits, impaired decision-making abilities and memory problems in the childhood years.

Working before Pregnancy

Hazards

Many workplace exposures, such as to X-rays and chemicals, could be harmful during pregnancy. Find out if this could be a problem for you during pregnancy by discussing it with your doctor *before* you get pregnant. If you wait to ask until after you find out you're pregnant, you may have already exposed your developing fetus to various dangers during the early and most important weeks of development.

Standing on the Job

Studies have shown that women who stand for a long time each day have smaller babies. If you have had premature deliveries or an incompetent cervix in the past, or if your job requires that you stand a lot, discuss the situation with your healthcare provider. You may need to modify your job.

Healthcare Insurance—Are You Covered?

Not every insurance plan includes maternity coverage. Some have a waiting period to pay for surgery or for having a baby. Some may not cover your doctor or the hospital you want. Find out about these things before trying to get pregnant. Having a baby costs a lot; know what your coverage is ahead of time. Planning ahead may save you money and save you the trouble of changing doctors or hospitals.

Your Pregnancy

Part

2

Your Health and 2 Medical Concerns

One of the first medical concerns you will probably have is finding out if you're *really* pregnant. For many women, the first sign they are pregnant is a missed menstrual period, but it could be different for you. Other signs and symptoms may make you *suspect* you are pregnant. As your pregnancy progresses, you may experience nausea (with or without vomiting), frequent urination, fatigue, breast changes and breast tenderness.

You have an incredible effect on the health of your growing baby. Planning for pregnancy is important. Even more important is how you treat yourself (and the developing fetus) *during* your pregnancy. Good nutrition, proper exercise, sufficient rest and taking care of yourself all have an effect on your pregnancy. Your health care affects your pregnancy and how well you tolerate being pregnant.

I cover many aspects of health care during pregnancy. In this chapter you will read what prenatal care is and what kind of care to expect during pregnancy, choosing whom you want to take care of you, how to deal with morning sickness, how your health affects your baby, discomforts you may experience, special pregnancy concerns and what to do about pre-existing medical conditions. It's a fairly long chapter, so read only those sections that concern you at this time. Then read about other areas as they become important to you.

To get the best medical treatment you can during pregnancy, call your doctor for an appointment as soon as you believe you might be pregnant.

Choosing Your Healthcare Provider

Depending on your HMO or insurance carrier, you may have choices when it comes to choosing your healthcare provider for pregnancy. You can choose an obstetrician, a family practitioner or a certified nurse-midwife to oversee your prenatal care.

Obstetrician

An *obstetrician* is a medical doctor or an osteopathic physician who specializes in the care of pregnant women, including delivering babies. He or she has completed further training in obstetrics and gynecology after medical school.

Family Practitioner

A *family practitioner*, sometimes called a *general practitioner*, often provides care for the entire family. Many family practitioners are experienced at delivering babies. If an obstetrician is not available in a community because it is small or remote, a family practitioner often delivers babies. If problems arise, your family practitioner may refer you to an obstetrician for prenatal care or delivery.

Certified Nurse-Midwife

A *certified nurse-midwife* is a trained professional who cares for women who have low-risk, uncomplicated pregnancies and delivers their babies. These professionals are *registered nurses* (RNs) who have additional professional training and certification in nurse-midwifery. They are supervised by a physician and call him or her if complications occur.

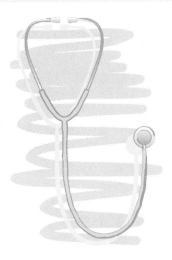

Perinatologist

A *perinatologist* is an obstetrician who specializes in high-risk pregnancies. Only about 1 in 10 pregnant women need to see one. If you have serious problems during pregnancy, you may be referred to a perinatologist. Or you may need to see one if you experienced problems with past pregnancies.

If you see a perinatologist, it still may be possible for you to deliver with your doctor. You may have to use a hospital other than the one you had chosen if the perinatologist will deliver your baby. This doctor may require specialized facilities or the availability of specialized tests for you or your baby.

How can I find the best caregiver for me?

If you have an obstetrician you like, you may not have to look further. If you don't have one, call your local medical society, and ask for a referral. Ask friends who have recently had a baby about their healthcare provider. Ask the opinion of a *labor-delivery nurse.* Sometimes another doctor, such as a pediatrician or internist, can refer you to an obstetrician. Ask your local librarian for publications that list physicians in your area.

Talk to Your Healthcare Provider

It's important to communicate freely with your healthcare provider so you can ask him or her anything about your condition. It's good to read articles and books, such as this one and my other books, *Your Pregnancy Week by Week* and *Your Pregnancy After 30.* They help you prepare questions to ask your healthcare provider. But never substitute information you receive from other sources in place of asking your provider particular questions about *your own pregnancy.* Your healthcare provider knows you, your history and what has occurred during this pregnancy. Always discuss your concerns with him or her!

Don't be afraid to ask your healthcare provider any question. He or she has probably already heard it, so don't be embarrassed. It's possible a situation is unwise or risky for you,

so be sure to check even the smallest details. It's better to take time to get answers to all your questions than to wait until a problem develops.

How Often Will I See My Doctor?

After your first visit, you will be scheduled for visits throughout your pregnancy. In most cases, you will go every 4 weeks for the first 7 months, then every 2 weeks until the last month, then once a week. If you have problems during your pregnancy, you may have to visit more frequently.

What kind of lab tests will I need?

You will probably have several tests during the first or second visit. These may include:

- a complete blood count (CBC)
- urinalysis and urine culture
- Pap smear
- cervical cultures
- blood-sugar test (for diabetes; may be done later in pregnancy)
- rubella titers (for immunity against rubella)
- blood typing
- Rh-factor
- test for syphilis
- test for hepatitis antibodies
- alpha-fetoprotein test
- triple screen
- quad screen, in some areas

What is Prenatal Care?

"Prenatal" means *before birth*. Prenatal care is the care you receive *during* pregnancy. You need this special care to help you uncover any problems before they become serious. Healthcare providers are trained to deal with pregnancy. They can and will answer your questions and address your concerns during this important time.

Prenatal care affects your pregnancy positively in several ways, so be confident you have the best you can find. With confidence in your healthcare provider, you will be able to relax and enjoy your pregnancy. It really is a special and an enjoyable time in your life. Do everything possible to make it the best 9 months for your growing baby. Getting good prenatal care is an excellent beginning!

Your First Visit

Your first visit may be the longest. You will be asked a lot of questions. You will have a physical exam. Lab tests may be ordered now or at your next visit.

You will be asked for your complete medical history, including information about your periods, recent birth-control methods and previous pregnancies. Tell your healthcare provider about any miscarriages or abortions. Be sure to include information about hospital stays or surgeries you have had.

Your doctor needs to know about any medications you take or any medications you are allergic to. Your family's past medical history may be important, such as the occurrence of diabetes or other illnesses. Be sure to tell him or her about any chronic medical problems you have. If you have medical records, bring them with you.

I hate having a pelvic exam. Will I need one?
Yes, probably. A pelvic exam helps your doctor determine if your uterus is the appropriate size for how far along you are in pregnancy, which can be helpful in determining your due date. You'll also have a Pap smear, if you haven't had one in the last year.

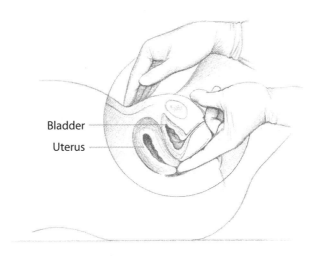

A pelvic exam is an important part of your gynecological and obstetrical care.

Bladder
Uterus

Dealing with Morning Sickness

An early symptom of pregnancy for many women is *nausea*. With or without vomiting, it is often called *morning sickness*. A more serious condition, *hyperemesis gravidarum*, results when a woman experiences a great deal of vomiting and the inability to eat foods or to drink fluids. A woman with this problem may need to be treated in the hospital with I.V.s (intravenous feeding) and medicines for nausea.

Nausea is typically the worst at the beginning of pregnancy; most often it is bad in the morning and improves during the day. Nausea and vomiting with pregnancy can occur at any time of the day or night, however; sometimes it lasts all day. Morning sickness usually begins around week 6 and lasts until week 12 or 13, when it lessens and disappears. A number of remedies can help ease the symptoms; see the box on page 26.

Take good care of your teeth if you have morning sickness. When nausea is accompanied by vomiting, stomach acid that enters the

You can ask your healthcare provider any question. He or she has probably already heard it, so don't be embarrassed.

mouth weakens tooth enamel. Brush your teeth after vomiting to remove any vomit residue.

What can I do about nausea?

A number of things might help you deal with the nausea and vomiting related to morning sickness. Try these suggestions, and use what works for you.

- Spread meals throughout the day so you eat several nutritious snacks instead of one large meal.
- Eat a snack before you get up, such as crackers or rice cakes. Or ask your partner to make you some dry toast.
- Avoid heavy, fatty foods.
- Keep up your fluid intake—fluids may be easier to handle than solids, and you want to avoid dehydration.
- Alternate wet foods with dry foods. Eat only dry foods at one meal, then liquids at the next.
- Try ginger—it's a natural remedy for nausea. Grate it on vegetables and other foods.
- Suck on a cut, fresh lemon when you feel nauseated.
- Avoid things that trigger your nausea, such as odors, movement or noise.
- Get enough rest.
- Avoid getting sweaty or overheated, which can contribute to nausea.

**I feel so nauseated that I can't eat anything.
Is this dangerous?**

Nausea, also called *morning sickness*, is usually not dangerous because it doesn't last too long. It becomes dangerous when you are unable to eat an adequate amount of food or to drink enough fluid.

Nausea is typically the worst at the beginning of pregnancy. It usually disappears after the first trimester, and you feel better for the rest of your pregnancy.

Severe Symptoms

If you get dehydrated or lose a substantial amount of weight with morning sickness, you may have to be hospitalized and fed intravenously. Caregivers can help you keep up your fluid intake and be sure you get the nourishment you need through I.V. feedings. Usually after only a couple of days or less in the hospital you can resume eating solids.

How Your Health Affects Your Growing Baby

Your baby depends on you *completely* for its needs. To make sure he or she gets the best possible start in life, eat right, get enough rest and stay as healthy as possible throughout your pregnancy.

Some infections and illnesses you have can affect your baby's development. That's why it is so important to remind your doctor you are pregnant when you call him or her with a medical problem. See the chart on page 34, which lists some illnesses and the effects each can have on a developing fetus.

Fever

A fever, particularly a high fever, may hurt your baby. Your baby relies on you for its temperature control. A prolonged high fever, especially in the first trimester (first 13 weeks), can affect a developing fetus.

To bring down a high fever, drink lots of liquids, take acetaminophen (Tylenol®) and dress appropriately to help you cool down. If your physician prescribes medication for a cold, bladder infection or other illness, take it as prescribed.

To bring down a high fever, drink lots of liquids, take acetaminophen (Tylenol) and dress appropriately to help you cool down.

Hepatitis

Hepatitis is a viral infection of the liver. *It is one of the most serious infections that can occur during pregnancy.* Your doctor will probably test you for hepatitis B antibodies at the beginning of your pregnancy.

Hepatitis B is spread from one person to another by the re-use of intravenous needles and by sexual contact. It is responsible for nearly 50% of the hepatitis cases in North America.

Flulike symptoms, nausea and pain in the area of the liver or upper-right abdomen are signs of this infection. The person may appear yellow (jaundiced), and urine may be darker than normal.

It is now recommended that all newborns receive hepatitis vaccine shortly after birth.

A developing baby can get hepatitis B from its mother. Hepatitis affects the liver; a fetus that gets hepatitis is at serious risk for liver damage or stillbirth.

A baby born to a mother who tests positive for hepatitis at the beginning of pregnancy may have to receive immune globulin against hepatitis after it is born. It is now recommended that all newborns receive hepatitis vaccine shortly after birth. Ask your pediatrician if the vaccine is available in your area.

Group-B Streptococcus Infection

Group-B streptococcus (GBS) rarely causes problems in adults but can cause life-threatening infections in newborns. You get an infection when your immunity or resistance is down.

You get an infection when your immunity or resistance is down.

You can "carry" the bacteria in your vagina (soon to be "birth canal") and not feel sick. There may not be symptoms. Sometimes a woman will have a vaginal discharge. GBS is treated with antibiotics.

At this time, there is no ideal screening test for GBS; however, your doctor may recommend taking a swab of your vagina or rectum at around 28 or 36 weeks of pregnancy. This is cultured to test for the presence of GBS. The test identifies 90% of all women who will carry the bacteria at the time of birth. Although faster tests are available that can be used during labor to detect GBS, they are not as accurate.

The risk of passing GBS to your baby increases with premature labor, premature rupture of membranes or a previous GBS infection.

Fifth Disease

Fifth disease, also called *parvo virus B19,* is a mild, moderately contagious airborne infection that spreads easily through groups, such as classrooms or day-care centers. (It is *not* the same infection that affects dogs.) A rash develops that looks like skin reddening caused by a slap. Reddening fades and recurs, and lasts from 2 to 34 days. There is no treatment, but it is important to distinguish it from rubella, especially if you are pregnant.

Fifth disease is a moderately contagious infection that spreads through groups, such as classrooms or day-care centers.

Fifth disease is something to know about. *This virus is important during pregnancy because it interferes with the production of red blood cells.* If you are exposed to fifth disease, contact your doctor. A blood test can determine whether you have had the virus before. If you have not, your doctor can monitor you to detect fetal problems. Some fetal problems can be dealt with before the baby is born.

Bacterial Vaginosis

Bacterial vaginosis (BV) is a vaginal infection that affects pregnant and nonpregnant women. Some researchers estimate that up to 20% of all pregnant women have BV. It can cause problems for a pregnant woman by increasing her risk of having a low-birthweight baby or of going into premature labor. It occurs when undesirable bacteria multiply due to suppression or killing of good bacteria. Most women are *not* routinely screened for BV.

It is possible to have BV without symptoms, but symptoms you may notice include:
- mild vaginal irritation
- a fishy odor
- increased creamy discharge from the vagina

Your doctor can do a vaginal swab if BV is suspected. Creams and oral antibiotics are used to treat BV. Treatment may increase a woman's chances of carrying her baby to full term.

Lyme Disease

Lyme disease is an infection carried and transmitted to humans by ticks. Lyme disease crosses the placenta. Treatment includes long-term antibiotic therapy. Many medications used to treat Lyme disease are safe to use during pregnancy.

Many medications used to treat Lyme disease are safe to use during pregnancy.

Lyme disease has several stages. In most people, a skin lesion with a distinctive look, called a *bull's eye*, appears at the site of the bite. Flulike symptoms appear, and after 4 to 6 weeks there may be signs of heart or neurologic problems. Arthritis may become a problem later.

To help avoid exposure to Lyme disease, stay out of areas known to have ticks, such as heavily wooded areas. If you can't avoid those areas, wear long-sleeved shirts, long pants, socks and boots or closed shoes. Immediately on entering your house, check your hair for ticks; they often attach themselves to the hair or the scalp. Researchers are working on a vaccine to prevent Lyme disease. It may be available in the near future.

Lupus

Lupus (systemic lupus erythematosus or SLE) is a disease of unknown cause that affects women more often than men (about 9 to 1). Women with lupus have a large number of antibodies in their bloodstream that are directed toward the women's own tissues. This can affect various parts of the body, including the joints, skin, kidneys, muscles, lungs, brain and central nervous system.

Lupus is a concern during pregnancy because it occurs most often in young or middle-aged women who may become pregnant. Miscarriage, premature delivery and complications around the time of delivery are increased in women with lupus.

The most common symptom of lupus is joint pain. Other symptoms include rashes or sores on the skin, fever, kidney problems and hypertension.

The drug of choice to treat lupus is steroids; the most commonly prescribed steroid is prednisone. Many studies on the safety of prednisone during pregnancy have found it to be safe.

Streptococcus A

Toxic streptococcus A, the "flesh-eating bacteria," is a bacterial infection that usually starts in a skin cut, not as a sore throat. The skin turns red and becomes swollen, painful and infected. Strep A spreads quickly and can soon involve the entire body.

Symptoms of streptococcus A are
• fever above 102F (39C)
• an inflamed cut or scratch
• flulike symptoms
• unusually cold extremities (feet, hands, legs and arms)

You can take steps to prevent toxic strep-A infection. Any time you get a scratch, clean the affected area with soap and water, alcohol or hydrogen peroxide. All are safe to use during pregnancy. After careful washing, apply triple antibiotic cream or ointment (available over the counter) to the area. Use a light bandage, if necessary. Keep the area clean, and cleanse and reapply antibiotic ointment as needed. IMPORTANT: *Use these measures with every member of your family.*

Diarrhea

Diarrhea during pregnancy can be a concern. If the diarrhea doesn't go away in 24 hours, or if it keeps returning, contact your healthcare provider. He or she may prescribe medication. *Do not take medication for diarrhea without discussing it first with your healthcare provider.*

One of the best ways to help yourself if you have diarrhea is to increase your fluid intake.

One of the best ways to help yourself if you have diarrhea is to increase your fluid intake. Drink a lot of water, juice and other clear fluids, such as broth. (Avoid apple juice, because it acts as a laxative.) You may feel better eating a bland diet, without solid foods, until your diarrhea stops.

Going without solid food for a few days isn't harmful if you keep up your fluid intake. Food may actually cause you more gastrointestinal distress. Avoid milk products while you have diarrhea; they can make it worse.

If You Have a Cat

At one of your prenatal appointments, your doctor may ask you if you own a cat. If a cat lives at your house, you may be exposed to *toxoplasma gondii*, a protozoa that causes *toxoplasmosis*. The disease is spread by contact with infected cat feces or by eating raw, infected meat. You can pick up protozoa from an infected cat's litter box, from counters and other surfaces the cat walks on or from the cat itself when you pet it.

Get someone else to change the kitty litter. Keep cats off counters.

A toxoplasmosis infection during pregnancy can cause miscarriage or an infected infant at birth. Usually an infection in the mother has no symptoms.

To protect yourself, avoid exposure to cat feces as a precaution. Get someone else to change the kitty litter. Keep cats off counters and other areas where you could pick up the protozoa. Wash your hands thoroughly after touching your cat or after handling raw meat. Keep counters clean, and cook meat thoroughly. Hygienic measures prevent transmission of the protozoa. If possible, have your cat cared for by a friend during your pregnancy.

Cytomegalovirus

Cytomegalovirus (CMV) is a member of the herpes-virus family. It is transmitted in humans by contact with saliva or urine. Day-care centers are a common source of the infection. CMV can also be passed by sexual contact. Most CMV infections do not cause symptoms. When symptoms do occur, they include a fever, sore throat and joint pain.

This virus can cause problems in an infant, including low birth-weight, eye problems, jaundice and anemia.

Rubella

Rubella, also called *German measles*, is a viral infection that causes few problems in the nonpregnant woman. It is more serious during pregnancy, especially in the first trimester. The most common symptom of rubella is a skin rash. You may also experience flulike symptoms.

Rubella infection during pregnancy can increase the rate of miscarriage and cause malformations in the baby, especially deafness and heart defects.

Rubella vaccine has been in use for a long time. One of the initial blood tests you will receive is to check for antibodies to rubella. Problems with rubella occur infrequently.

Chickenpox

If you have had chickenpox in the past, it shouldn't be a problem now. If you haven't had chickenpox, exposure during the first trimester can result in birth defects, including heart problems. Exposure close to delivery (within 1 week) can result in chickenpox in the baby.

Adults don't tolerate chickenpox as well as children. They may have serious symptoms, including painful lesions, high fever and severe flulike symptoms.

If you are not sure if you have been exposed to chickenpox in the past, avoid exposure to the disease if you can.

Varicella (Shingles)

Varicella (sometimes called *varicella-zoster*) is another in the herpes-virus family and is in the same family as chickenpox. Varicella may remain latent for years, only to be reactivated as shingles.

Varicella is in the same family as chickenpox.

Pain is the main symptom of shingles, which may be accompanied by a rash or lesions. If you get shingles while you're pregnant, it can cause severe pain and even breathing problems. Fortunately, it is rare.

Shingles may cause birth defects if you are exposed early in pregnancy. If you are exposed within 2 weeks of delivery, the baby may catch the disease.

Possible Prenatal Effects of Mother's Illness

Illness in Mother	Possible Effect on Fetus
Chickenpox	Heart problems
Cytomegalovirus	Microcephaly, brain damage, hearing loss
Group-B streptococcus	Pneumonia, meningitis, cerebral palsy, damage to lungs or kidneys
Hepatitis	Liver damage, death
Lupus	Miscarriage, premature delivery
Lyme disease	Preterm labor, fetal death, rash in newborn
Rubella (German measles)	Cataracts, deafness, heart lesions; can involve all organs
Syphilis	Skin defects, fetal death
Toxoplasmosis	Possible effects on all organs
Varicella	Possible effects on all organs

Environmental Poisons and Pollutants

Environmental poisons can be dangerous to a pregnant woman. Environmental poisons and pollutants that can harm a developing fetus include lead, mercury, PCBs and pesticides.

Lead

Lead exposure increases the chance of miscarriage. Lead is readily transported across the placenta to the baby. Poisoning occurs as early as the 12th week of pregnancy.

How could I be exposed to lead?
Lead exposure can come from many sources, including water pipes, solders, storage batteries, some construction materials, paints (especially older paints), dyes and wood preservatives. You may also be exposed in your workplace; find out if there is a risk.

Mercury

Mercury exposure has been linked to cerebral palsy and microcephaly. Exposure usually occurs from contaminated fish. Grain contamination by mercury has also been reported.

PCBs

PCBs (polychlorinated biphenyls) are not single compounds but mixtures of several compounds. Most fish, birds and humans have small, measurable amounts of PCBs in their tissues. PCBs have been blamed for miscarriage and fetal-growth retardation. We are exposed to PCBs through some foods we eat, especially fish.

Pesticides

Pesticides have been held responsible for an increase in miscarriage and fetal-growth retardation. Pesticides include a large number of agents used to control unwanted plants and animals. Human exposure is common because of the extensive use of pesticides. Those of most concern include DDT, chlordane, heptachlor and lindane.

The safest course is to *avoid* exposure, whether through the foods you eat or the air you breathe. Thoroughly wash all fruits and vegetables before eating. It may not be possible to eliminate all contact. If you know you will be around certain chemicals, wash your hands thoroughly after every exposure.

Common Discomforts of Pregnancy

Hemorrhoids

During pregnancy, you may get hemorrhoids, even if you haven't before. Hemorrhoids are dilated blood vessels around the area of the anus or inside the anus. They can itch, bleed and be painful. Hemorrhoids are caused by increased blood flow in the pelvis and the increased weight and size of the uterus, which congests or blocks blood flow.

If you have hemorrhoids, eat adequate amounts of fiber, and drink lots of fluid. Sitz baths help, and suppository medications, available without a prescription, can provide relief. You may need to use stool softeners. Apply ice packs or cotton balls soaked in witch hazel to the affected area. Discuss the situation with your doctor if hemorrhoids become a major problem for you.

I Have Heartburn!

Heartburn discomfort is a common complaint during pregnancy. It may begin early in pregnancy, although generally it becomes more severe as pregnancy progresses. Heartburn is caused by reflux (regurgitation) of stomach contents into the esophagus.

Heartburn occurs more frequently during pregnancy because of two factors—decreased gastrointestinal function and compression of the stomach by the uterus as it grows larger and moves up into the abdomen.

Can I do anything about heartburn?
Yes. Antacids may provide considerable relief. Follow the directions relating to pregnancy on the package or your doctor's instructions. Don't overdo it. You can use antacids, such as Amphojel®, Gelusil®, milk of magnesia and Maalox, without much concern. Avoid sodium bicarbonate because it could cause you to retain water. In addition to antacids, try the following tips for heartburn relief.
  • Eat smaller, more frequent meals.
  • Avoid eating before bedtime.
  • When lying down, elevate your head and shoulders.

The foods you eat may affect heartburn. Find foods (and amounts) that don't cause discomfort. Eliminate foods that cause problems. Add foods you tolerate well that benefit you and your growing baby.

Heartburn *is a burning discomfort felt behind the lower part of the sternum (breastbone).* **Indigestion** *refers to the inability to digest food or difficulty digesting food. If you have indigestion, eat foods that "agree" with you; avoid spicy foods. Eat small meals frequently. If you need them, take antacids after meals, but don't overmedicate.*

Headaches

It's a good idea to try to deal with headaches without medication. Several methods you can try are medicine-free.

- Use deep-breathing exercises and relaxation techniques to help you relax.
- Close your eyes and rest in a quiet place.
- Eat regularly. Avoid foods or substances such as caffeine that might cause a headache.
- Apply an ice pack to the back of your head.
- Get enough sleep.

If your headaches don't go away using these techniques, acetaminophen (Tylenol) is recommended. You can take the regular or extra-strength version. If this doesn't help, contact your healthcare provider.

If you suffer from migraine headaches, try the techniques described above. If they don't help, discuss the problem with your physician. Do *not* take any medications for a migraine headache without discussing it first with your physician.

Nasal Stuffiness

I have problems with allergies. Will they cause me problems during pregnancy?
Your allergies may change during pregnancy. Sometimes they get worse, but other times they improve.

Some women complain of nasal stuffiness or nosebleeds during pregnancy. We believe these occur because of circulation changes caused by the hormonal changes involved in pregnancy. The mucous membranes of the nose and nasal passages swell and bleed more easily.

Do *not* use decongestants or nasal sprays to relieve stuffiness without first asking your doctor. Many are combinations of several medications that should not be used during pregnancy. Try a humidifier to relieve stuffiness. Increase your fluid intake, and use a gentle lubricant, such as petroleum jelly. If these remedies don't provide relief, discuss the matter with your healthcare provider.

Pregnancy Precautions

Pregnancy is a time to reevaluate some activities that you might not worry about when you are *not* pregnant. I frequently hear questions from my patients about the following issues.

Hot Tub

Your baby relies on you to maintain correct body temperature. Research has shown that an elevated temperature for an extended time may harm a developing fetus. It's best to avoid hot tubs, saunas, steamrooms and spas during pregnancy.

Tanning Booth

Researchers have not studied the effects on a growing fetus when a pregnant woman lies in a tanning booth. Until we know there is no reason for concern, avoid tanning while you're pregnant.

Risky Sports

During pregnancy, avoid these risky sports:
• scuba diving
• water-skiing
• surfing
• horseback riding
• downhill or cross-country skiing
• any contact sport

The best exercises during pregnancy are walking and swimming.

See chapter 5 for a full discussion on exercise and exercise precautions during pregnancy.

Douching during Pregnancy

Most doctors agree douching can be dangerous during pregnancy. Don't do it.

Using a douche may cause an infection or bleeding or even break your bag of waters (rupture your membranes). It can cause more serious problems, such as an *air embolus*. An air embolus results when air gets into your circulation from the pressure of the douche. It is rare but can be a serious problem.

I love to have a massage because it relaxes me so much. Can I continue to have massages while I'm pregnant?
It's probably OK to have a massage during pregnancy. You may find it more difficult as your pregnancy progresses and you get bigger. If you want to have a massage when you are further along in your pregnancy, lie on your side instead of on your stomach or back. Always be careful not to get overheated in any activity.

I've heard a pregnant woman shouldn't have her hair colored or get a permanent. Is there any reason to avoid these?
It's a good idea to avoid these activities during the first trimester, especially if you have morning sickness. Fumes from the hair dye or the permanent solution could make you feel ill.

Electrolysis, Leg Waxing
No one knows for sure whether electrolysis is safe during pregnancy. Because no information is available, I suggest you wait until after your baby is born to have facial hair removed.

I don't believe leg waxing poses any risk to you. Just be sure not to get overheated while having it done. You shouldn't raise your body temperature above 102F (39C) for more than 15 minutes.

Tattoo Removal
Many tattoos are removed using lasers, and we are unsure how safe it might be for you to have this done during pregnancy. Get the tattoo removed *before* becoming pregnant or wait until after your baby is born to have it removed.

Spa Treatment
Definitely wait until after your baby is born to have spa treatments such as an herbal wrap. Being wrapped in hot towels causes your body to become very hot, which is not advisable during pregnancy.

Electric Blankets
There has been controversy about using electric blankets during pregnancy. At this time, no one knows if it is safe for your unborn baby. Until we know more, the safest thing to do is not to use an electric blanket. Find other ways to stay warm, such as with down comforters or extra blankets.

How safe is it for me to take a bath during pregnancy?
Most healthcare providers believe it is safe to bathe during pregnancy. The only precaution is to be careful to avoid slipping and falling as you get in or out of the tub.

There is no medical reason to choose showering over bathing during pregnancy. In the last few weeks of pregnancy, as you get bigger, you must be careful about slipping in the shower or the tub. If you think your water has broken (ruptured membranes), your doctor may recommend that you not bathe.

Allergies

If you suffer from allergies while you're pregnant, drink plenty of water, especially during hot weather. If you're sensitive to certain foods, be careful about what you eat. Avoid whatever else you might be sensitive to, such as animal dander or cigarette smoke.

Drink plenty of water.

You may or may not be able to take your regular allergy medications while you are pregnant. Ask your doctor or pharmacist *before* you take a medication, whether it's a prescription or over-the-counter (OTC) medication. Don't assume it's OK to take. It's safer and easier to ask ahead of time rather than to take a chance with a medication and have problems later.

Special Concerns

Your pregnancy may increase the need to deal with certain conditions that may have existed previously or developed in pregnancy. In this section, I discuss some of these conditions and their importance to your pregnancy.

Incompetent Cervix

An incompetent cervix is a condition in which painless stretching (dilation) of the cervix occurs prematurely. The woman usually doesn't notice it happening. Membranes may rupture without warning, and it usually results in premature delivery of the baby.

The problem is not usually diagnosed until after one or more deliveries of a premature infant without any pain before delivery. If it's your first pregnancy, you can't know if you have an incompetent cervix.

Some researchers believe the situation occurs because of previous trauma to the cervix, such as a D&C (dilatation and curettage) for an abortion or a miscarriage. It may also occur if surgery has been performed on the cervix.

Treatment for an incompetent cervix is usually surgical. Sewing the cervix shut can reinforce a weak cervix. After 36 weeks of pregnancy or when the woman goes into labor, the suture is removed and the baby can be born normally.

Your Rh-Factor

Your blood type—such as A, B or AB—contains a factor that determines if it is *positive* or *negative*. In the past, Rh-negative women who carried an Rh-positive child faced complicated pregnancies that could result in a very sick baby. Today, most of these problems can be prevented. If you are Rh-negative, you and your doctor need to know it. You will require additional attention during pregnancy and after your baby is born.

If you are Rh-negative and your baby is Rh-positive, if you have had a previous pregnancy, a blood transfusion or have received blood products of some kind, you could become Rh-sensitized (isoimmunized). This could affect the baby.

Isoimmunized. An Rh-negative woman becomes isoimmunized (sensitized) when Rh-positive blood gets into her bloodstream. This can happen with a blood transfusion, the previous birth of an Rh-positive baby, a miscarriage or an ectopic pregnancy.

If you are isoimmunized, certain antibodies are circulating inside your system. They won't harm you, but they can attack the blood of an Rh-positive fetus. Your antibodies can cross the placenta and attack your baby's blood. This can make your baby anemic while it is still inside the uterus. *That condition can be very serious.*

Preventing problems. Most problems can be prevented with the use of RhoGAM®, which is Rh-immune globulin, a blood product. If you are Rh-negative and pregnant, an injection of RhoGAM is given at 28 weeks of pregnancy to prevent sensitization before delivery. You will be given a second injection of RhoGAM within 72 hours after delivery if your baby is Rh-positive.

If you cannot use blood products for personal, religious or ethical reasons, discuss this with your doctor.

Not all babies are Rh-positive, are they?
No. Some women who are Rh-negative carry a child who is also Rh-negative. In this case, no RhoGAM injection is given after delivery.

RhoGAM is also used if you have an ectopic pregnancy and are Rh-negative. This also applies to miscarriages and abortions. If you are Rh-negative and have amniocentesis, you will also receive RhoGAM.

Your Blood Pressure

It's normal for your blood pressure to change a little during pregnancy. It often decreases a little during the second trimester of pregnancy and increases toward the end of pregnancy.

If you have high blood pressure, resting in bed on your side can help. If your blood pressure is still too high, you may need medications to lower it.

Low Blood Pressure

There are two causes of *hypotension* (low blood pressure) in pregnancy. It can be caused by the enlarging uterus putting pressure on large blood vessels, such as your aorta and vena cava. This is called *supine hypotension* and may happen when you lie down. It can be alleviated or prevented by not sleeping or lying on your back.

The second cause is called *postural hypotension*. When you rise rapidly from a sitting, kneeling or squatting position, gravity causes blood to leave your brain. This may result in a drop in blood pressure. Avoid postural hypotension by getting up slowly from a sitting or lying position.

I'm dizzy a lot. Should I worry?
Feeling dizzy while you're pregnant is fairly common. Anemia can cause dizziness any time during pregnancy and can be checked with a blood count, also called a *hematocrit*. Another cause of dizziness is *hypotension* (low blood pressure). Hypotension in pregnancy usually occurs during the second trimester.

Blood-sugar problems can cause dizziness. High blood sugar (*hyperglycemia*) *or* low blood sugar (*hypoglycemia*) can make you feel dizzy or faint. Many doctors routinely test pregnant women during their pregnancies for problems with blood sugar.

If you have a problem with blood sugar, eat a balanced diet, don't skip meals and *don't go a long time without eating*. Many do better with eating 4 or 5 smaller meals a day, rather than 3 larger meals. If the condition is more serious, you may need to see a dietitian.

Pregnancy-Induced High Blood Pressure

Pregnancy-induced hypertension is high blood pressure that occurs *only* during pregnancy. It disappears after the baby is born. It develops in about 3% of women under age 40, and in 10% of women over 40.

This condition is treated by resting in bed on your side, by drinking lots of fluid and by avoiding salt and foods containing large amounts of sodium. Medications to lower blood pressure may be prescribed. For further information, see the discussion of pre-eclampsia in chapter 14.

Pregnancy-induced high blood pressure disappears after the baby is born.

Urinary-Tract Infections and Bladder Infections

The terms *UTI* (urinary-tract infection) and *bladder infection* are often used interchangeably. *Bladder infection* refers to an infection in the bladder only, sometimes also called *cystitis. UTI* refers to an infection *anywhere* in the urethra, bladder or ureters (the tubes going from the kidney to the bladder).

You may get more bladder infections now that you are pregnant. This happens because of changes in your urinary tract. The uterus sits directly on top of the bladder and on the tubes leading from the kidneys to the bladder, called *ureters*. As the uterus grows, its increased weight can block the drainage of urine from the bladder, causing a bladder infection. Between 5 and 10% of all pregnant women experience bladder infections.

Usually your doctor will do a urinalysis and a urine culture at your first visit to check for bladder infection. He or she may also check your urine for infections on subsequent visits.

Symptoms of bladder infection. Symptoms of a bladder infection include:

- frequent urination
- burning on urination
- feeling as though you need to urinate and nothing will come out
- blood in your urine (with severe infection)

Pyelonephritis. A more serious urinary-tract infection is called *pyelonephritis.* Pyelonephritis is an infection of the urinary tract that also involves the kidneys. It occurs in 1 to 2% of all pregnant women. Pyelonephritis often begins as a bladder infection that spreads to the kidneys. The enlarging uterus blocks urine flow from the kidneys through the ureters and out of the bladder, increasing the likelihood of infection.

In addition to the symptoms of a bladder infection, symptoms of pyelonephritis include:
- high fever
- chills
- back pain

This condition may require hospitalization and treatment with intravenous antibiotics.

Kidney Stones

Kidney stones, also called *urinary calculi*, occur about once in every 1500 pregnancies. Symptoms usually include severe pain in the back and blood in the urine. In pregnancy, ultrasound is usually used to diagnose a kidney stone.

Kidney stones are usually treated during pregnancy with pain medication, antibiotics and by drinking lots of fluid or receiving I.V.s.

Anemia

Anemia is a common medical problem among pregnant women. The number of red blood cells in your blood is low; the quantity of these cells is not enough to carry the oxygen needed by your body.

Anemia occurs often in pregnancy because of the developing fetus's demand for iron *and* because your blood volume increases by about 40% during pregnancy. Blood is made up of fluid and cells. The fluid usually increases faster than the cells. This may cause a drop in your hematocrit (the volume, amount or percentage of red cells in the blood). The drop can result in anemia.

It is important to treat anemia during pregnancy. If you are anemic, you won't feel well during pregnancy. You'll tire more easily. You may feel dizzy. If you're anemic when you go into labor, you're more likely to need a blood transfusion after your baby is born. Pregnancy anemia can increase the risk of preterm delivery, growth retardation (not the same as "mental retardation;" it refers to the baby's physical growth) in the baby and low birthweight. Your healthcare provider will check you for anemia and if you are anemic, she may prescribe a course of treatment for you.

Iron-Deficiency Anemia

The most common type of anemia is called *iron-deficiency anemia.* While you're pregnant, your baby uses some of your iron stores. With iron-deficiency anemia, your body does not make enough red blood cells to keep up with the increased demand.

Several other factors may cause this condition, including:
• bleeding during pregnancy
• multiple fetuses
• recent surgery on your stomach or small bowel
• frequent antacid use
• poor dietary habits

Fortunately, iron-deficiency anemia is usually easy to control. Iron is contained in most prenatal vitamins, or your may receive iron supplements as well as your prenatal vitamins. If you can't take a prenatal vitamin, you may be given iron supplements. Eating certain foods, such as liver or spinach, also helps increase your iron intake.

Sickle-Cell Anemia

Sickle-cell anemia is different from iron-deficiency anemia. It occurs when a person's bone marrow makes abnormal red blood cells. Sickle-cell anemia occurs most often in people of African or Mediterranean descent or those of mixed-black descent. Your doctor can perform a blood test to see if you have this disease.

Sickle-cell anemia can cause pain in the abdomen or limbs of the mother-to-be if she has a *sickle crisis.* (This can happen at any time in her lifetime, not just during pregnancy.) In addition to a painful sickle crisis, a pregnant woman can suffer from more frequent infections. Risks to the fetus include miscarriage and stillbirth.

I've heard of a new treatment for sickle-cell disease that relieves severe pain. Can a pregnant woman take it?

You probably mean *hydroxyurea,* which has proved to be the first effective treatment of sickle-cell anemia. It reduces some of the excruciating pain, but its use carries some risk and is not for all sickle-cell sufferers. Because we do not know its long-term effects, women who are pregnant are advised not to use it.

Thalassemia

Thalassemia is a type of anemia that occurs most often in people of Mediterranean descent. The body doesn't produce enough globulin, which makes up red blood cells, and anemia results. If you have a family history of thalassemia, discuss it with your doctor.

Pre-existing Medical Conditions

Pre-existing medical conditions may or may not affect your pregnancy, depending on the problem. In some cases, medical advances have made pregnancy possible or safer for those with certain conditions. If you have a pre-existing medical condition, discuss the matter with your own doctor as early as possible.

Diabetes

Diabetes was once a very serious medical problem during pregnancy. It continues to be an important complication of pregnancy, but today most women can have a safe pregnancy with proper medical care, a good diet and by following their doctor's instructions. Using a glucometer to measure blood sugar is essential for diabetes control during pregnancy.

Symptoms of diabetes include:
- an increase in urination
- blurred vision
- weight loss or weight gain
- dizziness
- increased hunger

Diabetes can cause medical problems that could be serious to you and your baby. If diabetes is not treated, you will expose your baby to a high concentration of sugar called *hyperglycemia*, which is not healthy for the baby.

If you have uncontrolled diabetes, you also face a significantly higher risk of miscarriage and problems at the time of birth. The most common fetal problems are heart problems, genitourinary problems and gastrointestinal problems. Diabetes can also cause large babies.

Diabetes is diagnosed with blood tests, called a *glucose-tolerance test* or a *fasting blood sugar*. Some patients ask me if sugar in the urine is a sign of diabetes. The answer is, "Not necessarily." It is common for normal, pregnant, nondiabetic women to have a small amount of sugar in their urine, a condition called *glucosuria*. This occurs because of changes in your sugar levels and changes in the way the kidneys process sugar during pregnancy.

Epilepsy

If you have epilepsy and have just found out you are pregnant, call your physician immediately; tell him or her you are pregnant and you have epilepsy. Most medications to control seizures can be taken during pregnancy. However, some medications are safer than others.

During pregnancy, phenobarbital is often used to control seizures. Dilantin® is occasionally recommended. It carries a higher risk of birth defects.

Asthma

Many women have fewer problems with asthma if they increase their fluid intake during pregnancy.

Most women who have asthma can have a safe pregnancy. If you have severe asthma attacks before pregnancy, you may have them during pregnancy also. Usually the medications you use before pregnancy can be used while you are pregnant. Discuss medication use with your healthcare provider.

I've found that many women feel better and have fewer problems with asthma if they increase their fluid intake during pregnancy. Try it—you should increase your fluid intake during pregnancy anyway.

Cancer

Cancer during pregnancy is rare. However, it does occur occasionally during pregnancy.

It's not a pleasant subject to think about or to discuss, and most women do not need to be concerned about cancer during pregnancy. However, it's better to be aware that these problems do occur than to know nothing about them.

The most common cancer found in pregnancy is breast cancer. Gynecologic cancers, leukemia, lymphoma, melanoma and bone tumors are also found. Researchers believe there are a couple of reasons cancers could appear during pregnancy.

- Some cancers arise from tissues or organs that are influenced by the increase in hormone levels caused by pregnancy.
- Increased blood flow and changes in the lymphatic system may contribute to the spread of cancer to other parts of the body.

Cancer treatment during pregnancy can cause problems because a pregnant woman may experience side effects from the treatment. In particular, if you have been having chemotherapy and just found out you are pregnant, it's very important to talk to your doctor immediately! What you do depends on the medications you are taking.

Breast Cancer

I've heard it's harder to find breast cancer during pregnancy. Why?
Changes in the breasts, including breast tenderness, increased size and even lumpiness, may make it harder to discover this type of cancer. Of all women who have breast cancer, about 2% are pregnant when it is diagnosed.

How is breast cancer treated during pregnancy?
Treatment for breast cancer during pregnancy varies. Treatment could be surgery, chemotherapy, radiation or a combination of treatments.

If a woman has breast cancer, can she breastfeed?
Most doctors recommend a woman not breastfeed if she has breast cancer.

Other Medical Concerns

Many of my patients report discomforts that seem to appear frequently during pregnancy. Here are a few of the more common situations I'm asked about, with information on what you can do to relieve them.

Leg Cramps

Leg cramps can be bothersome, especially at night. The following may help you deal with leg cramps you experience at any time.
- Wear support hose during the day.
- Take warm baths.
- Have your partner massage your legs at the end of the day or whenever you feel like it.
- Wear comfortable clothing.

- Take acetaminophen (Tylenol) for pain.
- Rest on your side.
- Use a heating pad for up to 15 minutes when you experience pain.

Your activities may affect the degree to which your legs cramp. Avoid standing for long periods. Rest on your side as often as possible. Make sure clothing is not restrictive.

Back Pain

Low-back pain is common during pregnancy—nearly half of all pregnant women suffer from it. If you have problems you believe might be helped by chiropractic manipulation, discuss it with your regular physician before you do anything! Be sure to avoid X-rays of your pelvis and lower-back area.

Age

Today, more couples are waiting to start their families, so if you are in your late 30s or early 40s and pregnant, you're not alone. The older mother-to-be and her baby face a few more risks, but it's more likely you and your baby will be OK. My book *Your Pregnancy After 30* is written specifically for the older pregnant woman.

Some of my older patients who are pregnant with their second or third child comment that they feel more tired with this pregnancy than previous ones. It's harder to be pregnant when you're 35 than it is when you're 25. It doesn't mean anything is wrong necessarily; you just have more demands on your time and more to do.

With all the news reports I've heard about older women having more babies, what is the average age for a woman to give birth in North America? A recent study showed that about age 27 is the average at which women give birth. More women give birth in their 20s than at any other age.

Risk of Down Syndrome

Frequently women ask me about the risk of having a baby with Down syndrome. As you get older, the risk of delivering a baby with Down syndrome increases, as the following statistics show:

- at age 25 the risk is 1 in 1,300 births
- at 30 it is 1 in 965 births
- at 35 it is 1 in 365 births
- at 40 it is 1 in 109 births
- at 45 it is 1 in 32 births
- at 49 it is 1 in 12 births

But you can look at these statistics in a more positive way: Even at age 49, you have a 92% chance of delivering a child *without* Down syndrome.

Down syndrome is a condition in which a baby is born with mental disabilities and often physical deformities too. A person with Down syndrome may have a sloping forehead, short, broad hands, a flat nose and low-set ears. There may also be heart problems, gastrointestinal defects or leukemia. Down syndrome is caused by an extra chromosome.

Down syndrome can be diagnosed before the baby is born. Traditionally amniocentesis has been used to diagnose the condition. Other tests that may prove useful include alpha-fetoprotein, triple screen, quad screen, chorionic villus sampling and, in some cases, ultrasound.

Tests for You and Your Growing Baby 3

Pregnancy is an important time to pay attention to your health. One way you and your doctor will keep an eye on you is to perform various tests during your pregnancy. Some tests tell your doctor about your health. Other tests tell the doctor certain things about your baby.

Most tests are routine—every pregnant woman has them. A few tests are done if your doctor thinks he or she could learn more about your health or your baby's health from them.

Your first test will probably be a pregnancy test. You can do this yourself at home, or take care of it in your doctor's office. Home pregnancy test kits are very accurate.

Once you know you're pregnant, a lot of tests will be done at your first or second visit with your doctor. These tests tell your doctor how healthy you are at this time and whether he or she needs to caution you about things to avoid or to watch out for. Some tests are repeated during pregnancy, if necessary.

Because tests during pregnancy are important, cooperate with your doctor about having them. Keep your appointments for tests, and always check with your doctor's office about test results.

Pregnancy Tests

Pregnancy tests are very sensitive and can be positive (show you're pregnant) even before you miss a menstrual period. Most tests are positive 7 to 10 days after you conceive; this includes blood, urine and home pregnancy tests. Most doctors recommend you wait until you miss your period before having a test. This saves you money and emotional energy.

I did a home pregnancy test last night, and it was positive. How soon should I see my doctor?
Most doctors will want to see you within a few weeks, 8 weeks would be average, unless you are having problems and need to be seen right away. Good prenatal care is an important part of having a healthy baby. Don't wait for weeks or months to see your doctor; starting early is essential for your health and the health of your baby.

Quantitative HCG Test

A quantitative HCG (human chorionic gonadotropin) test is a blood test done in the first trimester if there is concern about miscarriage or ectopic pregnancy. The test measures the hormone HCG, which is produced early in pregnancy and increases rapidly. Two or more tests done a few days apart are more useful than one test because the change in the amount of the hormone present is significant. An ultrasound is also often done when a quantitative HCG test is ordered.

Tests after Pregnancy Is Confirmed

Your doctor will probably order several tests at the first or second visit. These may include:

- complete blood count (CBC)
- urinalysis and urine culture
- test for syphilis
- cervical cultures
- rubella titers (for immunity against rubella)
- blood type
- Rh-factor
- test for hepatitis-B antibodies
- alpha-fetoprotein test
- ultrasound
- Pap smear
- mammogram (if you are at least 35 and a mammogram has not been done before); many doctors will not do this test during pregnancy

See the chart on page 54 for a description of some common tests done during pregnancy.

Results of these tests give your doctor information he or she needs to provide the best care for you. For example, if testing shows you have never had rubella (German measles) or rubella vaccine, you will know you need to avoid exposure during pregnancy and you should receive the vaccine before your next pregnancy. Rubella can be responsible for miscarriage or birth defects if a woman contracts the disease during pregnancy.

Questions to Ask Your Doctor

Some tests are fairly routine, and you probably won't ask many questions about those. But for procedures that are more involved, you will want more information. Your goal in asking these questions about any test procedure is to ensure the benefits of the test outweigh any risks. You may want to ask your doctor some of the following questions before any test.

- Will my insurance cover the test?
- Why are you doing this test?
- How will the test be performed?
- What risk does this test pose to me or the baby?
- How experienced is the person doing the test?
- How experienced is the lab doing the test?
- How dependable are the results?
- When will I get the results?
- What happens after I get the results?
- What is the possibility of false-positive or false-negative results?
- What will happen if we don't do the test?
- How will the results affect my pregnancy?
- Is there any other way to get the same information?
- What is the cost of the test?

Tests Given or Repeated Later

Many doctors repeat some tests or perform new tests at other times during pregnancy. For example, the 28th week of pregnancy is the best time to uncover blood-sugar problems. Also at this point in your pregnancy, RhoGAM is given to an Rh-negative woman to protect her from becoming sensitized.

Some Common Tests at a Glance

Test	How It Is Done	What You and Your Doctor Can Learn
Alpha-fetoprotein	Blood sample drawn from mother	May indicate neural-tube defects (spina bifida) or risk of Down syndrome
Amniocentesis	Sample of amniotic fluid drawn by needle from uterus	Early in pregnancy, indicates chromosomal problems (Down syndrome), neural-tube defects (spina bifida), genetic disorders (cystic fibrosis), sex of fetus; late in pregnancy, indicates whether baby's lungs are developed
Biophysical profile	Variety of tests, including ultrasound for monitoring and observation	Used to show fetal well-being or to look for signs of fetal stress
Chorionic villus sampling	Sample of placental tissue drawn from placenta through abdomen or vagina	Used to determine many diseases, such as Down syndrome; some biochemical diseases, such as Tay-Sachs disease; and other fetal conditions, such as cystic fibrosis
Stress/nonstress test	Fetal activity is monitored by expectant mother and fetal monitor	Used to show fetal well-being or to look for signs of fetal stress
Ultrasound	Sound waves produce picture of uterus, placenta and fetus on screen	Age of fetal growth, fetal position, heart rate, movement, number of fetuses, some birth defects, fetal sex (sometimes)

What about Genetic Counseling?

Not everyone needs genetic counseling. Those who do usually have had an infant with abnormalities, have a family history of inherited diseases, have had recurrent miscarriages (usually three or more) or will be 35 or older at the time of their baby's birth.

If you are a candidate for genetic counseling, you and your partner participate together. Detailed questions are asked about your medical history, other pregnancies, medication usage and the medical history of your family and your partner's family. If chromosome tests are necessary, blood samples are taken from both of you. You are advised about the potential or possibility for problems in a pregnancy.

Ultrasound

Ultrasound is a test that gives a 2-dimensional picture of the developing embryo or fetus. It involves the use of high-frequency sound waves made by applying an alternating current to a transducer. This transducer is placed on the abdomen or in the vagina. Sound waves projected from the transducer travel through the abdomen or vagina, bounce off tissues and bounce back to the transducer. Reflected sound waves are translated into a rough picture, although the newest, most sophisticated ultrasounds show very clear pictures. These machines are new to ultrasound testing and are not in widespread use at present.

Many doctors routinely perform ultrasounds on their patients, but not every doctor does them with every patient. Some doctors perform them only when there is a definite reason for doing one.

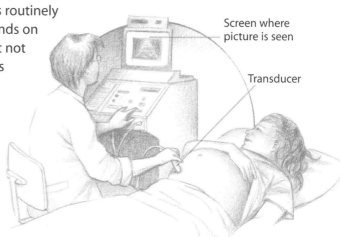

Screen where
picture is seen

Transducer

Ultrasound examination is a useful tool your healthcare provider may order for you.

There are three main reasons a doctor orders an ultrasound:
- to help confirm or determine the due date by measuring the baby
- to determine whether there is more than one baby
- to see if major physical characteristics of the fetus are normal

Who Has an Ultrasound?

You will not be given an ultrasound automatically. Whether you have one during your pregnancy depends on several factors, including:
- problems during pregnancy, such as bleeding
- previous problem pregnancies
- your healthcare provider
- your insurance company

Most doctors like to do at least one ultrasound during a pregnancy, but not all agree on this. If your pregnancy is "high risk," you may have several ultrasounds.

I'm confused about ultrasound and sonograms. What's the difference?
Ultrasound, sonogram and sonography refer to the same test.

Other reasons for ultrasound. Some other reasons for doing an ultrasound are
- identifying an early pregnancy
- showing the size and growth of the embryo or fetus
- measuring the fetal head, abdomen or thighbone to determine how far along in pregnancy the woman is
- identifying some fetuses with Down syndrome
- identifying some fetal abnormalities, such as hydrocephalus
- measuring the amount of amniotic fluid
- identifying the location, the size and the maturity of the placenta
- identifying abnormalities of the placenta
- detecting an IUD (intrauterine device)
- differentiating between miscarriage, ectopic pregnancy and normal pregnancy

• helping to find a safe location to perform an amniocentesis
• identifying a miscarriage

How early in pregnancy you may have an ultrasound depends on problems with your pregnancy, such as bleeding or cramping. If you're having problems, your healthcare provider may want to do an ultrasound fairly early in pregnancy.

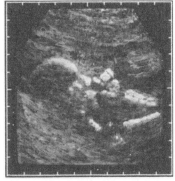

An ultrasound may help determine when your baby is due. Measurements can be taken of the baby with an ultrasound. Your doctor can compare these measurements against charts with averages to help approximate your due date.

This ultrasound picture shows a baby sucking its thumb inside the uterus.

Will I be able to find out if I am having a boy or girl when I have my ultrasound?
This is by far the most common question expectant parents ask me. If you are 18 weeks or more when you have an ultrasound, you *may* be able to determine the sex of your baby, but don't count on it. It isn't always possible to tell the sex if the baby has its legs crossed or is in a breech presentation.

Even if your doctor makes a prediction as to the sex of your baby, remember that ultrasound is a test, and tests are sometimes wrong. Most doctors recommend you not start buying for one sex or the other based on an ultrasound. If you do buy anything, save the receipts!

Vaginal ultrasound. This type of ultrasound can be helpful in evaluating problems early in pregnancy, such as possible miscarriage or an ectopic pregnancy. The instrument (a probe or transducer) is put just inside the opening of the vagina. It does not touch the cervix and will not cause bleeding or miscarriage. This type of ultrasound can sometimes give better information earlier in pregnancy than an abdominal ultrasound.

Is Ultrasound Safe?

Yes. The possibility of ultrasound having adverse effects has been studied many times without evidence that the test causes any problems.

Drink Water Beforehand

Your bladder lies in front of your uterus. When your bladder is full, your uterus is pushed up out of the pelvis and can be looked at more easily by ultrasound. When your bladder is empty, your uterus is farther down in your pelvis, where it is harder to see. The full bladder acts as a window between the outside of your abdomen and your uterus. You will probably be asked to drink 32 ounces (960ml) of water before you have the ultrasound and not to empty your bladder. With a vaginal ultrasound, your bladder doesn't have to be full.

Where Ultrasound Is Done

Some doctors have an ultrasound machine in their office and have ultrasound training. Other doctors prefer that you go to the hospital to have the ultrasound done and read by a radiologist. In certain high-risk situations, your doctor may send you to an ultrasound specialist. Ask your doctor about where your ultrasound will be done.

Videotape of Ultrasound

Most ultrasounds include black-and-white photos. Baby pictures before you have a baby!

When your ultrasound is scheduled, ask whether you can get a videotape of the film. Not all ultrasound machines are capable of making a video recording. Ask ahead of time if you need to bring a videotape, or if your partner can videotape it.

Cost

Cost of this test varies, depending on where the test is done and where you live. An average cost is about $150, but it can range from $100 to $300. With many insurance plans, ultrasound is an "extra" and not part of the normal fee for prenatal care. Ask about cost and coverage before having an ultrasound. Some insurance plans require pre-approval before an ultrasound is done.

Partner May Accompany You

The ultrasound is something your partner will probably want to see, so arrange to have the procedure when he can come. You may want others, such as your mother or older children, to come with you when possible. Ask about it when your ultrasound is scheduled.

Amniocentesis

Amniocentesis is a test that can reveal certain fetal abnormalities. Amniotic fluid is obtained for study from the fluid surrounding the fetus. The amniotic fluid must be withdrawn by needle. Ultrasound is used to locate a pocket of fluid where the fetus and placenta are out of the way. Skin over the abdomen is cleaned and numbed with a local anesthetic. A long needle is then passed through the abdomen into the uterus, and fluid is withdrawn from the uterus with a syringe.

Amniocentesis does not need to be performed on every pregnant woman. It is usually offered to women

- who will deliver after their 35th birthday
- who have had a previous baby with a birth defect
- with a family history of birth defects
- who have a birth defect themselves
- whose partners have a birth defect

This test is usually performed for prenatal evaluation between 16 and 18 weeks of pregnancy. Some doctors are using amniocentesis at 11 or 12 weeks of pregnancy; however, risks are higher when it is done at this time. A study in the medical journal *Lancet* reports that miscarriage and a higher incidence of babies born with a clubfoot have been noted.

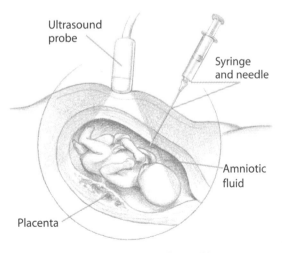

Amniocentesis is usually performed between the 16th and 18th weeks of pregnancy.

Amniotic Fluid

Only about 1 ounce (30ml) of amniotic fluid is needed to perform tests. Fetal cells that float in the amniotic fluid can be grown in cultures. These cells are used to identify fetal abnormalities or to reassure you that your baby is healthy.

We know of more than 400 abnormalities a child can be born with. Amniocentesis can identify about 40 problems. The problems a physician can identify include the following:

- chromosomal problems, particularly Down syndrome
- skeletal diseases, such as osteogenesis imperfecta
- fetal infections, such as herpes or rubella
- central-nervous-system disease, such as anencephaly
- blood diseases, such as erythroblastosis fetalis
- chemical problems or deficiencies, such as *cystinuria* or maple-syrup-urine disease

Amniocentesis can determine the baby's sex. However, the test is not used for this purpose, except in cases in which the sex of the baby could predict a problem, such as hemophilia. It may also be used later in pregnancy to determine if the baby's lungs are mature. See the discussion that begins on page 71.

Risks

Risks are relatively small; fetal loss from complications is estimated to be between 0.5 and 3%. Discuss the risk with your doctor before you have the test.

Who Performs Amniocentesis?

The test should be performed only by someone with experience doing it, such as a physician at a medical center. Your healthcare provider can give you more information if the test is to be performed on you.

About Down Syndrome

Down syndrome is a condition caused by an extra chromosome. A baby is mentally retarded and may have a somewhat dwarfed appearance, with a sloping forehead, short, broad hands, a flat nose and low-set ears. He or she may also have heart problems, gastrointestinal defects or leukemia. Down syndrome can be diagnosed during pregnancy by amniocentesis.

Other tests that can help diagnose Down syndrome include alpha-fetoprotein (AFP), the triple-screen test, chorionic villus sampling and ultrasound (in some cases). Amniocentesis or chorionic villus sampling (CVS) is done to confirm the diagnosis when "screening tests" such as AFP indicate a potential problem.

Bringing Others to Your Prenatal Appointments

It's a great idea to bring your partner along to a prenatal appointment! It will help him realize what is happening to you and to feel a part of the pregnancy. And it's nice for your partner and your doctor to meet before labor begins.

It's also all right to take your mother or mother-in-law to an appointment with you to hear the baby's heartbeat. Things have really changed since your mother carried you; she might enjoy a visit. If you want to bring anyone else, discuss it with your healthcare provider first.

Children at prenatal appointments. Many offices don't mind if you bring your children with you; other offices ask that you not bring children along. Ask about office policy. If you're having problems and need to talk with your doctor, it can be difficult to talk if you're also trying to take care of a young child.

Suggestions for bringing children along. Suggestions for bringing children to an office visit include the following:

• Ask about office policy ahead of time.
• Don't bring them on your first visit, when you will probably be having a pelvic exam.
• If you're bringing your children to hear the heartbeat, don't bring them the first time your doctor tries to hear it; wait until after you have heard it first.
• Bring one or two children at a time rather than a large group.
• Bring something to entertain your child in case you have to wait—not all offices have toys or books for kids.
• Be considerate of other patients; don't bring a child who has a cold or is sick. I've had patients bring their children with them, then tell me the child had chickenpox or strep throat! This could be very serious for other pregnant women sitting in the waiting room.
• Don't bring other people's children to your appointment.

Alpha-fetoprotein Test

The maternal alpha-fetoprotein (AFP) test is a blood test done on you to determine abnormalities in your baby. Measurement of the amount of alpha-fetoprotein in your blood can help your doctor predict problems, such as Down syndrome and spina bifida.

At this time, it is not performed on all pregnant women. However, some states require it, such as California and New York. If the test is not offered to you, discuss it with your doctor.

The AFP test is usually performed between 16 and 20 weeks of pregnancy, and test results must be correlated with the mother-to-be's age and weight, and the gestational age of the fetus. If AFP detects a problem, additional testing is usually ordered.

The test is designed to detect babies with

- neural-tube defects
- severe kidney disease
- severe liver disease
- esophageal or intestinal blockage
- Down syndrome
- urinary obstruction
- osteogenesis imperfecta (fragility of the baby's bones)

High Error Rate

The test is not specific enough to be relied on by itself. For example, if 1,000 women are tested, 40 tests will come back abnormal. Of those 40 tests, only one or two actually have a problem. If you have an AFP test and your test result is abnormal, don't panic! Another AFP test will be done to correlate results, and an ultrasound will be performed.

Neural-Tube Defect

AFP detects neural-tube defects, which are abnormalities in the bone surrounding the spinal cord, in the brain stem or in the brain itself. One of the most common neural-tube defects is spina bifida—an absence of vertebral arches, which allows the spinal membrane to protrude. Another abnormality is anencephaly; the brain develops only a rudimentary brain stem.

Triple-Screen and Quad-Screen Tests

These tests go beyond alpha-fetoprotein testing to help your healthcare provider determine if your child might have Down syndrome and to rule out other problems.

The **triple-screen test** helps identify problems using three blood components: alpha-fetoprotein, a pregnancy hormone called *human chorionic gonadotropin (HCG)* and a form of estrogen produced by the placenta called *unconjugated estriol*. Abnormal levels of these three blood chemicals can indicate Down syndrome. For older mothers, the detection rate is higher than 60%, with a false-positive rate of nearly 25%. Abnormal results of a triple-screen test are usually double-checked with ultrasound and amniocentesis.

The **quad-screen test** is used rarely at present. Only a few hospitals in the United States have laboratories equipped to conduct this test. The test is similar to the triple-screen but adds a fourth measurement—the blood level of inhibin-A, a chemical produced by the ovaries and the placenta. This fourth measurement raises the sensitivity of the triple-screen test by 20% in determining if a fetus has Down syndrome. The quad-screen test identifies almost 80% of fetuses with Down syndrome. It has a false-positive rate of 5%.

Chorionic Villus Sampling

Chorionic villus sampling (CVS) is a test that detects genetic abnormalities. Sampling is done early in pregnancy, usually between the 9th and 11th weeks.

Ultrasound is used to locate the fetus and the placenta. A small piece of tissue is removed from the placental area with an instrument placed through the cervix or with a needle inserted through the abdomen.

The advantage of CVS is an earlier diagnosis than amniocentesis of a problem, if one exists. The test can determine various fetal problems, such as Down syndrome, Tay-Sachs disease and cystic fibrosis. Some women choose to have this test because they want results earlier so they can make decisions about the pregnancy.

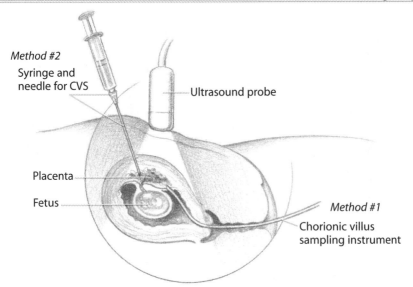

Method #2
Syringe and
needle for CVS

Ultrasound probe

Placenta

Fetus

Method #1
Chorionic villus
sampling instrument

Chorionic villus sampling can be done in either of two ways.
Tissue can be removed by a needle or by an instrument placed
through the cervix.

Risks

There is a small risk of miscarriage with this procedure. The test
should be performed only by someone who has experience doing it.

CVS or Amniocentesis?

CVS can be done much earlier in pregnancy than amniocentesis,
and results are available in about a week. If the woman decides to
terminate the pregnancy after learning results of the test, the
procedure can be performed earlier in pregnancy and may carry fewer
risks. On the other hand, the risk of disturbing a normal pregnancy is
slightly higher with CVS than with amniocentesis.

Each woman's pregnancy is different. Discuss CVS with your
doctor. He or she will be able to help you determine if your particular
case requires it.

Fetal Fibronectin

The fetal fibronectin (fFN) test can help predict if a woman will go
into labor early. fFN is a protein found in the amniotic sac and fetal
membranes during the first 22 weeks of pregnancy. If a doctor
believes a woman is going into premature labor, he or she can test the
woman's cervical-vaginal secretions; if fFN is present after 22 weeks, it

indicates increased risk for preterm delivery. If it is absent, the risk is low and the woman probably won't deliver in the next 2 weeks.

The test is performed like a Pap smear. A swab of cervical-vaginal secretions is taken from the top of the vagina, behind the cervix. Results are available from the lab within 24 hours.

Fetoscopy

Fetoscopy is performed on the fetus and placenta while both are still inside your uterus. It provides a view of the baby and placenta. The doctor can see the baby through the fetoscope and can detect some abnormalities and problems. This very specialized test is not performed very often.

A small incision is made in the mother's abdomen, and a scope similar to the one used in laparoscopy is placed through the abdomen into the uterus.

Risk of miscarriage is 3 to 4% with this procedure. The test should be done only by someone experienced in this technique.

Other Tests for the Mother-to-Be

Doppler

Doppler magnifies the sound of the baby's heartbeat enough to hear it. It is different from a stethoscope. You should be able to hear your baby's heartbeat at around the 12-week visit. If your healthcare provider doesn't offer it to you, ask about it.

I heard on the radio that some researchers are trying to develop a test that will predict Down syndrome from a pregnant woman's urine. Do you know anything about this?

Work is being done to develop a urine screen for Down syndrome. This test will measure urinary gonadotropin (UGD) in a pregnant woman's urine during the second trimester. The test is still experimental and requires more study.

Avoid X-ray Tests

Avoid exposure to X-rays during pregnancy unless it is an emergency. There is no known safe amount of radiation for a developing fetus. Dangers to the baby include an increased risk of birth defects and an increased risk of cancer later in life.

Greatest risk to fetus. Risk to a fetus appears to be the greatest between 8 and 15 weeks of pregnancy (between the fetal age of 6 weeks and 13 weeks). Some believe the only safe amount of radiation exposure for a fetus is *no exposure*.

Dental X-rays. If possible, avoid dental X-rays while you are pregnant. If you must have a dental X-ray, be sure your abdomen and pelvis are completely shielded by a lead apron.

Medical need for X-ray. There are medical reasons for X-rays, but the need for the X-ray must be weighed against the risk it poses to your pregnancy. If you have an injury to your foot or hand, it is fairly easy to shield the uterus with a lead apron while the area is X-rayed. However, if your injury is in your back or any place near the pelvic area, the risks increase. Discuss it with your physician before any X-ray is taken when you are pregnant.

Problems other than broken bones may occur that require X-rays. Pneumonia and appendicitis are two possibilities. Again, discuss the situation with your doctor.

CT scans. Computerized tomographic scans, also called *CAT scans*, are a very specialized type of X-ray. The technique involves the use of X-ray with computer analysis. Many researchers believe the amount of radiation received from a CT scan is much lower than a regular X-ray. However, it is probably wise to avoid even this amount of exposure, if possible.

MRI. Magnetic resonance imaging, also called *MRI*, is a diagnostic tool widely used today. It is not an X-ray. At this time, no harmful effects in pregnancy have been reported from its use, but pregnant women are advised to avoid an MRI during the first trimester of pregnancy for the safety of the fetus.

Pap Smear

A Pap smear removes some cells from your cervix and tests them for abnormal cells. You may have a Pap smear at your first prenatal appointment. If it has been a year or more since you had the test, you should have a Pap smear. If you had a normal Pap smear in the last few months, you won't need one. The goal of a Pap smear is to find problems early so they can be dealt with more easily.

Abnormal Pap smear. If you are told your Pap smear wasn't normal, you may or may not need a biopsy. It depends on how serious the problem might be. Usually a biopsy is not done while you're pregnant. Your doctor will probably wait until after your pregnancy for further testing. Instead of removing tissue for a biopsy, he or she may do a colposcopy (a very careful look at the cervix). An abnormal Pap smear during pregnancy must be handled carefully.

Home Uterine Monitoring

With home uterine monitoring, contractions of a pregnant woman's uterus are monitored in her home. This type of testing or monitoring is used when the doctor believes there could be a problem with premature labor.

A recording of uterine contractions is transmitted from the woman's home by telephone to a center where contractions can be evaluated. With the use of a personal computer, your doctor may be able to view the recordings at his or her own home or office.

Conditions that require home uterine monitoring include:
- previous preterm delivery
- infections in the mother-to-be
- premature rupture of membranes
- pregnancy-induced hypertension
- multiple fetuses

Nonstress Test

A *nonstress test* is a procedure done in the doctor's office, the labor room or the delivery room. While you are lying down, a fetal monitor is attached to your abdomen. Every time you feel the baby move, you push a button to make a mark on the monitor paper. At the same time, the fetal monitor records the baby's heartbeat on the same paper.

Information gained from a nonstress test gives reassurance that your baby is doing OK. If the test reports things are not OK, additional tests are done, including a biophysical profile or a contraction stress test.

Repeated Pelvic Exam

A pelvic exam is needed late in pregnancy because it reveals a lot of things, including:

- whether the baby is lying head-first or is in a breech position (presentation of the baby)
- how much the cervix has opened (dilation of the cervix)
- how much the cervix has thinned (effacement)
- shape and size of your birth canal or pelvic bones
- how low the baby is in your birth canal (station)

After my pelvic exam, my doctor said I was "2 and 50%." Why did she tell me this?
This information is important for two reasons. First, it tells you your cervix is open 2cm and thinned out 50% or halfway. (This is not an indication of when your baby will be born.) Second, this information is helpful if you go to the hospital thinking you're in labor. At the hospital, you'll be checked again. Knowing your measurements at your last pelvic exam can help determine if you are in labor.

If your healthcare provider does a pelvic exam and tells you that you are not dilated and your cervix has not thinned out, it doesn't mean you have a lot longer to wait for labor to begin. The pelvic exam tells you where you are at that particular moment. No matter what the condition of your cervix, labor may begin at any time.

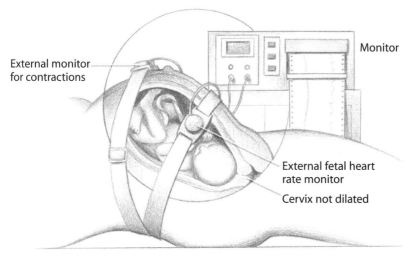

External monitor for contractions

Monitor

External fetal heart rate monitor

Cervix not dilated

External fetal monitoring with membranes intact (bag of waters has not broken).

Fetal Monitoring

In many hospitals, a baby's heartbeat is monitored throughout labor to detect problems early so they can be resolved. There are two types of fetal monitoring during labor—external fetal monitoring and internal fetal monitoring. See the illustrations at left and below.

External fetal monitoring. A belt with a receiver is strapped to your abdomen, and it records the baby's heartbeat. This type of monitoring can be done before your membranes rupture. See illustration, page 68.

Internal fetal monitoring. This is a more precise method of monitoring the baby. An electrode is placed on the fetal scalp to give a more exact reading of the fetal heart rate than external monitoring provides. Your membranes must be ruptured for internal monitoring. See illustration, below.

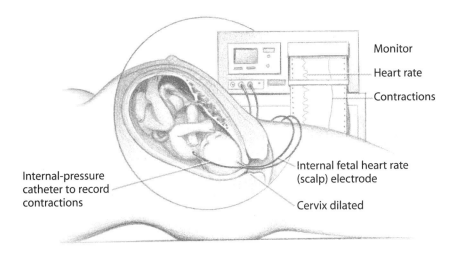

Monitor

Heart rate

Contractions

Internal fetal heart rate (scalp) electrode

Internal-pressure catheter to record contractions

Cervix dilated

Internal fetal monitoring during labor. Membranes (bag of waters) have ruptured.

Tests for Your Developing Baby

Biophysical Profile

This comprehensive test examines the fetus while it is still in your uterus. It helps determine the baby's health. The test is useful in evaluating an infant with intrauterine-growth retardation, when the mother-to-be is diabetic, with a pregnancy in which the baby doesn't move very much, in high-risk pregnancies and in overdue pregnancies.

This test measures and records
- fetal breathing movements
- body movements of the fetus
- fetal tone (tightening or contractibility of muscles)
- reactive fetal heart rate (increase in heart rate when baby moves)
- amount of amniotic fluid

Ultrasound, external monitors and observation are used to perform the test and make the different measurements.

Scoring. Each area is given a score of 0, 1 or 2. A total is obtained by adding all five scores together. The higher the score, the better the baby's condition. A low score may indicate problems.

If a baby receives a low score, the situation will be evaluated—the baby may need to be delivered immediately. If the score is reassuring, the test may be repeated at intervals. It may be necessary to repeat the test the following day. Your doctor will evaluate the scores, your health and the pregnancy before any decisions are made.

Contraction Stress Test

A *contraction stress test* (CST), also called a *stress test*, is another test that evaluates the baby's well-being in the womb.

If a woman has had problem pregnancies in the past or experiences medical problems during this pregnancy, her doctor may order the contraction stress test in the last few weeks of pregnancy. This is done when the nonstress test is not reassuring.

A monitor is placed on the woman's abdomen to record the fetal heart rate. Sometimes nipple stimulation is used to make the woman's uterus contract, or an I.V. is started and oxytocin is given in small amounts to make the uterus contract. Results indicate how well a baby will tolerate contractions and labor. If the baby doesn't respond well to the contractions, it can be a sign of fetal distress.

Fetal Blood Sampling

This test is another way of evaluating how well a baby is tolerating the stress of labor. To conduct the test, the membranes must have ruptured, and the cervix must be dilated at least 2cm. An instrument is placed inside the mother to make a small nick in the baby's scalp. The baby's blood is collected in a small tube, and its pH (acidity) is checked.

The pH level helps determine whether the baby is having trouble during labor and is under stress. The test helps the physician decide whether labor can continue or if a C-section is necessary.

Tests for Fetal Lung Maturity

A couple of tests can evaluate the maturity of fetal lungs. When a baby is born prematurely, a common problem is immaturity of the lungs, which can lead to development of respiratory-distress syndrome in the baby. This means the lungs are not completely mature at birth, and the baby cannot breathe on its own without assistance.

The respiratory system is the last fetal system to mature. If your doctor knows the baby's lungs are mature, it helps him or her in making a decision about early delivery, if it must be considered.

Two tests give doctors this information. Both are performed by amniocentesis. The **L/S ratio** measures the ratio of *lecithin* to *sphingomyelin*, two substances found in amniotic fluid. Results give the doctor an index of the maturity of the baby's lungs.

The **phosphatidyl glycerol (PG)** test gives either a positive or negative result. If the result shows *phosphatidyl glycerol* is present, there is greater assurance that the baby will *not* develop respiratory-distress syndrome.

If tests reveal the baby's lungs aren't mature enough, the first consideration is to avoid premature delivery, if possible. If premature delivery cannot be prevented, tests are done immediately after birth to determine if the baby has surfactant in its lungs. *Surfactant* is a chemical essential for respiration. If it is not present, the baby's doctor may introduce surfactant directly into the lungs of the newborn, preventing respiratory-distress syndrome. The baby will not have to be put on a respirator—it can breathe on its own!

Medications and Treatments for You 4

One of the most important pieces of advice I can give you during pregnancy is to be *extremely careful* about any medications you use. By "medications," I mean prescriptions your doctor may write for you *and* over-the-counter preparations, vitamins, minerals and herbs. Any of these substances may affect a developing baby. What may seem like only a little to you could pass through the placenta to your developing fetus.

If possible, discuss the medications you must take for medical conditions *before* you get pregnant. If you were unable to do this, discuss all medications (prescription and over-the-counter) you take on a regular basis at your first visit. Dosages may need to be adjusted, or you may have to stop taking a particular substance. However, *never* stop taking any medication you need for a chronic problem without consulting your doctor first! Some medication cannot and should not be stopped during pregnancy. Talk to your doctor before making any decisions about medication use.

Various medications you take affect the developing baby. See the chart on page 74, which lists some of these substances and their effects.

*Be **extremely** careful **about any medications you use—not only prescriptions your doctor may write for you, but also over-the-counter preparations, vitamins, minerals and herbs. Any of these substances may affect a developing baby.***

Possible Effects of Some Medications on the Fetus

Medication	Possible Effects
Androgens (male hormones)	Ambiguous genital development (depends on dose given and time when given)
Anticoagulants (warfarin)	Bone and hand abnormalities, intrauterine-growth retardation, central-nervous-system abnormalities, eye abnormalities
Antithyroid drugs (propylthiouracil, iodide, methimazole)	Hypothyroidism, fetal goiter
Chemotherapeutic drugs (methotrexate, aminopterin)	Increased risk of miscarriage
Isotretinoin (Accutane)	Increased miscarriage rate, nervous-system defects, facial defects, cleft palate
Lithium	Congenital heart disease
Phenytoin (Dilantin)	Growth retardation, mental retardation, microcephaly
Streptomycin	Hearing loss, cranial-nerve damage
Tetracycline	Hypoplasia of tooth enamel, discoloration of permanent teeth
Thalidomide	Severe limb defects
Trimethadione	Cleft lip, cleft palate, growth retardation, miscarriage
Valproic acid	Neural-tube defects

There are so many different kinds of medicine. How can I remember which are safe to take? You don't have to remember them all. Ask your doctor about those you use. Much of the information in this chapter probably won't apply to you, but it's good information to have at hand. The important thing is to call your doctor about any medication before you take it. And read labels!

Vitamin Usage during Pregnancy
(Also see the discussion of vitamins in chapter 5)

Prenatal Vitamins

It's very important to take your prenatal vitamins for your entire pregnancy. Sometimes late in pregnancy a woman stops taking them—she gets tired of taking them or she decides they aren't necessary. The vitamins and iron in prenatal vitamins are essential to your baby's well-being, so take them until your baby is born.

Folic Acid

Most women don't need to take extra folic acid during pregnancy if they follow a good diet and take prenatal vitamins as directed. Folic acid is found naturally in green leafy vegetables. Prenatal vitamins have 0.8 to 1mg of folic acid in each pill, which should be sufficient for a normal pregnancy.

Studies indicate a woman who has had a baby with a neural-tube defect, such as spina bifida, may be able to reduce her chances of having another baby with the same problem if she takes extra folic acid before pregnancy and throughout early pregnancy.

As of 1998, many products have been enhanced with folic acid. These foods include staples, such as some bread products, rice, cereals, noodles, farina and cornmeal. Read labels.

Prescription and Nonprescription Medications during Pregnancy

Prescription Medications

Discuss *all* medications (prescription and over-the-counter) you take on a regular basis at your first prenatal visit. This is an extremely important part of your prenatal care. You may need to have your dosage adjusted, you may have to stop taking a particular substance, or certain conditions may require additional medication.

Thyroid medication. It's important to continue taking your thyroid medication throughout your pregnancy. Be sure your doctor knows what you take. Thyroid hormone is made in the thyroid gland. This hormone affects your entire body and is important in

your metabolism. Thyroid hormone is also important in your ability to get pregnant. Don't stop taking or change your dose of thyroid hormone without talking with your doctor.

Thyroxin (medication for low thyroid or hypothyroid) is safe to take during pregnancy.

Propylthiouracil (high-thyroid or hyperthyroid medication) passes to the baby; you will probably be given the lowest amount possible during your pregnancy.

Lupus medication. The medication used to treat lupus is steroids; the primary steroid given is prednisone. Many studies have been done on the safety of prednisone during pregnancy, and it has been found to be safe.

Prozac™. Studies indicate Prozac is safe for use during pregnancy.

Skin medication. Accutane® (retinoic acid isotretinoin) is a common treatment for acne. However, pregnant women must *not* take it! There is a higher frequency of miscarriage and malformation of the fetus if a woman takes Accutane during the first trimester of pregnancy.

Tetracycline, also commonly used to treat acne, should not be taken during pregnancy because it can cause discoloration of your baby's permanent teeth later in life. (For that reason, tetracycline must not be prescribed for any child under age 8.)

Any type of medication you use can get into your bloodstream and could be passed to your baby. Retin-A, which some women use on their skin, should be avoided during pregnancy because we do not know its effects on the fetus at this time.

> **I occasionally use a steroid cream for a skin condition. Can I use it during pregnancy?**
> Discuss this with your doctor. There may be another preparation you can use that is considered safer during pregnancy.

Nonprescription or Over-the-Counter Medications

Although they do not require a prescription, over-the-counter (OTC) medications should be taken with care during pregnancy. Many OTCs contain aspirin, caffeine or phenacetin—all should be avoided during pregnancy. Limit your use of cough syrups, which may contain as much as 25% alcohol.

Be careful with medications containing ibuprofen, such as Advil®, Motrin® and Rufen®. Avoid newer medicines, such as Aleve® and Orudis®, until we know more about them and their safety in pregnancy.

Read package labels and ask your doctor or pharmacist before taking anything.

Any type of medication you use can get into your bloodstream and could be passed to your baby.

Safe nonprescription preparations. OTC medications that are safe include acetaminophen (Tylenol), some antacids (Amphojel, Gelusil, Maalox, milk of magnesia), throat lozenges (Sucrets®), some decongestants (Sudafed®) and some cough medicines (Robitussin®).

Aspirin. Almost any medication you take when you are pregnant passes to your baby or has some effect on your pregnancy. Discuss aspirin use with your doctor.

> **Won't my doctor or the nurses get mad if I call them about every medication I'm thinking of taking?**
> No. They would rather answer a question about medication use before you take something have you than worry about its effect on your baby after you have taken it.

I usually take a lot of vitamins, but my doctor advised me to take only a prenatal vitamin during pregnancy. Why? Too much of a good thing can be harmful. Some vitamins accumulate in body tissues when taken in megadoses and can have an adverse effect on you and your baby. Researchers believe that megadoses of vitamin A can cause birth defects when taken during pregnancy. In addition, vitamins D, E and K in megadoses can be harmful. Follow your doctor's advice, take a prenatal vitamin and eat nutritious, well-balanced meals to get the vitamins and minerals you and your baby need.

Can Birth-Control Methods Affect Pregnancy?

Some women who discover they are pregnant have been practicing birth control. They worry about the effect birth-control pills, IUDs and spermicide may have on their pregnancy.

Birth-Control Pills

Some women who discover they are pregnant have been practicing birth control.

If you get pregnant while taking birth-control pills, stop taking the pills, and notify your doctor. Any method of contraception can fail; the chance of failure with birth-control pills is between 1 and 3%. There is a small increase in problems for the fetus if you take birth-control pills while you're pregnant. It is not cause for great alarm, but discuss it with your doctor.

IUDs

If you become pregnant while using an IUD, notify your doctor immediately. You will need to discuss whether the IUD should be removed. Most doctors usually attempt to remove the IUD, if possible. The risk for miscarriage is higher if your IUD is left in place. The risk for ectopic pregnancy is also higher if you get pregnant with an IUD.

Spermicides

Spermicides have not been shown to be harmful to a developing fetus.

Immunizations and Vaccinations in Pregnancy

Be careful about immunizations and vaccinations during pregnancy. Some immunizations may harm the developing fetus and should not be received by a pregnant woman. The risk of exposure to various diseases is an important consideration. Not all vaccines harm the fetus. That's why it is so important to discuss this concern with your doctor.

Sometimes immunization is needed. Once your doctor determines you have been exposed to a disease, or exposure is possible, he or she will weigh the risk of the disease against the potential harmful effects of the immunization.

Some vaccines are not harmful to a fetus and may be used without problems.

There are vaccines you should never receive if you are pregnant. Avoid vaccinations for measles, mumps and rubella (MMR), poliomyelitis and yellow fever. You should receive primary vaccine against polio only if your risk of exposure is high; for example, if you are traveling to a high-risk area.

Few vaccines are considered safe for a pregnant woman. The only vaccines generally regarded as safe during pregnancy are tetanus, diphtheria and rabies. Others may be safe, but we are unsure about them at this time, so avoid them.

If you are unsure if you might need a vaccine and are pregnant, talk to your healthcare provider. If you don't think you are pregnant, it would still be wise to have a pregnancy test and to be using reliable contraception before receiving a vaccine.

Nutrition, Exercise and Weight Management 5

Eating healthfully, exercising and controlling your weight during pregnancy go a long way toward giving your baby a healthy start in life. The foods you eat help your baby develop and grow. By eating healthfully, you will provide your baby with the nutrients it needs to build its bones and organs. Exercising during pregnancy keeps you in good shape and ready to do the work of labor and delivery. Controlling your weight (not gaining too much weight but gaining enough) makes sure your developing baby is getting the nutrients it needs.

One study showed 95% of the women who had good-to-excellent diets delivered babies in good-to-excellent health. Only 8% of those women who ate poor diets (lots of junk food) had babies in good-to-excellent health. One of your main goals in pregnancy is to give birth to the healthiest baby you can. Your nutrition during pregnancy has a great effect on your baby's health. Exercise and weight control add to your overall health and thus to the health of your baby.

I've heard that during pregnancy I'm "eating for two." What does that mean?

The old adage "a pregnant woman is eating for two" means you must provide good nutrition for yourself and for your growing baby. However, many women think it means they can eat twice as much, which is incorrect!

Some women get the false idea they can eat all they want during pregnancy. Don't fall into this trap! You don't want to gain more weight than your doctor recommends during pregnancy—it can make you uncomfortable and it is harder for you to lose the extra pounds after your baby is born.

Most experts agree a normal-weight pregnant woman needs to increase her caloric intake by 300 to 800 calories a day.

Increase the number of calories you consume now you're pregnant. Most experts agree a normal-weight pregnant woman needs to increase her caloric intake by 300 to 800 calories a day. These extra calories are important for tissue growth in you and your baby. Your baby uses the energy from your calories to create and to store protein, fat and carbohydrates, and to provide energy for its own body processes. Expect some weight gain during your pregnancy—it's natural and normal.

Eat a variety of foods every day to supply you with the nutrients you need. You'll want to eat dairy products, protein foods, fruits and vegetables, and breads and cereals.

I'm 11 weeks pregnant and had my cholesterol checked. It was higher than the last time I had it checked. Is that normal?
Yes. Cholesterol levels usually increase during pregnancy and nursing because of hormonal changes.

Cravings

For many women, cravings during pregnancy are normal. Cravings for particular foods during pregnancy can be both good and bad. If you crave foods that are nutritious and healthy, eat them in moderate amounts. If you crave foods that are high in sugar and fat, and loaded with empty calories, be very careful about eating them.

No one knows why some women develop cravings during pregnancy, especially cravings for foods they might not normally eat. But many believe it is because of the hormonal and emotional changes that occur during pregnancy. It's not uncommon during pregnancy to be nauseated by foods you love to eat normally.

The hormones of pregnancy have a significant impact on the gastrointestinal tract, which can affect your reaction to certain foods.

I've found I want to eat late at night, even though I've never felt hungry at night before. Should I?
Late-night nutritious snacks are beneficial for some women, especially if they must eat many small meals a day. However, many women should not snack at night because they don't *need* the extra calories. Food in the stomach late at night may also cause more distress if heartburn or nausea and vomiting are problems.

Artificial Sweeteners

Aspartame and saccharin are the two most widely used artificial sweeteners. Recently there has been controversy over the safety of aspartame. I advise you to substitute foods that do not contain the sweeteners for products you usually use because currently we just don't know about its safety for pregnant women and their developing babies.

Also, aspartame is a source of phenylalanine in the diet. Pregnant women who suffer from phenylketonuria must follow a low-phenylalanine diet or their babies may be born mentally retarded and suffer from delayed development.

Saccharin is not used as much today as in the past, but it is still found in many foods, beverages and other substances. The Center for Science in the Public Interest reports saccharin is not safe for use during pregnancy. Without further evidence, it is probably better to avoid using this product while you're pregnant.

Is it OK to use the microwave during my pregnancy?
We don't know for sure if there is danger to your pregnancy from being around a microwave oven, so follow the directions provided with your microwave oven. Don't stand next to or directly in front of it while it's in use.

A Healthy Eating Plan

**It's a good idea to eat a variety of foods throughout your pregnancy.
Below is a list of daily servings from six food groups.**

Dairy products—4 to 5 servings a day
Vegetables—at least 4 servings a day
Fruits—2 to 4 servings a day
Protein sources—3 to 4 servings a day
Carbohydrates (breads, cereal, pasta and rice)—6 to 11 servings a day
Fats/flavorings—3 to 5 servings a day

Dairy Products

Foods you might choose from this group, and their serving sizes, include:

- *3/4 cup (336g) cottage cheese*
- *2 ounces (56g) of processed cheese (such as American cheese)*
- *1-1/2 ounces (42g) natural cheese (such as Cheddar)*
- *1 ounce (28g) hard cheese (such as Parmesan or Romano)*
- *1 cup (240ml) pudding or custard*
- *1 cup (240ml) milk*
- *1 cup (240ml) yogurt*

To keep the fat content low, choose skim milk, low-fat yogurt and low-fat cheese instead of whole milk and ice cream.

I know milk products are a good source of calcium, but I've heard I could get something called "listeriosis" from some milk products. Is this true?

I advise you to avoid unpasteurized milk and any foods made from unpasteurized milk. Also avoid soft cheeses, such as Brie, Camembert, feta and Roquefort. These products are a common source of a form of food poisoning called *listeriosis*.

In addition, undercooked poultry, meat, seafood and hot dogs can contain listeriosis. Cook all meat and seafood thoroughly before eating to avoid this problem.

Vegetables

Foods you might choose from this group, and their serving sizes, include:

- *3/4 cup (180ml) vegetable juice*
- *1/2 cup (120ml) broccoli, carrots or other vegetable, cooked or raw*
- *1 medium baked potato*
- *1 cup (240ml) raw, leafy vegetables (salad greens)*

Eating a variety of vegetables gives you a good nutritional balance. Eat at least one vegetable a day that is high in folic acid, such as green leafy vegetables.

Fruit

Some foods you might choose from this group, and their serving sizes, include:

- *1/2 cup (120ml) canned or cooked fruit*
- *3/4 cup (180ml) grapes*
- *1/2 cup (120ml) fruit juice*
- *1 medium banana, orange or apple*
- *1/4 cup (60ml) dried fruit*

Include one or two servings of a fruit rich in vitamin C, such as orange

Orange juice is high in folic acid.

juice or orange slices. Fresh fruits are also a good source of fiber. Fiber is important during your pregnancy if you suffer from constipation.

Protein

During pregnancy, you need protein for growth and development of the embryo/fetus and growth of your placenta, uterus and breasts. The recommended amount of protein in pregnancy is 6 to 7 ounces (168 to 196g) a day.

Foods you might choose from this group, and their serving sizes, include:
- 2 tablespoons (30ml) peanut butter
- 1/2 cup (120ml) cooked dried beans
- 2 to 3 ounces (56 to 84g) cooked meat
- 1 egg

Poultry, fish, lean cuts of red meat, dry beans, eggs, nuts and seeds are all good sources of protein.

I really love protein foods that have a lot of fat, like bacon and cheese. What can I substitute for them?
Choose foods that are high in protein but low in fat, such as skinless chicken and turkey, tuna packed in water, cod, ground turkey and low-fat (1%) or fat-free (skim) milk.

Carbohydrate—Bread, Pasta, Cereal, Rice

There is no recommended dietary allowance (RDA) for carbohydrate intake during pregnancy. Most physicians believe carbohydrates should make up about 60% of the total number of calories in your diet. If you

eat 2000 calories a day on average, you would consume about 1200 calories as carbohydrate calories.

Foods you might choose from this group, and their serving sizes, include:
- 1 large tortilla
- 1/2 cup (120ml) cooked pasta, cereal or rice
- 1 ounce (28g) ready-to-eat cereal
- 1/2 bagel
- 1 slice of bread
- 1 medium roll

I love junk food. Do I have to give it up completely?
Consider not eating most junk food while you're pregnant. The foods we consider "junk food" are usually high-calorie, high-fat foods that contain little nutrition for you or your baby. It's probably OK to eat junk food once in a while, but *don't make it a regular part of your diet.*

Fat/Flavorings

Foods you might choose from this group, and their serving sizes, include:
- 1 tablespoon (15ml) sugar or honey
- 1 tablespoon (15ml) olive oil or other type of oil
- 1 pat butter or margarine
- 1 tablespoon (15ml) jelly or jam
- 1 tablespoon (15ml) prepared salad dressing

Everyone's diet has to include a little fat. Don't avoid all fats, but include them only in moderate amounts. Measure how much you use of each, and use them sparingly!

Inadequate fat intake is rarely a concern for most people; usually fat intake is excessive. There is no recommended daily amount for fat intake during pregnancy.

Drink Your Water!

Drink 6 to 8 glasses (64 ounces; 1.9 liters) of liquid every day. Water is the best choice.

I advise all my patients to drink plenty of water every day. Some patients tell me they don't like drinking so much water, but it really is *important* during pregnancy. Water is necessary for your body to process nutrients, develop new cells and sustain blood volume. You will probably feel better if you drink more fluid than you normally do. Your blood volume increases during pregnancy; drinking extra fluids helps you keep up with this change.

Drinking water throughout the day can help you in other ways too. Many women who suffer from headaches, uterine cramping and various other problems during pregnancy find increasing their fluid intake helps resolve some of their symptoms. It also helps avoid bladder infections.

Drink 6 to 8 glasses (64 ounces; 1.9 liters) of liquid every day. Water is the best choice. When your urine is light-yellow to clear, you're getting enough water. Dark-yellow urine is a sign you need to add more fluid to your diet.

If I drink beverages that normally act as diuretics, such as coffee, will it counteract the increase in fluids?
No, it will not.

It's not too hard to drink this much extra fluid. Some women drink water, one glass at a time, throughout the day. (Decrease your intake later in the day so you don't have to go to the bathroom all night long.)

Eating Out

More people eat out at least some of their weekly meals. It's OK to eat out at restaurants; just be a little more careful about what you eat. Avoid raw meats or raw seafood, such as sushi. You may find certain foods do not agree with you; avoid them.

Fish, fresh vegetables and salads are usually your best bets, but be careful with calorie-loaded salad dressings if excessive weight gain is a concern. Avoid highly spicy foods or foods that contain a lot of sodium, such as some Chinese food and soy sauce. You may experience water retention after eating these foods.

About Caffeine

Drinking as few as 4 cups of coffee a day (800mg of caffeine) by a pregnant woman has been associated with decreased birthweight and a smaller head size in newborns. Although an exact "toxic" amount for caffeine has not been determined, it makes sense to limit your caffeine intake.

Some medications, such as cough medicines and headache medicines, contain a lot of caffeine. It's important to read labels.

Caffeine is found in many beverages and foods, including coffee, tea, cola drinks and chocolate. Some medications, such as cough medicines and headache medicines, also contain a lot of caffeine. It's important to read labels.

Caffeine is a central-nervous-system stimulant. There are no known benefits for you or your unborn fetus from caffeine. Caffeine can also affect calcium metabolism in both you and your baby.

Limit your caffeine intake during pregnancy and if you breast-feed. Read labels on foods, beverages and over-the-counter medications to find out about caffeine content. Eliminate as much caffeine from your diet as possible.

Where can I get more information on nutrition while I'm pregnant?
The **National Center for Nutrition and Dietetics' Consumer Nutrition Hotline** is a toll-free number you can call to speak directly with a registered dietitian: **(800) 366-1655**. This excellent resource can provide you with information on all aspects of nutrition, whether or not you are pregnant.

Vitamins and Minerals

As I said before, it's very important to take your prenatal vitamin *throughout* pregnancy. Prenatal vitamins contain the recommended daily amounts of vitamins and minerals you need during pregnancy. They are taken to ensure your health and your baby's health. However, they aren't a substitute for food or a good diet.

The main difference between prenatal vitamins and multivitamins is that prenatal vitamins also contain iron and folic-acid supplements.

The only mineral that needs to be supplemented during pregnancy is *iron*. The average woman's diet seldom contains enough iron to meet the increased demands of pregnancy. Blood volume increases by 50% in a normal pregnancy, and iron is an important part of blood production in your body.

Iron

You may be advised to take iron supplements during pregnancy. Prenatal vitamins contain some iron but you may need to take extra iron. Your healthcare provider will test you for anemia early in your pregnancy. If he or she determines you need an iron supplement, you must take it for your health and your baby's health. Most prenatal vitamins contain 60mg of elemental iron.

Some women worry that taking iron may cause constipation. Constipation can be a side effect. Work with your doctor to find the correct amount of iron to help lessen side effects.

Fluoride

The use of fluoride and fluoride supplementation during pregnancy is controversial. Some researchers believe fluoride supplementation during pregnancy results in improved teeth in your child, but not everyone agrees. However, no harm to the baby has been shown from fluoride supplementation in a pregnant woman. Some prenatal vitamins contain fluoride.

Sodium

Sodium is a chemical that works to maintain the proper amount of fluid in your body. During pregnancy, it can also affect your baby's system. Sodium is found in salty foods (such as potato chips and dill pickles) and in processed foods, from soups to meats. You need some sodium; you just don't need too much. Read food labels to discover just how much you're getting!

During pregnancy, keep your consumption of sodium under 3g (3000mg) a day. Too much sodium causes water retention, swelling and high blood pressure. Any of these can be a problem for you.

It's difficult to avoid something unless you know where to find it. With sodium, that can be tricky. It's in the salt shaker and in salty-tasting foods, such as pretzels, chips and salted nuts. (Table salt is about half sodium.) You may be surprised by the amount of sodium present in foods that don't taste salty.

Sodium is found in canned and processed products, fast foods, cereals, desserts and even soft drinks and some medications! See the chart opposite for a listing of the sodium content in a variety of foods. Read labels!

Sodium Content of Some Foods

Fresh or Minimally Prepared Foods

1 cup apple juice	2mg
3 apricots (fresh)	1mg
1 medium banana	1mg
8 ounces of bluefish	170mg
1 head Boston lettuce	15mg
1 medium carrot	35mg
1 large egg	70mg
1 cup green beans (frozen)	2mg
3 ounces ground beef	60mg
1 lemon	1mg
1 cup whole milk	120mg
1 cup oatmeal (long-cooked)	10mg
1 cup orange juice	2mg
1 peach	1mg
3 ounces pork	65mg

Prepared Foods

3 ounces bacon	1400mg
1 cup baked beans	100mg
1 slice white bread	100mg
1 frozen chicken dinner	1400mg
1 cup chicken-noodle soup	1050mg
1 cinnamon roll	630mg
1 tablespoon cooking oil	0mg
3 ounces corned beef	1500mg
1 cup corn flakes	305mg
1 cup green beans (canned)	320mg
1 cup all-purpose flour	2mg
1 cup self-rising flour	1565mg
1 tablespoon Italian dressing	250mg
1 tablespoon catsup	155mg
1 olive	165mg
1 dill pickle	1930mg
1 cup pudding, instant	335mg
1 cup puffed rice	1mg
1 cup tomato juice	640mg

Fast Foods

1 Arby's turkey sandwich	1060mg
1 Burger King Whopper	675mg
1 Dairy Queen hot dog	990mg
1 KFC dinner (3 pcs chicken)	2285mg
1 Taco Bell Enchirito	1175mg
1 McDonald's Big Mac	1010mg

Exercise

Experts agree that exercise during pregnancy is safe and beneficial for most pregnant women, if it is done properly. This is definitely an area to discuss with your healthcare provider at the beginning of your pregnancy.

Regular, moderate exercise during pregnancy can benefit you in many ways. It can help

- relieve backache
- prevent constipation and varicose veins
- strengthen muscles needed for delivery
- leave you in better shape after delivery
- help you feel better about yourself

The goal of exercising during pregnancy is overall good health. It will make you feel better physically, and it can give you an emotional boost.

Exercise was not always approved for a pregnant woman. In the past, doctors were concerned about the redirection of blood flow from the fetus to the pregnant woman's muscles during exercise. This does occur to a small degree, but it is not harmful to the fetus in a normal pregnancy.

Starting a Program

Some women become interested in exercising during pregnancy to help them feel better. **If you've never exercised before, you must discuss it with your doctor before you begin. Pregnancy is not the time to begin a vigorous exercise program.**

If you've never exercised before, walking and swimming are excellent forms of exercise. Riding a stationary bike or walking on a treadmill can also be enjoyable and beneficial.

Don't be afraid that exercise might cause you to do something to hurt your pregnancy. It's a good idea to be fit and to exercise when you're pregnant. If you're fit, you'll do better with weight gain during pregnancy, be able to do the work of labor and delivery better, and feel better sooner after the birth.

Most experts recommend reducing your exercise to 70 to 80% of your prepregnancy level. If you have problems with bleeding or cramping, or have had problem pregnancies before, you will need to modify your exercise with your doctor's advice.

Someone told me exercising can cause early labor. Should I believe her?
It was once believed exercise could cause preterm labor because there is a temporary increase in uterine activity following exercise. However, in a normal pregnancy, this does not cause a problem.

Exercise and Heart Rate

During pregnancy, your heart rate is higher; you don't have to exercise as vigorously to reach your target-heart-rate range. Be careful not to stress your cardiovascular system. If your heart rate is too high, slow down but don't stop exercising completely. Continue exercising, but exercise at a more moderate rate.

If your heart rate is low, and you don't feel too winded, pick up the pace a bit, but don't overdo it. Check your pulse rate again in a few minutes to make sure you aren't overexerting. During pregnancy, check your pulse rate fairly often when you exercise. You'll be surprised at how fast your pulse can increase during a pregnancy workout.

I read that my baby's heart rate increases when mine does during exercise. Can this cause a problem?
The fetal heart rate increases somewhat during and immediately after exercise, but it stays within the normal fetal range of 120 to 160 beats a minute. This should not cause problems for you or your baby.

Discuss exercise with your healthcare practitioner at your first prenatal visit. If you decide later to start or to change your exercise program, consult your physician before you begin. Some women should not exercise during pregnancy. If you experience any of the following symptoms, do not exercise during pregnancy:

- a history of an incompetent cervix, preterm labor or repeated miscarriages
- high blood pressure early in pregnancy
- multiple fetuses
- diagnosed heart disease
- pre-eclampsia
- vaginal bleeding

As your pregnancy progresses and your body changes, you need to change your exercise habits. Your center of gravity changes, so you have to adapt your exercise to account for that. As your abdomen grows larger, you won't be able to do some activities comfortably. You may have to stop other activities entirely.

How do I figure out my heart rate?
When you're pregnant, your pulse rate (heart rate) should not exceed 140 beats a minute for more than 15 minutes during a workout. Check your pulse with the following steps.
- Look at a clock with a second hand.
- Place the index and middle fingers of one hand on the side of your neck where you can feel your pulse.
- After finding your pulse, watch the second hand until it reaches the 12.
- Begin counting the pulse beats until the second hand reaches the 2 (10 seconds).
- Multiply that number by 6 to find your heart rate.

Feeling Out of Breath

Your growing abdomen can put a strain on your respiratory system, causing you to feel out of breath sooner than normal. When you exercise, don't work to the point that you can't talk and you have trouble breathing. This indicates you're working too strenuously; cut back on your workout.

Feeling Warm

When you're pregnant, you normally feel warmer than usual. You'll feel warmer still when you exercise, so try to avoid becoming overheated during workouts. Work out in a well-ventilated room, and drink lots of water while you exercise.

I'm 9 weeks pregnant and haven't exercised in years. Can I start now?
It is possible to start exercising now, but take it slowly. Discuss your desire to exercise with your healthcare provider before you begin any program. If you don't have problems with your pregnancy, you should be able to exercise as long as you are comfortable. The key is not to try to do too much too fast. The best exercises for you are walking and swimming.

Sports

If you are used to playing a competitive sport, such as tennis, you should be able to continue to play, but expect to reduce the competition level. The point to remember is *don't get carried away or overwork yourself.*

Some less strenuous sports are listed below. Most are generally considered safe for a normal, low-risk pregnancy:

The best exercises during pregnancy are walking and swimming.

- walking
- swimming
- low-impact aerobics designed especially for pregnancy
- water aerobics
- stationary bicycling
- regular cycling (if you're experienced)
- jogging (if you jogged before pregnancy)
- tennis (played moderately)
- walking on a treadmill
- using a stair stepper or stair climber
- riding a recumbent bike
- using a Nordic Track® ski machine
- weight training, if you have been active in it before pregnancy

Pregnancy is a time to maintain your workout and not increase it. After the first half of the pregnancy, as the uterus enlarges, it is better not to lie flat on your back.

During pregnancy, avoid the riskier sports listed below:

- scuba diving
- water-skiing
- surfing
- horseback riding
- downhill skiing or cross-country skiing
- any contact sport

Aerobics

Aerobics classes specifically designed for pregnant women are a good choice. They concentrate on the unique needs of the pregnant woman, such as strengthening abdominal muscles and improving posture. When choosing a class, be sure the instructor has proper training and the class meets the exercise guidelines developed by the American College of Obstetricians and Gynecologists. To obtain a copy of the guidelines, write to:

ACOG Exercise Program
4021 Rosewood Ave.
Los Angeles, CA 90004
Tel: (213) 383-2862

Eating and Exercise

Your nutrition needs increase during pregnancy, and you burn extra calories during exercise, so eat enough calories to ensure a balanced diet. As I've already discussed, a woman of normal weight before pregnancy needs to eat between 300 and 800 extra calories a day during pregnancy. Exercising may increase your needs.

Effects of Exercise on Labor and Delivery

Exercise during pregnancy should help you have an easier time with your labor and delivery. Many believe that women who exercise during pregnancy have a shorter recovery time after birth. Exercise keeps you fit so you can get back in shape more quickly.

Exercise Guidelines

As always, be sure you consult with your physician before you begin any exercise program. Follow the tips below to keep you healthy and in good shape.

- Stop immediately and consult your physician if you experience any problems.
- Exercise at least 3 times a week for 20 to 30 minutes each time.

- Start your exercise routine with a 5-minute warm-up and end with a 5-minute cool-down period.
- Wear comfortable clothes that offer support, including a support bra and good athletic shoes.
- Drink plenty of water during exercise.
- Don't exercise strenuously for more than 15 to 20 minutes.
- Check your pulse rate; keep it below 140 beats a minute.
- Don't exercise in hot, humid weather.
- After 16 weeks of pregnancy, avoid exercises that require you to lie on your back.
- Never allow your body temperature to rise above 100.4F (38C).

What kind of problems should I watch out for while I'm exercising?

Be aware of any unusual occurrences, and report them to your doctor immediately. Be careful about the following:

- pain
- bleeding
- dizziness
- extreme shortness of breath
- heart palpitations
- faintness
- abnormally rapid heart rate
- back pain
- pubic pain
- difficulty walking

Weight Management

Nearly all my patients are interested in their weight during pregnancy. Many have a difficult time seeing their pregnancy weight gain in a positive light. But proper weight gain at this time is vitally important to your baby's health—and your own. Below are some of the most important and interesting facts to know regarding weight management during pregnancy. Don't hesitate to discuss with your own doctor any "weighty" questions you may have.

Normal Weight Gain

Weight gain for a normal-weight woman during pregnancy is 25 to 35 pounds (11.25 to 15kg). This sounds like a lot, but if you add up weight for the baby, placenta, amniotic fluid and changes in you, it really isn't that much. See the chart on this page for general guidelines to weight gain during pregnancy.

Sometimes patients ask me how they are supposed to watch their weight and still eat 300 to 800 extra calories a day.

General Weight-Gain Guidelines for Pregnancy

Current Weight	Acceptable Gain
Underweight	28 to 40 pounds (12.6 to 18 kg)
Normal weight	25 to 35 pounds (11.25 to 15.75 kg)
Overweight	15 to 25 pounds (6.75 to 11.25 kg)

Sometimes patients ask me how they are supposed to watch their weight gain and still eat 300 to 800 extra calories a day. The answer is, not every woman needs to increase her food intake by 300 to 800 calories; that's a general guideline only. Take your individual situation into account. If you are underweight when you begin pregnancy, you may have to eat more than 800 extra calories each day. If you're overweight when you get pregnant, you may have less need for extra calories.

Underweight before pregnancy. If you start your pregnancy underweight, the normal weight gain is 28 to 40 pounds (12.6 to 18kg). It is important for you to eat regularly and nutritiously, even if you are not used to doing so.

Overweight before pregnancy. If you're overweight before pregnancy, you probably should not gain as much as other women during pregnancy. Acceptable weight gain is 15 to 25 pounds (6.75 to 11.25kg). This is an individual situation to discuss with your doctor. It is important for you to eat nutritious, well-balanced meals during your pregnancy. Do not diet!

The key to good nutrition and weight management is to eat a balanced diet throughout pregnancy.

The key to good nutrition and weight management is to eat a balanced diet throughout your pregnancy.

Eat the foods you need to help your baby grow and develop, but choose wisely. For example, if you're overweight, avoid peanut butter and other nuts as a protein source; choose water-packed tuna or low-fat cheeses instead. If you're underweight, select ice cream and milkshakes as dairy-food sources.

Distribution of Weight Gained during Pregnancy

Weight	Location
7-1/2 pounds (3.38kg)	Baby
7 to 10 pounds (3.15 to 4.5kg)	Maternal stores (fat, protein and other nutrients)
4 pounds (1.8kg)	Increased fluid volume
2 pounds (0.9kg)	Uterus
2 pounds (0.9kg)	Amniotic fluid
2 pounds (0.9kg)	Breast enlargement
1-1/2 pounds (0.68kg)	Placenta

Fear of Fat

Getting on the scale and seeing your weight increase is hard for some women, especially those who have to watch their weight closely. Remind yourself it is a normal part of pregnancy, and it is necessary for your baby's health!

You can control your weight gain by eating carefully and nutritiously; you don't have to gain an extra 50 pounds (22.5kg). But you must gain enough weight to meet the needs of pregnancy. Be prepared to gain weight while you're pregnant.

Thirty years ago, it was fairly normal for pregnant women to be allowed to gain just 13 to 15 pounds for their entire pregnancy. We have learned a lot about pregnancy because of advances in technology and information from research and other sources. We realize today that it is good for a woman to gain a sufficient amount of weight during pregnancy. The normal weight gain today during pregnancy (25 to 35 pounds; 11.25 to 15.75kg) is quite a change from 13 pounds (5.85kg)!

You say I should gain 25 to 30 pounds (11.25 to 15.7 kg) with my pregnancy. That sounds like a lot to me when the baby only weighs about 7 pounds (3.15kg). Where does all that weight go? The weight you gain is distributed as shown in the chart (left). As you can see, some weight will be lost during the birth process. More weight is often lost as your body readjusts to its nonpregnant state.

Some Weight Gain Each Week

As an average for a normal-weight woman, many healthcare providers suggest pregnant women gain 2/3 of a pound (10 ounces; 300g) a week until 20 weeks, then 1 pound (0.45kg) a week from 20 to 40 weeks. However, this varies for each woman. Your doctor can guide you.

One exception: It is common not to gain weight or even to lose a little weight early in pregnancy. Your healthcare provider will keep track of the change in your weight during your pregnancy.

It's all right to gain weight— it's for the health of your baby.

Weigh-in at Each Office Visit

Many of my patients hate to be weighed when they come to my office. Some ask if they can't just weigh themselves at home, then report their weight to me when they get to the office. I have to tell them "no." It's best to be weighed at the office. It's one way your doctor can tell that everything is progressing normally with your pregnancy. Although you may be shy about being weighed, it's an important part of your visit to the doctor. Your healthcare team weighs you to make sure everything is OK with your pregnancy.

It's best to be weighed at the office. It's one way your doctor can tell that everything is progressing normally with your pregnancy.

Fatigue, Work and Pregnancy 6

One comment I hear frequently is, "I'm exhausted! Will I ever feel normal again?" Let me assure you the fatigue you feel at the beginning of your pregnancy will ease, and you will no doubt feel much better soon. *Fatigue is a normal part of pregnancy*—you're not experiencing anything abnormal.

Fatigue may continue during your pregnancy, but for most women, it's worst early in pregnancy; then it gets better. Eating right, taking your prenatal vitamins and getting plenty of rest helps.

You may also feel concern about working while you're pregnant. In the past, women were told they couldn't work, but that's changed. With so many women working outside the home, we've been able to study how this activity affects pregnancy. Studies show that working under normal circumstances does not harm the developing baby, as long as you don't have a job that causes you to stand for exceptionally long periods of time or that requires you to lift or carry heavy objects.

Sleep and Rest

A pregnant woman needs more sleep than she does when she's not pregnant. In most cases, 8 to 10 hours of sleep a night will help you feel better. When you see your doctor, one of the first tests he or she will do is a hematocrit (a blood test) to check for anemia, which can also be a reason for feeling tired.

Getting Comfortable

Most women find it's harder to get comfortable as their pregnancy progresses. Lying directly on your stomach isn't a good idea. It puts a lot of pressure on your growing uterus, which will be a comfort problem later. The bigger you get, the harder it is to lie on your stomach.

Experiment with different positions when you rest. Lie on your side, with a pillow under your abdomen. Elevate your head and shoulders. Try to find a comfortable position. See the box on this page.

If experimenting with different positions doesn't help much, and you can't sleep enough at night to make yourself feel better, try taking naps during the day. If you can't nap, sit down and relax—listen to music or read, if that helps. When you relax, prop your feet above your chest, if possible, to help with swelling and to ease discomfort in your legs.

What is the best position for sleeping?
Learn to sleep on your side—you'll be glad you did as you get bigger. Use extra pillows to support your back so you don't lie flat on your back. Rest your top leg on another pillow. A "pregnancy pillow" that provides support for your entire body may help.

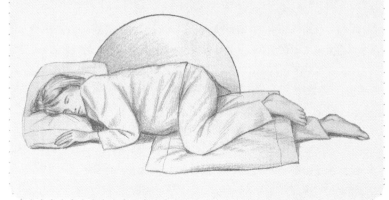

My sister said it's not good for me to lie on my back during pregnancy. Does she know what she's talking about?

It is best for you not to lie on your back when you sleep or rest after 16 weeks of pregnancy. As your uterus grows, lying on your back can place the uterus on top of important blood vessels (*inferior vena cava* and *aorta*) that run down the back of your abdomen. This can decrease circulation to your baby and to parts of your body. It may also be harder for you to breathe when you lie on your back.

Managing Stress

Feelings of stress aren't uncommon during pregnancy. They can make it hard to rest or sleep. Fortunately you can take steps to manage stress. The following breathing exercise can help you relax.

- Inhale slowly as you count to 4. Push out your abdomen as you breathe in.
- Let your shoulders and neck relax as you slowly exhale while counting to 6.
- Repeat as often as you need to.
- *Hint:* Play gentle, soothing music as you practice this exercise.

Another stress-reliever I recommend is to relax each muscle group with each deep breath. Start with the feet and work up through the legs, hands, arms, torso, shoulders, neck and face. Continue for 10 to 20 minutes. This exercise also helps when you're having trouble getting to sleep.

Swelling and Back Pain

Nearly every woman experiences backache at some time during pregnancy. It usually occurs as you get bigger. You may also experience backache after walking, bending, lifting, standing or excessive exercise. Be careful about lifting and bending. Do so correctly, lifting or bending from the knees while keeping your back straight.

You can treat backache with heat, rest and analgesics, such as acetaminophen (Tylenol). Special maternity girdles provide some support. Keep your weight under control, and participate in mild exercise, such as swimming, walking and stationary-bike riding. Lie on your side when resting or sleeping.

**My feet are huge—I can't wear any of my shoes.
What can I do?**
Some swelling in your feet is normal during pregnancy.
Wear sneakers, flats or shoes with low heels (no higher
than 2 inches). If swelling becomes extreme, especially
during the last trimester, consult your physician; it
could indicate a problem. Rest lying on your side as
frequently as possible. Expect to buy larger shoes
toward the end of your pregnancy.

Lower-back pain is common during pregnancy, but it could be an indication of a more serious problem, such as pyelonephritis or a kidney stone. If pain becomes constant or more severe, it's important to discuss with your doctor.

Sciatic-nerve pain may also be a problem during pregnancy. Sciatic-nerve pain is an occasional excruciating pain in your buttocks and down the back or the side of your leg. You may experience it as your pregnancy progresses. The sciatic nerve runs behind the uterus in the pelvis to your legs. We believe the pain is caused by pressure put on the nerve by the growing uterus. The best remedy is to lie on your *opposite* side to help relieve pressure on the nerve.

**Is it true that lying on my side in the third
trimester will help me control any swelling I have?**
Yes. By the third trimester, your uterus is large and
puts a lot of pressure on your blood vessels, which
blocks their flow. Lying or sleeping or your side
during the third trimester helps relieve this condition.

Working during Pregnancy

More than half of all women work outside the home; many pregnant women work and do well. If you are concerned about whether your job is safe for your pregnancy, discuss your particular situation with your healthcare provider. It may be difficult to know the specific risk of a particular job—the goal is to minimize the risk to you and your baby while still enabling you to work. The average healthy woman should be able to work at most jobs throughout her pregnancy.

My mother told me I shouldn't work during pregnancy. Is she right?
In the past, women were encouraged or even forced to stop working when they were pregnant. Today, many women work until they deliver their baby. Whether you work your entire pregnancy depends on your particular circumstances. If you are concerned, discuss it with your physician.

You will probably have to slow down if you continue to work. You may also have to take it a little easier; you may not be able to do some of the things you do when you aren't pregnant. You may have to ask for help with some of the tasks you are required to perform.

If possible, rest during your work day. Try to lie down during breaks or on your lunch hour. Even sitting in a quiet place such as in your car can be beneficial. Ten or 15 minutes of rest can make you feel better and restore your energy.

Can my work be hazardous to my pregnancy?
Certain factors may increase your risk of working during your pregnancy. If your job includes two or more of the following conditions, talk to your doctor:
• prolonged standing (more than 3 hours a day)
• work on an industrial machine, especially if it vibrates a great deal or requires strenuous effort to operate
• strenuous physical tasks, such as heavy lifting or heavy cleaning
• repetitious, tedious work, such as assembly-line jobs
• environmental factors, such as high noise levels or extreme temperatures
• long working hours
• shift changes

Stretch Your Legs

If you sit at a desk for your job, try to do some leg-stretching/foot exercises several times each hour. Remove your shoes before doing the following exercise: Extend your legs in front, then point your toes and flex your feet. Repeat this four or five times. It helps circulation in your feet and may prevent some swelling in your legs.

Benefit of Maternity Stockings

Whether you sit or stand at work, maternity stockings provide support for your legs. They can be helpful even if you don't work. Maternity stockings may be preferable to regular support stockings because they don't constrict your waist or abdomen. If you are concerned, discuss it with your healthcare provider. Maternity stockings are available at medical supply stores where you can be measured and fitted. A prescription may be necessary for your insurance to cover this cost.

Stay Calm!

Elevated hormones and the stress of being pregnant can trigger mood swings in you. You may also find you're more tired; it's normal. Take a break if any situation becomes more than you can bear.

Everybody at work seems to have advice for me. How do I handle this?
Unwelcome advice, unwarranted questions, even physical contact, are common during pregnancy. Use humor to deflect some of the questions. You can always listen, nod wisely and say "thanks," without making a commitment to follow unasked-for advice. You are in charge!

Special Situations

Standing. Studies show that women who stand all day have smaller babies. If you stand all day, you may have problems at the end of your pregnancy with your feet and ankles swelling. You may have to modify your work, lie down a couple of times during the day or work fewer hours.

Active jobs. If you have an active job—for example, working in a warehouse—avoid activities that involve climbing and balance, especially during the third trimester. Talk with your supervisor about eliminating these activities for now.

I know my center of gravity is changing. What's the best way for me to lift an object?
Do most of your lifting with your legs. Bend your knees to lift; don't bend at the waist. As your abdomen grows larger, don't lift anything weighing more than 30 pounds (13.6kg), including your older children.

Computer terminal. Some women worry about the effect working at a computer terminal might have on their baby. To date, there is no evidence that working at a computer terminal can harm a growing baby. However, if you work at a computer terminal, be aware of how long you sit and the way you sit.

Get up and move around regularly to stimulate your circulation— about once every 15 minutes. Take short walks frequently. Sit in a chair that offers good support for your back and legs. Don't slouch or cross your legs while sitting.

Harmful substances. According to Maureen Paul, M.D., M.P.H., director of the Occupational Reproductive Hazards Center at the University of Massachusetts, some substances can harm a developing fetus. The chart on page 108 describes various agents, their sources and the possible effects they may have on a growing baby.

You or your partner could bring home substances you are exposed to at work. This poses a potential danger. Substances may be brought into your home on your work clothes or the work clothes of someone else in your family. If you think you may be exposed to hazardous substances, be sure to discuss it with your physician.

Travel and Driving during Pregnancy

Travel during pregnancy can be fatiguing and frustrating, but if your pregnancy is normal, you should be able to travel during the first and second trimesters without too much trouble. Consult your physician if you plan to travel during your third trimester.

Take frequent breaks to stretch your legs during trips. Don't overdo—rest when possible. Avoid places where good medical care is not available or where changes in climate, food or altitude could cause you problems.

Driving is permitted, but always wear your seat belt!

Is it all right to fly?
Flying shouldn't cause you any problems. Try to reserve an aisle seat so you can stretch your legs and get up to walk more easily. Drink plenty of fluids, such as water and juice, because recirculated air in an airplane is extremely dry. Discuss any plans you have for flying with your physician. Some airlines may refuse to carry a pregnant passenger without written consent of her physician.

Travel in the First and Second Trimesters
Ask your doctor *before* you take a trip. Most will tell you it's OK to travel during pregnancy, but each situation is different. Some general considerations about traveling during pregnancy include the following.
- Don't plan a trip during your last month of pregnancy.
- If you're having problems, such as bleeding or cramping, don't travel.
- If you are uncomfortable or have problems with swelling, traveling, sitting in a car or doing a lot of walking may make things worse

(and it probably won't be much fun either).
- If your pregnancy is considered high risk, a trip during pregnancy is just not a good idea.
- Remember you are pregnant when you plan a trip. Be sensible in your planning, and take it easy.

Travel in the Third Trimester
In the third trimester, labor could begin at any time, your water could break or other problems could occur. Your doctor knows what has happened during your pregnancy and has a record of tests done—this knowledge is important. If you check into a hospital in a strange place, they don't know you and you don't know them. Some doctors won't accept you as a patient in this situation, and it can be awkward. It doesn't make sense to take a chance.

No one can predict when your labor will begin. No one can guarantee you can go on a trip and not go into labor or have other problems. You can't guarantee it even if you're at home! Plan ahead, and discuss it with your doctor *before* you make plans or buy airplane tickets.

What are the greatest risks for me if I decide to travel during my pregnancy?
The biggest risk is the development of a complication while you are away from home and away from those who know your pregnancy history. Other concerns include your discomfort or trouble sleeping, especially if you are cooped up in a car for hours or are trying to sleep in a strange bed. Consider these things and discuss them with your doctor before making plans or buying tickets.

The same goes for your partner's travel plans. If you are within a month of your due date, your doctor can check you, but this only tells you where you are *at that very moment.* This is not a good time for either of you to travel.

Driving and Seat-Belt Use in Pregnancy

There is no reason not to drive while you're pregnant if your pregnancy is normal and you feel OK. Be sure to wear a seat belt throughout your pregnancy as well as at all other times.

Is it safe for me to drive during pregnancy?
Yes. It may become uncomfortable for you to get in and out of the car as pregnancy progresses, but being pregnant should not interfere with your ability to drive.

Many women are confused about wearing seat belts and shoulder harnesses during pregnancy. They wonder if wearing the restraints over their abdomen could cause a problem. *It is important to continue wearing your safety belt whenever you go out in a car.* These safety restraints are necessary during pregnancy, just as they are necessary when you're not pregnant. Seat-belt use is so important that the National Highway Safety Administration has designed a "pregnant" crash-test dummy. The dummy is used in simulated car crashes to record how an accident could affect a pregnant woman and her unborn baby.

There is no evidence use of safety restraints increases the chance of fetal or uterine injury. You have a better chance of survival in an accident wearing a seat belt than not wearing one.

Wear Seat Belts Properly

There is definitely a correct way to wear a seat belt. Place the lap-belt part of the restraint under your abdomen and across your upper thighs so it's snug and comfortable. Adjust your sitting position so the belt crosses your shoulder without cutting into your neck. Position the shoulder harness between your breasts; don't slip this belt off your shoulder.

Seat-belt use is extremely important during pregnancy. Always buckle up!

Workplace Hazards and Possible Effects on the Fetus

Agent	Sources	Possible Effects
Cytomegalovirus	Hospitals, day-care centers	Congenital malformation
Cytotoxic drugs	Hospital or pharmacy preparation of chemotherapeutic drugs	Miscarriage
Ethylene oxide	Surgical-instrument sterilization	Miscarriage
Ionizing radiation	X-rays and radiation treatments, radioactive implants, nuclear power plants	In very high doses, congenital malformation; lower doses may increase risk of childhood cancer
Lead	House, automotive and art paints made before 1980; battery manufacturing plants and radiator repair shops; ceramics and glass manufacturers; toll booths on heavily traveled roads	Preterm birth, delayed cognitive development
Organic solvents	Paint thinners, lacquers, adhesives; electronics and printing plants	Congenital malformation
PCBs	Electronic capacitors and transformers; hazardous waste industry	Delayed cognitive development
Rubella virus	Day-care centers, schools	Congenital malformation
Toxoplasmosis	Veterinary clinics, animal shelters, meat-packing operations	Congenital malformation

Your Legal Rights

United States. Women who work full time who need to take time off while they are pregnant may be made to feel their jobs are vulnerable. The Pregnancy Discrimination Act of 1978 prohibits job discrimination on the basis of pregnancy, childbirth or related disability. It guarantees equal treatment of all disabilities, including pregnancy, birth or related medical conditions, by companies that employ 15 or more people. If you have problems, ask your healthcare provider for help.

Most doctors will encourage you to work as long as the work isn't harmful to you or your baby.

Several elements of the law may apply to you.

- You must be granted the same health, disability and sick-leave benefits as any other employee for any other medical condition.
- You must be given modified tasks, alternate assignments, disability leave or leave without pay (depending on your company's policy).
- You are allowed to work as long as you can perform your job.
- You are guaranteed job security on leave.
- You continue to accrue seniority and vacation, and to remain eligible for pay increases and benefits.

Another law, the Family and Medical Leave Act, was passed in 1993 and also affects pregnant women. It allows you or your husband to take up to 12 weeks of unpaid leave in any 12-month period for the birth of your baby. Leave may be taken intermittently or all at the same time. You must be restored to an equivalent position with equal benefits when you return. However, the act applies only to companies that employ 50 or more people within a 75-mile radius of the job site. States may allow an employer to deny job restoration to those in the top 10% compensation bracket. Check with your state's labor office.

State employment laws differ, so check with your state's labor office. You may also receive a summary of state laws on family leave from:

The Women's Bureau Publications
U.S. Department of Labor
Box EX
200 Constitution Avenue, NW
Washington, DC 20210

Canada. Laws and benefits regarding pregnancy differ greatly
in Canada. Currently, Canadians who qualify may receive employment
insurance benefits while pregnant. You must have worked at least
700 hours for pay in the last 52 weeks. Benefits are of two types:
maternal and parental. Maternity benefits may only be paid to the
natural mother of a child. Parental benefits may be paid to both
natural and adoptive parents. Maternity benefits may be taken for
up to 15 weeks. Parental benefits may be taken for up to 10 weeks.
In either case, the benefits may be taken before and after the baby's
birth. Parental benefits may be claimed by one parent or split between
the two.

To apply, contact your nearest Human Resource Centre of Canada
(HRCC). You will need two pieces of information:

• Your Social Insurance Number (SIN)

• Your Record of Employment (ROE). Your employer must give you
this form. It states how long you worked and how much you
earned with that employer. If you have worked for more than
one employer in the last 52 weeks, you may have more than one
ROE.

Workplace discrimination because of pregnancy. It isn't
common, but it happens. If you feel discriminated against in the
workplace because of your pregnancy, you do have recourse. One
excellent booklet I know about is *Facts about Pregnancy
Discrimination.* It is available from the Equal Employment Opportunity
Commission. Call (202) 663-4900 for a free copy. In Canada, contact
your nearest Human Resource Centre of Canada for help.

More Than One Baby!

7

It seems almost common today for women to be pregnant with more than one baby. You read about it in the newspapers and magazines, and you hear about it on TV and the radio. Some women are giving birth to more babies than we could have imagined not long ago. This has occurred for many reasons, including the following:

- use of fertility drugs
- use of in-vitro fertilization
- women having babies later in life
- some women having more children

What does this mean for the typical woman? Some factors, such as being older, increase your chances of having more than one baby. If you have in-vitro fertilization, this also increases your chances for multiple fetuses.

No matter how it occurs, being pregnant with two or more babies affects you in many ways. In this chapter, I discuss what changes you may have to make in pregnancy and what adjustments you may be required to deal with in a multiple birth. These adjustments may be necessary for your health and your babies' health. If this happy event occurs in your life, work with your doctor and other healthcare professionals to help ensure your pregnancy is healthy and safe.

How does a multiple pregnancy occur?
The babies may come from a single egg that divides after fertilization (identical twins), or more than one egg may be fertilized (fraternal twins).

How Frequent Are Multiple Births?

Twins from one egg occur about once in every 250 births around the world. Twins from two eggs occur in 1 out of every 100 births in white women and in 1 out of 79 births in black women. In certain areas in Africa, twins occur once in every 20 births! The occurrence of twins in Asian populations is less common—about 1 in every 150 births. Hispanics also have a higher incidence of twin births.

Triplets are much less common; they occur only once in every 8,000 deliveries. I've been lucky to deliver two sets of triplets, but most doctors never deliver a set of triplets in their entire careers.

Fertility drugs and the growing number of women who are having babies at an older age are two major reasons for the increased incidence of twins. Fertility drugs can stimulate the ovaries to release more than one egg, increasing the chance of a multiple pregnancy.

The incidence of twins is highest among women between 35 and 39. This increase is attributed to higher levels of *gonadotropin*, the hormone that stimulates the ovaries to develop and to release eggs. As a woman gets older, the level of gonadotropin increases, and she is more likely to produce two eggs during one menstrual cycle.

Conjoined twins, until recently also called *Siamese twins,* are twins whose bodies are connected. It is a serious complication because these babies may share important internal organs, such as the heart, lungs or liver. Sometimes they can be separated; often they cannot. The birth of conjoined twins is very rare. When it happens, it is usually necessary to deliver conjoined twins by Cesarean section.

What is the difference between identical and fraternal twins?

Identical (*monozygotic*) twins develop from a single egg that divides after being fertilized. Babies are always the same sex, and they look alike. When two eggs are fertilized, the babies will be as different in appearance as any other brothers and sisters. They are called fraternal (*dizygotic*) twins. Most twins born to older women are fraternal twins—babies born from two different eggs.

Tendency Runs in Families

It's true that twin births can run in the family—on the *mother's* side. One study showed that if a woman was a twin, the chance of her giving birth to twins was about 1 in 58! If a woman is the daughter of a twin, she also has a higher chance of having twins. Another study reported that 1 out of 24 twins' mothers (4%) was also a twin, but only 1 out of 60 (1.7%) of the fathers was a twin.

More Common in Large Families

Research shows that the more pregnancies a woman has, the greater the chance of having twins. I know of one woman who had three single births, then twins, then triplets!

In-vitro Fertilization

With in-vitro fertilization, multiple embryos are placed in the uterine cavity in hopes that at least one will implant and grow to maturity. Sometimes more than one embryo implants, resulting in a multiple birth.

Pregnancy with Multiples

A twin pregnancy is usually confirmed during the second trimester. Ultrasound is the best way to determine if a woman is carrying more than one baby.

You may know of someone who was told early in pregnancy she was going to have twins. Then sometime later, one of the twins "disappeared." It happens sometimes. Early ultrasound exams revealed two babies; later ultrasounds of the same woman show one baby disappeared, but the other baby was OK. We believe one of the fetuses may die, then be absorbed in the mother's body. This is one reason many doctors prefer not to predict a twin birth before 10 weeks of pregnancy.

Protecting This Pregnancy

The possibility of problems increases slightly when a woman is carrying more than one baby. One of the most important things to remember with a multiple pregnancy is to take things more slowly, from the beginning of your pregnancy until delivery.

Get Ready for Twins!

The average delivery date for twins is about 36 weeks; for triplets, the average is about 33 weeks. I advise my patients not to wait too long to take care of their preparations for the babies' birth. This section gives you suggestions to help you get ready.

Nursery Items

Many expectant mothers wait until they are close to the delivery date of their baby to buy nursery items they will need. However, don't wait that long if you are the expectant mother of multiples—your second trimester is not too early to shop for these things. It may be better to choose them while you can get around easily than to wait until you are too big to move comfortably or even until after your babies are born!

Tip: If you're expecting twins, buy necessary nursery items in the second trimester—while you can still move around comfortably!

Maternity Leave

Often a physician will advise a woman expecting twins to stop working at least 8 weeks before her due date. Ideally, a woman should stop working at 28 weeks with a twin pregnancy—24 weeks if her job requires standing or physical exertion.

When is a twin pregnancy most often discovered?
A twin pregnancy is usually found during the second trimester because the woman is larger than expected and growth seems to be too fast.

We try to delay delivery of twins until about the 37th week of pregnancy, and triplets until about the 35th week. In many cases, these pregnancies deliver earlier.

Childbirth-Education Classes

It's a great idea to take these classes for any pregnancy. However, schedule your classes to begin at least 2 to 3 months before your due date if you're expecting more than one baby. If you have time, a brief course in Cesarean birth might also be worthwhile, if you can find one in your area.

Delivery

How multiple fetuses are delivered depends on how the babies are lying in the uterus. All possible combinations of fetal positions can occur. Some doctors believe two or more babies should *always* be delivered by Cesarean section. When twins are both in a head-first position, a vaginal delivery may be attempted. One baby may be delivered vaginally, with the second requiring a C-section if the baby turns, if the cord comes out first or if the second baby is distressed after the first baby is born.

Feeding More Than One Baby

Many of my patients who are expecting twins ask if they can breastfeed two babies. Yes, it's possible. It will be more demanding, but many women successfully breastfeed twins.

We know breast milk is especially valuable for small or premature infants; often twins are both. If you want to breastfeed, do try it.

It's certainly possible to breastfeed two babies, but it will be more demanding for you.

If you have triplets, it is possible to breastfeed all three babies. You'll find it is challenging, but it's important to try, if you want to. One way you may be able to do it is to let each baby breastfeed for a bit at a feeding, then supplement with formula. You can also express your milk, and divide it among the three babies. Because triplets are usually small and premature, your breast milk is especially valuable to them.

Heartburn

Women who carry more than one baby commonly experience heartburn more frequently than other pregnant women. Heartburn is caused by the larger uterus encroaching on the space the stomach usually enjoys by itself.

Taking care of yourself is the best way to take care of your developing babies. A multiple pregnancy is more stressful for your body than a single pregnancy, and your needs increase in many areas.

Eat more. A woman carrying multiples has to eat more—at least 300 more calories *per baby* each day. A woman needs more protein, minerals, vitamins and essential fatty acids.

Keep track of your weight. You are more likely to put on extra weight with multiple fetuses. For a normal-weight woman, a weight gain of 35 to 45 pounds (15.75 to 20.25kg) for a twin birth is recommended. However, some women do not gain as much weight because of the added stress on their bodies.

Get extra iron. Iron supplementation is essential. Often women who are pregnant with more than one baby have iron-deficiency anemia.

Check before exercising. Walking and swimming may be permissible for you while you're pregnant with multiple fetuses. Be sure to check out any exercise program with your doctor before you do anything. Don't do anything strenuous, and stop immediately if you feel overexerted. As much as you want to stay in shape, you may have to forgo all exercise until after your babies are safely delivered.

Care in the Last Trimester

Most complications in a multiple-fetus pregnancy arise in the last trimester, as the babies grow larger. The biggest problem with twins is premature labor and premature delivery. When you are carrying twins, you get "big" earlier and you get larger than you do with a single pregnancy. This can cause problems, such as difficulty breathing, back pain, hemorrhoids, varicose veins, pelvic pressure and pelvic pain.

Find People Who Will Support You

You will need extra help after you deliver your babies. Your time of greatest need will be immediately after your babies are born. Ask for help from family, neighbors and friends for the first 4 to 6 weeks after you bring your babies home. You may be fairly exhausted, so it's helpful to have extra pairs of hands available until your new family settles into a routine. You may want to arrange for this help ahead of time, before you deliver your babies.

There are some wonderful resource groups for parents and families of multiples. Contact them for information and assistance. See the box below for listings.

Resources for Parents of Multiples

National Organization of Mothers of Twins Clubs, Inc.
P.O. Box 23188
Albuquerque, NM 87192-1188
Tel: (505) 275-0955
Offers free information to expectant parents or new parents of multiples. Will also refer you to local Twins Clubs.

Twin Services
P.O. Box 10066
Berkeley, CA 94709
Tel: (510) 524-0863
Offers publications and information to parents. Will also refer to local groups.

Center for Study of Multiple Births
333 E. Superior St., Rm. 464
Chicago, IL 60611
Tel: (312) 266-9093
Will supply list of current resources and references for parents of multiples.

Twins magazine
5350 S. Roslyn St., Suite 400
Englewood, CO 80111
Tel: (800) 328-3211 or (303) 290-8500
customer.service@businessword.com
Bimonthly magazine for the parents of twins, triplets and more. Contact for information about subscribing.

Changes in Your Growing Baby 8

During your pregnancy, you will see many changes in your body (discussed in the next chapter). However, the most incredible changes are occurring in your developing baby. In 9 short months, your baby grows from a few small cells into a fully grown, fully developed little being that can live on its own outside of your body. For 9 months, your body has protected, nourished and nurtured the baby as it has grown to maturity, ready to begin its life. And although you won't be able to see much more than an enlarging abdomen, incredible things are happening inside your body.

This chapter attempts to give you an idea of some of the fascinating things that occur as your baby grows and develops. After reading it, you may agree with me that the growth of your baby is truly a miracle.

Your Baby's Due Date

Two Ways to Figure the Due Date

Most women don't know the exact date their baby was conceived, but they usually know the day their last menstrual period began. The doctor subtracts 2 weeks from the date of the last period as an estimate of when conception occurred. Your estimated due date is 38 weeks after the date of conception (40 weeks after the first day of your last period).

There is a second way to determine your due date. Add 7 days to the date of the beginning of your last menstrual period, then subtract

3 months. This gives you the approximate date of delivery. For example, if your last period began on January 20, your estimated due date is October 27.

Gestational Age and Fertilization Age

Gestational age, also called *menstrual age,* dates a pregnancy from the first day of the last menstrual period. It is 2 weeks longer than the fertilization age.

Fertilization age, also called *ovulatory age,* is 2 weeks shorter than gestational age and dates from the actual date of conception. This is the actual age of the fetus.

These dating techniques are confusing. When my doctor says I'm 12 weeks pregnant, how old is my baby?

Most doctors count the time during pregnancy in weeks. If your doctor says you're 12 weeks pregnant, he's referring to the gestational age. Your last menstrual period began 12 weeks ago, but you actually conceived 10 weeks ago, so the fetus is 10 weeks old.

Your Baby's Growth

Your baby grows and changes from a small group of cells to a fully developed baby ready to begin life. The designation between "embryo" and "fetus" is somewhat arbitrary. During the first 8 weeks of development (10 weeks of gestation), the developing baby is called an *embryo.* From 8 weeks of development until delivery, it is called a *fetus.* The great changes your baby goes through to become a fully developed baby are easier to follow if we look at them in each trimester.

How is it decided whether I will have a boy or a girl?

The sex of the baby is determined at the time of fertilization. If a sperm carrying a Y chromosome fertilizes the egg, it results in a male child; a sperm carrying an X chromosome results in a female child. It's all determined when the sperm fertilizes your egg.

Life-size

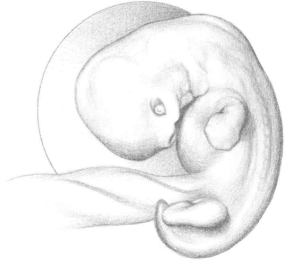

*The fetus at 6 weeks looks more
like a tadpole than a baby.*

Trimesters

The length of your pregnancy is divided into three trimesters, each about 13 weeks long.

First trimester development. The first trimester represents the greatest change for any developing fetus. In the first 13 weeks of development, your baby grows from a collection of cells the size of the head of a pin to a fetus the size of a softball. Organs begin developing, and your baby begins to look more like a baby.

Very few, if any, structures in the fetus are formed after the 12th week of pregnancy. This means your baby forms all of its major organ systems by the end of the first trimester. These structures continue to grow and to develop until your baby is born.

Second trimester development. At the beginning of the second trimester (14th week), your baby weighs less than 1 ounce (28g) and is only about 4 inches (10cm) long.

Third trimester development. Your baby weighs about 1-1/2 pounds (0.7kg) at the beginning of the third trimester (27th week), and its crown-to-rump length is under 9 inches (22cm). (*Crown-to-rump length* is the measurement from the top of the baby's head [crown] to the buttocks of the baby [rump].) When it is delivered, your baby will weigh close to 7-1/2 pounds (3.4kg) and be about 21 inches (53cm) long.

Baby's Size and Weight

Birthweight varies greatly from baby to baby. However, the average weight of a baby at term is 7 to 7-1/2 pounds (3.3 to 3.4kg).

Ultrasound is the test of choice to estimate fetal weight. A formula has been established to help estimate fetal weight using this technology. Several measurements are taken, including the diameter of the baby's head, circumference of the baby's abdomen and length of the femur (thighbone) of the baby's leg. Occasionally other fetal measurements are taken. A drawback of using ultrasound for estimating fetal weight is that estimates may vary as much as half a pound (225g) in either direction. However, the accuracy of predicting fetal weight with ultrasound continues to improve.

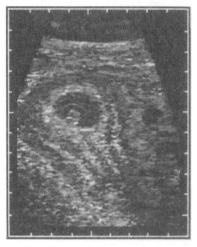

Early ultrasound done at 6 weeks.

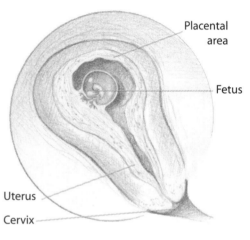

Placental area

Fetus

Uterus

Cervix

Illustration of what ultrasound at 6 weeks shows.

The size of the fetus's head surprises many of my patients. When you are 13 weeks pregnant, your baby's head takes up about half the crown-to-rump length (measurement from top of the head to the baby's buttocks). In 2 months, when you are 21 weeks pregnant, the head will be about one-third of the fetal body. At birth, your baby's head will be one-fourth the size of its body.

Can the doctor estimate from my size how big my baby will be?
It's hard to estimate the weight of any baby before birth. Many doctors will take a guess and give a range of a couple of pounds. Some of my estimates have really been off! It's not uncommon to estimate a baby will weigh 8-1/2 (3.8kg) pounds and find only a 7-pound (3.15kg) baby.

Your Baby's Heart

Your baby's heart starts beating very early. By the 6th week of pregnancy (age of fetus is 4 weeks), the heart tubes fuse and contractions of the heart begin. This can be seen on ultrasound.

When will I be able to hear my baby's heart beat?
With doppler ultrasound, it is possible to hear the heartbeat as early as 12 weeks. It may be possible to hear your baby's heart beat with a stethoscope at around 20 weeks of pregnancy. If you can't hear it, don't worry. It's not always easy, even for a doctor who does this on a regular basis.

Occasionally you may listen to your baby's heartbeat at the doctor's office and hear it skip a beat. An irregular heartbeat is called an *arrhythmia*. Arrhythmias in a fetus are not unusual, so don't be overly concerned. The equipment could be faulty or there may be some other problem transmitting the sound.

Arrhythmias are not usually serious in a baby before birth; many disappear after the baby is born. If an arrhythmia is discovered before labor and delivery, you may require fetal heart-rate monitoring during pregnancy. When an arrhythmia is discovered during labor, it may be decided to have a pediatrician present when the baby is born.

Your Baby in the Womb

Some of my patients are startled when they see an ultrasound of their baby and it appears that the baby has its mouth open. In addition to turning over and moving their hands and feet, babies do open and close their mouths in the womb. The fetus may also suck its thumb or finger.

Digestive System Develops

By 21 weeks, the fetal digestive system has developed enough to allow the fetus to swallow amniotic fluid. The fetus absorbs much of the water in the swallowed fluid. Hydrochloric acid and adult digestive enzymes are present in small amounts in the fetal digestive system at 21 weeks.

Researchers believe swallowing amniotic fluid may help growth and development of the fetal digestive system. It may also condition the digestive system to function after birth. By the time a baby is born, he or she may swallow large amounts of amniotic fluid, as much as 17 ounces (500ml) of amniotic fluid in a 24-hour period.

Eyes Open

Your baby can open its eyes inside the uterus. Eyelids cover the eyes and are fused or connected around 11 to 12 weeks. They remain fused until about 27 to 28 weeks, when they open.

Hearing Begins

A baby can hear inside the womb, before it is born. Life inside the womb may be like living near a busy freeway. The developing baby hears a constant background of digestive noises and the maternal heartbeat. The mother-to-be's voice is also heard, although the fetus may not hear higher-pitched tones.

Life inside the womb may be like living near a busy freeway.

There is evidence that by the third trimester the fetus responds to sounds it hears. Researchers have noted fetal heart-rate increases in response to tones it hears through the mother's abdomen. Newborns have been found to prefer their mother's voice to a stranger's, which suggests they recognize the mother's voice. They have also been found to prefer their mother's native language, and they respond strongly to a recording of an intrauterine heartbeat.

Problems for the Developing Baby

The first 10 weeks of pregnancy (8 weeks of fetal development) are called the *embryonic period;* it is a time of extremely important development in the baby. The embryo is most susceptible during this time to factors that can interfere with its development. Most birth defects occur during this period.

Birth Defects

When a birth defect occurs, we want to know why it happened. This can be frustrating because in most instances we cannot determine a cause. *Teratology* is the study of abnormal fetal development. A substance that causes birth defects is called a *teratogen* or is said to be *teratogenic.* Some things may have a bad effect (be teratogenic) at one point in pregnancy, then be safe at others.

The most critical time appears to be early in pregnancy, during the first trimester or first 13 weeks. An example of this is rubella (German measles). If the fetus is infected during the first trimester, abnormalities such as heart defects can occur. If infection happens later, problems are often less serious.

What is the chance of my baby having a major birth defect?
Every pregnant couple worries about birth defects. The risk of a birth defect is very low, only about 1 to 2%.

Effect of Medications on the Baby

Medications can be grouped into three main groups—safe, unsafe and unsure. It's best to avoid any medication during pregnancy unless you discuss it with your doctor. Some medications, such as thyroid medication, are necessary and important during pregnancy.

It's easier and safer to discuss medication use with your physician ahead of time rather than after you have taken a medicine and want to know if it is safe or if it could harm your baby. For a chart on how some medications can affect the developing fetus, see page 74.

Other medications, besides those listed on the chart, may also be harmful. If you take any of those listed on the next page during your pregnancy, don't panic! Exposure alone *doesn't* mean definite harm to the fetus. The effect on a developing fetus depends on when you took the medication, the amount you took and how long you took it. Talk to your doctor if you believe you took any of the medications listed below:

- angiotensin-converting enzyme (ACE) inhibitors
- aminopterin
- anticonvulsants
- benzodiazepines
- ethanol
- etretinate
- live vaccines
- methimazole
- penicillamine (not penicillin)
- ribavirin
- vitamin A (in large doses)

Cataracts

Congenital (present-at-birth) cataracts rarely happen and are usually genetic. With cataracts, the lens of the eye is not transparent. Children born to mothers who had German measles (rubella) around the 6th or 7th week of pregnancy may be born with cataracts.

We believe exposure to cigarette smoke may be harmful to an unborn baby.

Air Pollution

I am often asked if smog an expectant mother breathes will harm her unborn baby. This is rarely a problem and would be very hard to prove. Your lungs and airways filter the air you breathe, and that protects your baby. However, exposure to cigarette smoke—from the mother's smoking or from the mother's exposure to secondary smoke—*is harmful to a developing baby.*

Premature Birth

It is hard to believe, but many babies born at 25 weeks survive. Some of the greatest advances in medicine have been in the care of premature babies. However, don't start wishing for delivery now;

babies born this early are in the hospital a long time and often have serious problems. And the expenses are enormous!

It is very risky for a baby to be born very early. Premature birth increases the risk of physical and/or mental impairment in the baby. It also increases the risk of fetal death.

How early is "too early" depends on your particular situation. In many cases, 1 or 2 weeks is not going to make much difference in your baby—the baby may only be slightly smaller. However, the earlier the baby is born, the greater the risks.

Help Avoid Premature Labor

Some activities may increase your risk of going into premature labor. Taking the following precautions may help you reduce the risk of giving birth too early.

- **Sit whenever you can.** Standing may cause contractions as the body attempts to restore circulation to the uterine area.
- **Don't lift and carry heavy objects.** When you lift and carry something heavy, you cause abdominal muscles to tighten, which increases pressure on the uterus.
- **Don't smoke.** Research shows that women who smoke during pregnancy have a 20 to 50% higher risk of premature labor.
- **Don't drink alcohol.** Even in small amounts, alcohol may harm the baby.
- **Gain enough weight.** Underweight women who do not gain enough weight have a higher risk of having a baby born too early.
- **Get enough rest.** Resting, especially on your left side, improves circulation to your body and your baby.
- **Don't exercise too strenuously.** If you exercise too intensely or for too long, it can draw blood away from the uterus to your muscles.
- **Don't stoop, bend or climb stairs when you can avoid it.** These activities raise your blood pressure and draw blood away from your uterus.
- **Limit caffeine intake.** You increase your risk if you drink five or more cups of coffee a day.
- **Keep all prenatal appointments.** Your routine appointments with your doctor will help identify any problems early so they are more treatable.

Great medical advances have been made in the care of premature babies.

Fortunately, more premature babies are surviving today than ever before. Because of advances in technology, today fewer than 10 deaths per 1,000 are reported in premature births. However, survival is hard-won; the average hospital stay for a premature baby ranges from 50 days to more than 100 days.

In babies born extremely early, there is an increased rate of physical and mental disabilities; some are severe. This is the reason your doctor attempts to prolong your pregnancy as long as possible.

Hydrocephalus

Hydrocephalus is a developmental problem that causes the head to enlarge. It occurs in about 1 in 1,000 babies and is responsible for about 12% of all severe fetal malformations found at birth.

Hydrocephalus occurs with the development of the brain and central nervous system of the baby in early pregnancy. Spinal fluid circulates around the brain and spinal cord, and must be able to flow without restriction. If openings are blocked and the flow of fluid is restricted, it can cause hydrocephalus (sometimes called *water on the brain)*. Fluid accumulates and causes the baby's head to enlarge.

Hydrocephalus is a symptom and can have several causes, including spina bifida, meningomyelocele and omphalocele. Sometimes intrauterine therapy—treatment in some instances while the fetus is still in the uterus—can be performed.

There are two ways of treating hydrocephalus inside the uterus. In one method, a needle is passed through the mother's abdomen into the affected area of the baby's brain to remove fluid. In the other method, a small plastic tube is placed into the area of fluid in the fetal brain. This tube is left in place to drain fluid continuously from the baby's brain.

Meconium

The term *meconium* refers to undigested debris from swallowed amniotic fluid in the fetal digestive system. It is a dark substance that your baby may pass from its bowels into the amniotic fluid. This may happen before or at the time of delivery. Meconium is detected when your water breaks. Before this time, the only way to know about it is by amniocentesis.

Is meconium important?
The presence of meconium can be important at the time of delivery. If a baby has a bowel movement and meconium is in the amniotic fluid, the infant may swallow the fluid before birth or at the time of birth. If meconium is inhaled into the lungs, it may cause pneumonia or pneumonitis.

If meconium is detected during labor, it is removed from the baby's mouth and throat after delivery with a small suction tube so the baby won't swallow it. Meconium in the amniotic fluid may be caused by distress in the fetus. When meconium is present, it doesn't always mean distress, but it must be considered.

Intrauterine-Growth Retardation

Intrauterine-growth retardation (IUGR) occurs when a baby does not grow in size appropriately during pregnancy; the baby is too small. This can be a serious development because when the baby's weight is low, the risk of problems increases. Research has shown that a previous delivery of a growth-retarded infant makes it more likely to happen again in later pregnancies.

The word "retardation" causes some people some concern. Retardation in this sense does not apply to the development or function of the baby's brain. It does *not* mean the baby will be mentally retarded. It means the growth and size of the fetus are inappropriately small; growth and size are considered to be retarded or slowed.

When the baby's weight is low, the risk of problems increases.

Many conditions increase the chance of IUGR, including the following:

- maternal anemia
- smoking by the mother-to-be during pregnancy
- poor weight gain by the mother-to-be
- vascular disease in the mother-to-be, including high blood pressure
- kidney disease in the mother-to-be
- alcoholism or drug abuse by the pregnant woman
- multiple fetuses
- infections in the fetus
- abnormalities in the umbilical cord or the placenta
- small size of mother-to-be (probably not a cause for alarm)

The doctor usually discovers this problem by watching the growth of your uterus for a period of time and finding no change. If you measure 10.8 inches (27.4cm) at 27 weeks of pregnancy, and at 31 weeks you measure only 11 inches (28cm), your doctor might become concerned about IUGR. This is another good reason to keep all your prenatal appointments.

If IUGR is diagnosed, your doctor will advise you to avoid anything that can make it worse. Stop smoking. Stop using drugs or alcohol. Eat nutritiously. Bed rest may be prescribed. This allows your baby to receive the best blood flow from you and thus to receive as much nutrition as possible.

The greatest risk associated with IUGR is stillbirth (death of the baby before delivery). To avoid this, it may be necessary to deliver the baby before full term. The baby may be safer outside the uterus than inside. Because infants with IUGR may not tolerate labor well, the possibility of a C-section increases.

Umbilical-Cord Problems

We believe umbilical-cord knots form as the baby moves around early in pregnancy. A loop forms in the umbilical cord; when the baby moves through the loop, a knot forms. In some cases a baby may become entangled in its umbilical cord, but usually it isn't a problem.

A tangled cord only becomes a problem if the cord is stretched tightly around the neck or another part of the body, or if it is in a tight knot. You can do nothing to prevent it. Be reassured to know these knots do not occur often.

Changes in You 9

During your pregnancy, you will see many changes in your body. Your breasts get bigger, you may have food cravings and you'll probably have to go to the bathroom more often. You may experience changes in your emotions, too. These are all natural. By knowing what you can expect, you may be more comfortable with the changes you experience.

In the first part of your pregnancy, you won't look much different than you did before you were pregnant. It may even take awhile before you realize you are going to have a baby. You shouldn't gain much weight during this time—probably no more than 5 pounds (2.25kg) for the first few months. Your abdomen will grow a little, but though you may want to, you won't feel the baby move during this time. That won't happen until about the fourth month.

Getting Bigger

The length of your pregnancy is divided into three stages, or trimesters, each about 13 weeks long. Trimesters help group stages of development for you and your baby. Pregnancy is unique to each woman. Usually you don't have to worry if you don't look or feel exactly like another woman at the same point in pregnancy.

Trimesters

First trimester changes in you. You will see very little change in yourself, although your baby is growing and changing quite rapidly. You may not even realize you are pregnant until the middle or close to the end of this trimester! You will experience very little weight gain during this time—probably no more than 5 pounds (2.25kg) for the entire 13 weeks. Your abdomen will grow a little—you may be able to feel your uterus about 3 inches (7.6cm) below your bellybutton. You won't feel the fetus move during this time.

Second trimester changes in you. You will begin showing; others will be able to tell you are pregnant during this trimester. By the end of this trimester, you will feel your uterus about 3 inches (7.6 cm) above your bellybutton.

Average weight gain for this trimester is a total of 17 to 24 pounds (7.65 to 10.8kg), including weight from the first trimester. You will begin to feel your baby move during this time.

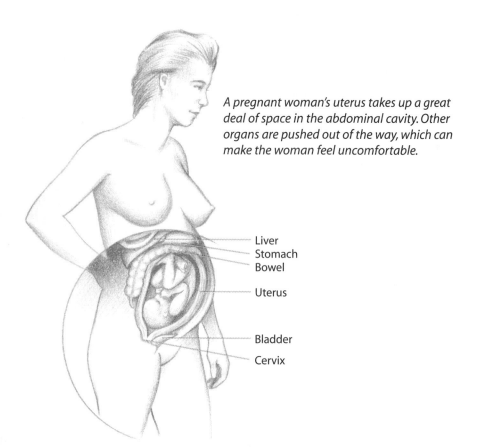

A pregnant woman's uterus takes up a great deal of space in the abdominal cavity. Other organs are pushed out of the way, which can make the woman feel uncomfortable.

Liver
Stomach
Bowel

Uterus

Bladder

Cervix

I'm 19 weeks pregnant and have only gained 4 pounds (1.8kg). Should I be concerned?
Weight gain varies among women a great deal. If you were sick a lot or had nausea during the first few months, you may have lost weight at first and may be behind in gaining weight. If you were overweight before you got pregnant, you may not have gained as much. At this point, you should be gaining weight steadily. Discuss it with your doctor if you are concerned.

Third trimester changes in you. You will experience a lot of physical change during this time because your baby will be growing so much. By delivery, your uterus is 6-1/2 to 8 inches (16.5 to 20.3cm) above your bellybutton.

Your baby will gain a great deal of weight during this time, even though you may not. Total weight gain by delivery is 25 to 35 pounds (11.25 to 15.75kg) for the average woman.

How You Look and Feel

Your body changes a lot during pregnancy. Get good prenatal care and follow your doctor's recommendations about nutrition, medication and exercise. Keep all your appointments. Establish good communication with your healthcare provider. Ask any question you have about how you look or feel.

Not showing yet. Don't be concerned if you are about done with the first trimester and don't show yet. A lot is happening with the development of your baby's organs and organ systems, but friends probably can't tell you're pregnant. You may be able to feel your uterus down by your pubic bone, or your clothes may be getting a little snug.

If this is your first pregnancy, it often takes longer to see a change in your tummy. You may not show until your second trimester. Don't despair—you'll be getting larger soon, and then everyone will know you're pregnant! If you have had other pregnancies, you will probably show sooner.

Showing "already." If you have had a baby before, you may notice changes in the way your body adapts to the pregnancy this time around. The way a woman's body responds to pregnancy is influenced by her previous pregnancies. Skin and muscles stretch to accommodate the enlarged uterus, placenta and baby. Stretched muscles and stretched skin are never exactly the same again. They may give way faster to accommodate the growing uterus and baby with subsequent pregnancies, which causes a woman to show sooner and to feel bigger. Some other reasons for looking bigger are that you are farther along than you think, or you are carrying twins.

Everyone tells me I'm too big. What's wrong?
Before you become too concerned, discuss it with your doctor. Friends may tell you you are too big or too small; probably nothing is wrong. Women and babies are different sizes and grow at different rates. Most important is the continuous change and continuous growth of the fetus.

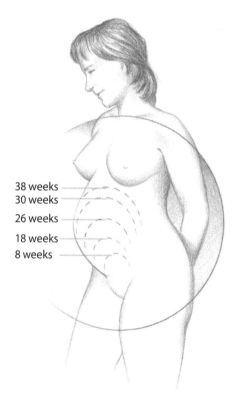

38 weeks
30 weeks
26 weeks
18 weeks
8 weeks

This illustration shows how a woman's uterus grows during pregnancy. The dotted lines represent growth from about 8 weeks through the end of the third trimester (about 38 weeks).

Changes in Your Skin

Hormonal changes in pregnancy can cause changes in your skin. Most of these changes are not serious, but some may require a doctor's attention.

Linea Nigra

You may notice a dark vertical line on your abdomen. It is called the *linea nigra* and appears on many women during pregnancy. It often fades markedly after pregnancy, but it may never fully disappear.

Chloasma

In pregnancy, some women notice brown patches on their face they never had before. These patches are called *chloasma* or *mask of pregnancy*.

Chloasma is believed to be caused by the hormonal changes brought about during pregnancy. Usually these dark patches disappear completely or lighten after your baby is born. (Oral contraceptives often cause similar pigmentation changes.)

I don't usually use sunscreen, but a friend suggested it's important during pregnancy. Why?
Sunscreen lessens the likelihood of getting the "mask of pregnancy," which is a darkening of skin pigment on cheeks, forehead and chin. Use products with an SPF of 15 or higher. If you are prone to acne breakouts, use a water-based or oil-free product.

Small Red Elevations

During pregnancy, you may experience vascular changes to your skin. These small red elevations, with branches extending outward, are called *vascular spiders, telangiectasias* or *angiomas*. They usually occur on the face, neck, upper chest and arms, and disappear after delivery.

Red Palms

Some women in pregnancy develop a harmless condition in which the palms of their hands turn red. The condition is called *palmar erythema*; it is fairly common. It occurs in 65% of pregnant white women and 35% of pregnant black women. It is probably caused by increased estrogen in the system. It's OK to use lotions but the redness of your palms may not disappear until after you deliver. Vascular spiders and red palms often occur together.

Moles and Skin Tags

Pregnancy can cause many changes in your skin. Moles may appear for the first time, or existing moles may grow larger and darken during pregnancy. If you have a mole that changes, be sure to have your doctor check it.

If your doctor says you have a precancerous spot, you can have it removed. This is usually done in the doctor's office. You don't have to wait until after your baby is born.

Skin tags are small lumps or bumps of skin that may appear for the first time during pregnancy. If you already have them, they may grow larger while you are pregnant. Don't worry too much about them. If they are in an area, such as the waist, that is rubbed frequently by clothing, you may want to have them removed.

Itchy Skin

Itching, also called *pruritis gravidarum*, is a common symptom during pregnancy. It usually occurs later in pregnancy, and about 20% of all pregnant women suffer from it. Itching does not indicate a problem in your pregnancy.

The skin over your abdomen may itch the most. As your uterus grows and fills your pelvis, abdominal skin and muscles must stretch to accommodate it. Stretching of the skin causes abdominal itching in many women.

Scratching the skin can make it worse, so try not to scratch. Lotions can help reduce itching. Occasionally cortisone creams are used. Ask your healthcare provider about relief.

Pimples

Most women experience some changes in their skin while pregnant. Some women find their skin breaks out more often. Some lucky women find their skin becomes less oily and softer. These changes are due to the hormones of pregnancy; your skin will probably return to normal after your baby is born.

Stretch Marks

Stretch marks, also called *striae distensae*, are areas of stretched skin that may be discolored. They usually occur on the abdomen as your growing uterus stretches the skin. They can also occur on the breasts, hips or buttocks.

Stretch marks usually fade and won't be as noticeable after your pregnancy, but they won't go away completely.

No one has found a reliable way to avoid stretch marks. Women have tried many kinds of lotions with little success. There is no harm in trying lotion products, but they probably won't help.

Varicose Veins

Varicose veins (also called *varicosities* or *varices*) are dilated blood vessels that fill with blood. They usually occur in the legs but also may be seen as hemorrhoids or appear in the birth canal and in the vulva. Pressure from the uterus and the change in blood flow make varices worse.

My mother had varicose veins during her pregnancies. Will I?
Varicose veins occur to some degree in most pregnant women. If your mother had varicose veins, you are more likely to have them, too.

What They Look Like

Symptoms vary. For some women varicose veins are only a blemish or purple-blue spot on the legs. They cause little or no discomfort, except in the evening. For other women, varices are bulging veins that require elevation of the legs at the end of the day and compression stockings during the day; they can be very uncomfortable.

Varicose veins may get worse during pregnancy. In most cases, they become more noticeable and more painful as pregnancy progresses. Increasing weight (from your growing baby), clothing that fits tightly at the waist or legs and standing a great deal cause them to worsen.

What Helps

Many women wear maternity support hose to relieve the problem; various types are available. Clothes that don't restrict circulation at the knee or groin may also help. Spend as little time as possible on your feet. Elevate your feet above the level of your heart or lie on your side when possible to help the veins drain. Wear flat shoes. Don't cross your legs when you sit down. If you continue to have problems after your pregnancy, surgery may be required.

Maternity Hose

Maternity support hose, also called *compression hose*, are not the support hose you buy at the store. A specialist fits them for you. Try these two tricks for putting them on more easily.

First, turn stockings inside out. Starting at the toe, unroll the stockings up your legs.

Second, put your support hose on before you get out of bed in the morning—your legs may tend to swell as soon as you get up.

Prevention

You can do several things to lessen your chances of developing varicose veins in pregnancy. Some practices are the same ones you would use if you already suffered from varicose veins.

- Exercise.
- Don't cross your legs at the knee.
- Don't stand for long periods.
- If you must stand, bounce gently on the balls of your feet every few minutes.
- Lie on your side several times a day.
- Keep your total pregnancy weight gain in the normal range— from 25 to 35 pounds (11.25 to 15.75kg) for a normal-weight woman.

Emotional Changes

Crying easily, mood swings, energy lows and fatigue are all normal aspects of pregnancy. During the first trimester, your body experiences an increase in hormones that are needed to support a pregnancy. Some women are more sensitive than others to these changes, especially those who are sensitive to a similar hormonal shift before menstruation. If you become weepy or edgy around your menstrual period, you may experience similar emotions as your body adjusts to pregnancy.

It also takes time to adjust to the notion of the fetus as your very own baby. When this happens is different for everyone. Some women begin to feel this way as soon as they know they are pregnant. For others, it occurs when they hear their baby's heartbeat, around 12 or 13 weeks, or when they first feel their baby move, between 16 and 20 weeks.

Conflicting Feelings about the Pregnancy

It is quite normal to have conflicting feelings about your pregnancy. Your feelings arise from your adjustment to your pregnancy—you are taking the first steps toward an incredible role change that will involve many aspects of your life. Your feelings come from your attempts to deal with all the questions and concerns you have.

Medication for Depression

Antidepressant medication is not usually prescribed during pregnancy. However, if it is necessary, most physicians prefer to use tricyclic antidepressants, such as amitriptyline and desipramine. Prozac has also been shown to be acceptable. Treatment must be done on an individualized basis. Your doctor and possibly a psychiatrist or psychologist will discuss the situation with you.

Emotional Build-up

As your pregnancy grows, your emotions may become more pronounced, too. By the third trimester, you may feel very emotional much of the time. You're normal! You may be getting a little anxious about the upcoming labor and delivery. Mood swings may occur more frequently, and you may be more irritable. Relax and don't focus on your feelings. Talk to your partner about how you are feeling and what you are experiencing.

I find it annoying when people (even total strangers) pat my pregnant abdomen. How do I stop them from doing this?
Ask people to look but not touch! When someone reaches out to touch your abdomen, it's OK to tell them you are uncomfortable with that.

Aches and Pains

As your uterus grows during pregnancy, you may feel slight cramping or even pain in your lower abdominal area on your sides. Your uterus tightens or contracts throughout your pregnancy. If you don't feel this, don't worry. However, if contractions are accompanied by bleeding from the vagina, call your doctor immediately!

Braxton-Hicks contractions. Braxton-Hicks contractions are painless, nonrhythmical contractions you may be able to feel when you place your hands on your abdomen. You may also feel them in the uterus itself. These contractions may begin early in your pregnancy and are felt at irregular intervals. They are not signs of true labor.

"Pins and needles" feeling. My patients sometimes report a "pins and needles" feeling in their pelvic area during pregnancy. This is another feeling associated with increased pressure as the baby moves lower in the birth canal. Tingling, pressure and numbness are common at this time.

To alleviate some of the discomfort, lie on your side to help decrease pressure in your pelvis and on the nerves, veins and arteries in your pelvic area.

Round-ligament pain. Ligaments lie on either side of the uterus; as your uterus gets bigger, these ligaments stretch and get longer and thicker. Quick movements can stretch the ligaments and cause discomfort. This is not harmful to you or your baby, but it can be uncomfortable.

Be careful about making quick movements. If you experience discomfort, you may feel better if you lie down and rest. Most doctors recommend acetaminophen (Tylenol) if the pain is bothersome. Tell your doctor if it gets worse.

Feeling Your Baby Move

The time you first feel your baby move is different for every woman. It can also be different from one pregnancy to another. One baby may be more active than another, so movement is felt sooner.

My friend was talking about "quickening." What is it?

"Quickening" is feeling your baby move. It usually occurs between 16 and 20 weeks of pregnancy.

Many women describe their baby's first movements as a gas bubble or fluttering in their abdomen. It may be something you notice for a few days before you realize what it is. Movements will become more common and occur fairly frequently—that's how you'll know that what you're feeling is your baby moving. The movement will be below your bellybutton. If it's your first baby, it may be 19 or 20 weeks before you are sure you feel movement.

Baby's Activity Level

After an initial period of activity, a fetus may grow quiet again. Probably nothing is wrong. It is unusual to feel the baby move every day at first. As your baby grows, movements become stronger and occur quite often. Between 20 and 32 weeks of pregnancy, the fetus can move between 200 and 500 times a day, including kicking, rolling or wiggling.

Every baby is different. Sometimes women ask me how often their baby should move, frequently after they have compared notes with a pregnant friend who feels her baby move a lot. Your sensation of your baby moving will be different from anyone else's, and the movement of every baby is different. It is not unusual for one baby to move less than another. If your baby has been very active, then is very quiet for a while, you may want to discuss it with your doctor.

It's all right if you have not felt your baby move in the early part of your second trimester. The most common time to feel first movements is between 16 and 20 weeks.

Active at night. You may find your baby is extremely active at night and keeps you awake. There isn't much you can do about this. You might try changing your position in bed. Avoid exercising just before bed—it may cause your baby to move more. If these tips don't work, you may have to be patient and endure it until your baby is born.

If your baby kicks a lot, try changing your position or lie on your side. You may still be uncomfortable. Taking acetaminophen or relaxing in a warm (not hot) bath may also help.

A growing baby may cause mild pain or pressure under your ribs. There isn't much you can do about the pain or the pressure you feel when your baby moves. You might lie on your side and rest for a while. For example, if you feel pressure under your right ribs, lie on your left side.

Keeping Track of Baby's Movements

A doctor may have a pregnant woman monitor her baby's movements at around 26 weeks if she has had a difficult pregnancy or a previous stillbirth or if she has a medical condition, such as diabetes. Recording movements at certain times each day may provide the doctor with additional information about the status of the fetus.

Baby Is "Floating"

Your healthcare provider may tell you at some point your baby is "floating." This means the baby can be felt at the beginning of the birth canal, but it has not dropped into the birth canal. That is, the baby is not engaged (fixed) in the birth canal yet. The baby may even move away from your healthcare provider's fingers when you are examined.

Can Your Baby Fall Out?

No, it can't, although it may feel that way. What you are probably experiencing is the pressure of your baby as it moves lower in the birth canal. If this occurs, bring it to your doctor's attention. He or she may want to do a pelvic exam to check how low the baby's head is.

Constipation

Bowel habits may change during pregnancy. Most women notice an increase in constipation, often accompanied by irregular bowel habits and an increased occurrence of hemorrhoids. These problems are usually the result of a slowdown in the movement of food through the gastrointestinal system and iron supplements or iron in prenatal vitamins.

Do not use laxatives to relieve constipation, other than those mentioned in the box below, without consulting your healthcare provider. If constipation is a continuing problem, discuss it with him or her.

Natural Ways to Relieve Constipation

Increase your fluid intake, and exercise three or four times a week. Many doctors suggest prune juice or a mild laxative, such as milk of magnesia. Certain foods that are high in fiber, such as bran and prunes, increase the bulk in your diet and may help relieve constipation.

Take Care of Your Teeth

It's important to maintain your regular dental checkup schedule during pregnancy. Recent research has shown that women with gum disease are seven times more likely to deliver a premature baby. Take care of any gum problems you may experience during pregnancy.

If you need dental treatment, advise your dentist you are pregnant before anything is done. Some dental anesthetics might harm your baby. In most cases, a pregnant woman should not have a general anesthetic.

Bleeding Gums

Pregnancy can cause sore, bleeding, swollen gums because of hormonal changes. Your gums are more susceptible to irritation and may bleed more often when you floss or brush your teeth. Ask your dentist to check for this. Your gums usually clear up by themselves after the baby is born. Talk to your dentist if the problem becomes too uncomfortable.

You may notice a small nodule on your gum. It is called a *pregnancy tumor* or *pyogenic granuloma* and may bleed when you brush your teeth or eat. This condition usually clears up after pregnancy, but don't ignore it if it causes you problems.

Special Procedures

I usually advise a pregnant woman to wait until after the baby is born to have any elective dental procedure, such as dental bonding. However, if you have a dental trauma, such as an abscess or a broken tooth, take care of it immediately!

X-rays. If your dentist wants to take an X-ray of your teeth, be sure you tell him or her you're pregnant *before* you begin your exam. In most cases, avoid dental X-rays while you are pregnant. If there is a particular need for them, discuss the problem with your dentist and your doctor before proceeding any further. If you must have an X-ray, shield your pregnancy with a lead apron.

Antibiotic treatment. Before a procedure such as a root canal, your dentist may want you to take an antibiotic medication to protect you from infection. Discuss this situation with both your dentist and your doctor ahead of time. They will be able to decide the best course of action. Taking care of this kind of problem is important—an infection you have might possibly harm your baby. Together, your dentist and doctor will plan the safest course of treatment for you and your baby.

Good Dental Hygiene

Here are some tips to help you keep your teeth in good shape.
- Brush your teeth after every meal.
- Floss teeth at least once a day.
- Have at least one checkup and dental cleaning during pregnancy, preferably after the first trimester.
- Watch your diet. Eat foods rich in vitamin C (good for gums) and calcium (to keep teeth healthy).
- If you have morning sickness, rinse teeth thoroughly after vomiting.

Discomforts You May Experience

Frequent Urination

One of the first symptoms of early pregnancy is frequent urination. This problem continues off and on throughout pregnancy; you may have to get up to go to the bathroom at night when you never did before. It usually lessens during the second trimester, then returns during the third trimester, when the growing baby puts pressure on the bladder.

It seems like I am always going to the bathroom since I found out I'm pregnant. Is this normal?
More frequent urination is common in pregnancy.

Urinary-Tract Infections

It is more common to get urinary-tract infections during pregnancy. They are also called *bladder infections, cystitis* and *UTIs*. Symptoms include painful urination, a burning sensation during urination, the feeling of urgency to urinate, blood in the urine and frequent urination.

You can help prevent urinary-tract infections by not "holding" your urine. Empty your bladder as soon as you feel you need to. Drink plenty of fluids. Cranberry juice helps acidify your urine (kills bacteria) and may help you avoid infections. For some women, it helps to urinate after having intercourse.

A urinary-tract infection may be a cause of premature labor and low-birthweight infants. If you think you have an infection, discuss it with your healthcare provider. If you do have an infection, take the entire prescription of antibiotics prescribed for you.

Vaginal Discharge

It's normal to have an increase in vaginal discharge or vaginal secretion during pregnancy, called *leukorrhea*. The discharge is usually white or yellow and fairly thick. It probably isn't an infection if it's not irritating.

We believe the discharge is caused by the increased blood flow to the skin and muscles around the vagina, which also causes Chadwick's sign in early pregnancy. This symptom is visible to your doctor as a violet or blue coloration of your vagina when he or she does a pelvic exam. (It's one of the reasons your doctor performs a pelvic exam on you in early pregnancy.)

Do *not* douche if you have a heavy vaginal discharge during pregnancy. Wear sanitary pads for protection. Avoid wearing pantyhose and nylon underwear—choose cotton underwear or underwear with a cotton crotch.

You can learn to tell the difference between vaginal discharge and a vaginal infection. The discharge that accompanies a vaginal infection is often foul-smelling, with a greenish or yellowish color, and causes itching or irritation around or inside the vagina. If you have any of these symptoms, notify your healthcare provider. Treatment is often possible with creams and ointments that are safe to use during pregnancy.

Breast Changes

Your breasts undergo many changes during pregnancy. After about 8 weeks, it's normal for your breasts to start getting larger. You may notice they are lumpy or nodular. These are all normal changes in pregnancy.

Your breasts will enlarge during your pregnancy. However, a very large increase in size is extremely unlikely. On average, women gain between 1 and 1-1/2 pounds in each breast.

Breast Tenderness and Color

Tenderness, tingling or soreness of your breasts early in pregnancy is common. Before pregnancy the areola, which surrounds the nipple, is usually pink. It turns brown or red-brown and may get larger during pregnancy and lactation (when you are producing milk).

My breasts are really sore. Is this normal?
Changes in your breasts may begin early in your pregnancy; it isn't unusual for them to tingle or be sore. You may also notice your breasts getting larger, or see a darkening area or an elevation of the glands around the nipple.

Your Maternity Wardrobe

When your clothes don't fit well and you're uncomfortable, it's time for maternity wear! By the beginning of the second trimester (around the 14th week of pregnancy), maternity clothes will probably be a necessity. If this is your first pregnancy, you may not need maternity clothes until a little later.

Now that I know I'm pregnant, I look forward to wearing maternity clothes. When will I need them? It's hard to predict exactly when you'll need to start wearing maternity clothes. You may have some clothes that are loose enough to wear for a while. You might be able to wear some of your partner's shirts. When you become uncomfortable wearing your regular clothes, it's time to start wearing maternity clothes.

Comfort and Fit

Natural fabrics. Choose natural fabrics when possible—avoid synthetic fabrics. During pregnancy, your metabolic rate increases, and you may feel warmer than usual. Wear fabrics that "breathe," such as cotton in the summer and wool in the winter. Layer your clothing in winter.

Wear fabrics that "breathe," such as cotton in the summer and wool in the winter.

Comfortable style. Fashion is a matter of personal preference, but I'll share with you some tips my patients have given me. They have found the following styles added to their comfort:

• wide, elastic bands or panels that fit under your abdomen to provide support
• wrap-around openings that tie and are easy to adjust
• elastic waists that expand
• button or pleated waistbands that are adjustable
• waistbands with sliders to adjust fit

Maternity underwear. Undergarments that add support to your abdomen, breasts or legs may make you feel more comfortable during pregnancy. These undergarments include maternity bras, nursing bras, maternity panties and maternity support hose. Be sure to choose panties and support hose with a cotton crotch.

Maternity bras. Maternity bras are designed to provide your enlarging breasts the extra support they need during pregnancy. They have wider sides and stretchier backs than regular bras. They usually have four sets of hooks on the back, instead of two or three, providing more room for you to grow.

You may be tempted to buy a regular bra in a larger size instead of buying a maternity bra, but it's probably better to buy a maternity bra. They provide better support for your heavier breasts.

Nursing bra. A nursing bra is worn for breastfeeding; it has cups that open so you can breastfeed without having to undress. Buy a nursing bra only if you plan to breastfeed your baby. You won't need one if you bottlefeed. Wait until the final weeks of your pregnancy to buy a nursing bra; don't buy one before the 36th week of pregnancy. It may be difficult to get a correct fit before then.

Choose a nursing bra with about a finger's width of space between any part of the cup and your breast. This allows for the enlargement of your breasts when your milk comes in.

Choose a nursing bra with about a finger's width of space between any part of the cup and your breast. This allows for the enlargement of your breasts when your milk comes in. Take nursing pads with you when shopping for a nursing bra for a better fit. Choose a bra that is comfortable when fastened on the loosest row of hooks to allow for shrinkage in your ribcage after pregnancy.

Maternity panties. These panties provide support for your enlarging abdomen. Some have panels for your abdomen; others have a wide elastic band that fits under your abdomen to provide support. These panties may be most comfortable in the last trimester of pregnancy.

Maternity support stockings. Many women do not have to wear maternity support hose during pregnancy. However, if you have a family history of varicose veins or if you develop them during pregnancy, you may need to wear maternity support stockings. You may not be able to depend on over-the-counter support hose. If you need to visit a vein specialist to have maternity support stockings personally fitted, discuss it with your doctor. See chapter 9 for additional information on varicose veins and compression support stockings.

If you don't have a problem with varicose veins, regular pantyhose are OK to wear. Choose hose with a stretchy, wide, nonbinding waistband, and wear them over or under your abdomen, whichever is more comfortable. You might be able to buy maternity pantyhose.

Leaky Breasts

During the second trimester, the breasts produce *colostrum*, a thin yellow fluid that is the precursor to breast milk. Sometimes it leaks from the breasts or can be expressed by squeezing the nipples. This is normal. It is usually best to leave your breasts alone; don't try to express the fluid. Wear breast pads if you have problems with leakage.

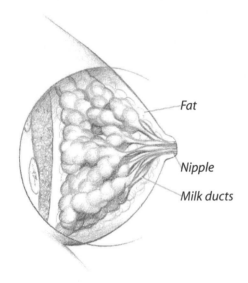

Fat

Nipple

Milk ducts

A pregnant woman's breasts change a lot during pregnancy. One of the greatest changes is the increase in the number of milk ducts, which prepares the breast for nursing.

Inverted Nipples

Inverted nipples are flat or invert (retract) into the breast. Women with inverted nipples may find it more difficult to breastfeed. Devices are available to help prepare inverted nipples for nursing and make it possible for women with inverted nipples to breastfeed their baby. Ask your doctor about this.

To see if you have inverted nipples, place your thumb and index finger on the areola, the dark area surrounding the nipple. Gently compress the base of the nipple. If it flattens or retracts into the breast, you have inverted nipples.

One device to help with inverted nipples is a breast shell you wear on each breast during the last few weeks of pregnancy. These plastic shells are worn under your bra to create a slight pressure at the base of the nipple. This pressure helps draw out the nipple. Ask your doctor for further information.

Other Changes You Experience

Around the 14th week of pregnancy, you may notice your clothes aren't fitting very well. You still may not "show" a lot, but it's important to wear clothes that you feel comfortable in. Pregnant women have a lot of clothing choices these days, so you should be able to find clothes that are comfortable and will allow you to grow bigger. See pages 146 to 147 for tips about buying maternity clothing.

Hair and Nails

Pregnancy hormones circulating through your body often trigger changes in your hair. You may notice less hair loss than usual. Unfortunately, after your baby is born, the hair you have retained during pregnancy is lost. Don't worry if it happens to you—you're not going bald!

The same hormones that stimulate hair growth also temporarily influence your nails. You may find that you have problems keeping your nails filed to a practical length during pregnancy. Enjoy them while you're pregnant!

Facial Hair

Some women notice they have more facial hair during pregnancy. Usually it's not a problem, but check with your healthcare provider if it worries you. Facial hair will probably disappear or decrease after pregnancy, so wait before making any decisions about permanent hair removal.

Body Temperature

During pregnancy, your metabolism increases; your body uses more energy when you're pregnant. You may feel overheated or hot.

Pregnancy hormones elevate your body temperature, which may lead to greater perspiration. Use absorbent talc to help keep you dry because excess moisture can result in a heat rash. Don't get over-heated. Wear layers of clothing, and peel them off if you have to. If you perspire heavily, keep up your fluid intake to avoid dehydration.

A Different Bulge (Not the Baby)

When you lie down and look at your stomach, you may notice a bulge you didn't have before (not the baby). Abdominal muscles are stretched and pushed apart as your baby grows. Muscles that are attached to the lower portion of your ribs may separate in the midline. Called a *diastasis recti*, it isn't painful, and it does not harm the baby.

This condition may still be present after the birth of your baby, but the separation won't be as noticeable. Exercising can strengthen the muscles, but a small bulge or gap may remain.

Measuring Your Abdomen

As you progress in your pregnancy, your doctor needs a point of reference to measure how much your uterus is growing. Your abdomen will probably be measured at each office visit during your pregnancy. Some doctors measure from the bellybutton to the top of the uterus. Others measure from the *pubis symphysis*, the place where pubic bones meet in the middle-lower part of your abdomen, to the top of the uterus.

These measurements reveal a great deal. If at 20 weeks, you measure 11.2 inches (28cm), your doctor may be alerted to the possibility of twins or an incorrect due date. If you measure 6 inches (15cm) at this point, your due date may be wrong or there may be a concern about intrauterine-growth retardation or some other problem. If there is a question, your doctor will have you evaluated further by ultrasound.

A couple of my friends got pregnant at about the same time I did, but we all look as if we're at different stages of pregnancy. Is anything wrong?
No, not usually. Every woman's pregnancy is different, and every woman reacts to pregnancy differently. A lot of what you look like depends on your size (how tall you are, your weight) and the size of your growing baby. Don't expect to look the same as other women or to have the same experiences as your friends.

When "Lightening" Occurs

Often a few weeks before labor begins or at the beginning of labor, your baby's head begins to enter the birth canal, and your uterus seems to "drop" a bit. This is called *lightening*. It's normal.

One benefit of lightening is an increase in space in your upper abdomen, which gives you more room to breathe. However, as your baby descends, you may notice more pressure in your pelvis, bladder and rectum, which may make you uncomfortable.

Center of Gravity Changes

When your uterus grows, it grows out in front of you, so your center of gravity moves forward over your legs. Your joints are looser, and it may feel as if they are slipping. Your posture may suffer, which may cause backaches.

Your Partner and Your Pregnancy 10

Your partner's support before, during and after your pregnancy is important to you. Having someone to talk with, share concerns with and plan your future as a family with increases the joy and happiness you feel as you go through your pregnancy. While you are probably excited, your partner may feel some anxiety. It's probably important to your partner to share his feelings and concerns with you, too.

Your pregnancy is the beginning of big changes in your life. After the birth of your baby, you will be a family. You will have wonderful experiences to share and perhaps also some hard times to weather. Knowing you can count on one another helps when everything may seem overwhelming. Establishing communication and caring for each other during this "pregnant" time can strengthen the bonds of your relationship and will help you in your future together.

Involving Your Partner

Getting pregnant and having a baby involves *both* of you. Talk together about the decision to get pregnant, your health and your partner's health. Do this before you try to get pregnant.

During the pregnancy, your partner can be an important source of support. It's probably good to involve him as much as he is willing to be involved. Make him feel he's a part of what's going on.

Is it OK for my husband to go to prenatal appointments with me?
It's a great idea for him to accompany you! It will help him realize what is happening to you and may help him feel more like he's a part of the pregnancy. It's also good for your husband and your doctor to meet before labor begins.

Your partner may feel increased anxiety as your pregnancy progresses. He may be concerned about your health, the health of the baby, sex, labor and delivery, and his abilities to be a good father. Share your own concerns with him. Hearing how you feel may help calm his anxieties. Let him know how he can help you and be involved in the pregnancy (see box below).

Many fathers-to-be experience some sort of physical problem during their wife's pregnancy, a condition called *couvade*. It was first noticed in a Carib Indian tribe in which every expectant father engages in rituals that enable him to understand what his wife is experiencing. In our culture, a father-to-be may experience nausea, headache, back and muscle aches, insomnia, fatigue and depression.

How to Help Your Pregnant Partner

Men, you can be a great help to your pregnant partner!
Here are some ideas patients have told me helped them a lot.

- Keep stress to a minimum.
- Communicate about everything.
- Be patient and supportive.
- Promote good nutrition.
- Encourage exercise.
- Help around the house when possible, and do the more strenuous chores.
- Attend prenatal checkups when possible.
- Plan for the baby's arrival.
- Learn about the birth process.

If He Is Not as Enthusiastic about the Pregnancy

Not every expectant father is as excited about the impending birth as the mother-to-be is. A woman is directly involved in the pregnancy because she is carrying the baby. Her partner is less involved, so she may have to adjust her expectations somewhat. If this sounds like your situation, you may need to take an active role in encouraging your partner to become more involved, such as asking him to accompany you to a prenatal visit. Discuss with him his feelings about the pregnancy. He may have fears and uncertainties he hasn't told you. Be open and direct with each other about your feelings—it will help both of you.

We've been considering names for our baby; some of them are unusual. Should we discuss our choices with others?

I had one patient tell me she and her husband decide on a name together, but don't tell anyone else until after the baby is born. She said it's very easy for people to criticize a name when you're thinking about it, but few people will tell you they don't like a name when you've already named your baby!

How can I involve my partner more in my pregnancy?

Because the pregnant woman is the focus during pregnancy, a man may feel left out. Educate him so he understands what you and the baby are going through. Share this book and other books and information you receive with him. Take him with you to see the doctor.

Delivery of Your Baby

Your husband can help you a lot during labor and the delivery of your baby. You and your partner may want to discuss his level of participation well before labor begins. Some men prefer not to be involved in the birth itself; it's a personal choice. Other couples view labor and the delivery of their child as a very special experience to share. See the first box on page 156 for some of the most important ways your partner can help you during labor and delivery.

Who Cuts the Umbilical Cord?

Many couples today discuss the possibility of having the father cut his baby's umbilical cord after delivery. Cutting the cord is something many men enjoy doing. Talk to your doctor in advance about your husband's participation in your labor and delivery.

My doctor said my husband can be very important to me during labor and delivery. How?

Your husband can help you in several ways. He can help prepare you for labor and delivery and can support you as you labor. You can both attend a childbirth-education class to learn how. He can share in the joy of the delivery of your baby. He can also support you emotionally, which is very important to you both.

Being Helpful at Home

It's better for both partners to share the responsibilities and chores of parenthood. Form an equal-parenthood partnership with your husband. Encourage him to take equal responsibility for parenting your new baby. He'll enjoy being a father much more if he is actively involved in the care and decision making for his new daughter or son.

Dad Can Bond with Baby, Too

The baby's father can begin bonding with the baby before birth and continue after the baby is born. Encourage your partner to try the following suggestions.

- Have your partner talk to the baby while it is in the uterus.
- Encourage your partner to talk to the baby soon after birth. Babies bond to sound quickly.
- Have your partner hold the baby close and make eye contact; a baby relates to people through sight and smell.
- Let your partner feed the baby. It's easy if you bottlefeed.
- If you breastfeed, let him give the baby a bottle of your expressed breast milk.
- Encourage him to help with daily baby chores, such as changing diapers, holding the baby when it is restless, dressing and bathing the baby.
- Ask your partner to get up occasionally at night with the baby.

Father's Health

Studies show that reproduction and fetal development may be affected if a man is exposed to various substances. Exposure by the father-to-be to alcohol, cigarettes, certain drugs and some environmental hazards could cause problems for the unborn baby. Problems include miscarriage, stillbirth, birth defects, low-birthweight babies, a greater risk of childhood cancer and even subtle learning disabilities. Exposure could also affect the man's ability to father a child.

Usually such exposure on the male's part is harmful if it occurs before and around the time of conception. However, we also know a father-to-be's smoking throughout his partner's pregnancy has been linked to some problems.

Alcohol Use

Researchers have shown that heavy alcohol consumption by the baby's father may produce a condition called *fetal alcohol syndrome* (FAS) in the baby. See chapter 12 for further information on FAS. Alcohol intake by the father has also been linked to intrauterine-growth retardation (see page 129).

Drug Use

Your partner's drug habits may affect your pregnancy if he was using "recreational drugs" when you became pregnant. If this is your situation, tell your doctor and see what can be done to reassure you about your baby's well-being.

Environmental Hazards

You need to be concerned if your partner is exposed to harmful chemicals or other substances at work. Substances may be brought into your home on your partner's work clothes. If you think you may be exposed to hazardous substances in this manner, be sure to discuss it with your partner and your healthcare provider.

He Smokes, You Don't

When a nonsmoking pregnant woman and her unborn baby are exposed to secondary smoke, both are exposed to harmful chemicals. It's a good idea to ask your partner to stop smoking during your pregnancy or at least not to smoke inside your home.

His Age

We now have information indicating the age and health of the father of your baby does make a difference in the baby's health. Some researchers believe there may be a slight increase in the risk of Down syndrome if the baby's father is over 50.

Sex during Pregnancy

When a woman's partner comes to her prenatal appointments with her, the man often asks if it is safe for him and his partner to have sex during pregnancy. I'm always glad to be asked this question because it gives me an opportunity to discuss something very important to this couple. As we all know, sexual intimacy is a wonderful way to express love for each other. Just because pregnancy has occurred doesn't mean this form of closeness has to stop.

In most instances, my response is, "Yes, it's OK to have sex." In all but a few instances, sexual intercourse or other forms of lovemaking present few problems for the woman or the baby. Occasionally caution must be used, however. Your own doctor, who knows your pregnancy so well, will be able to advise what is best in your case.

Common Concerns

If you and your husband are concerned about sexual activity during pregnancy, discuss it with your doctor. You need to rule out any complications and ask for individual advice. Most doctors agree sex can be a part of a normal pregnancy.

Frequent sexual activity should not be harmful to a healthy pregnancy. Usually a couple can continue the level of sexual activity they are used to. If you are concerned, discuss it with your healthcare provider.

Fear for the Baby

It's common for a couple to worry about having sex because "it might hurt the baby." However, sexual activity doesn't usually harm a growing baby. Neither intercourse nor orgasm should be a problem if you have a healthy pregnancy. The baby is well protected by the amniotic sac and amniotic fluid. Uterine muscles are strong and protect the baby, and a thick mucus plug seals the cervix, which helps protect against infection. Often it's the man who asks about sex during pregnancy. You might want to discuss this with your doctor if your partner goes with you to your appointments. If he doesn't, assure him there should be no problems if the pregnancy is normal.

If you feel the baby move more after sexual intercourse, it doesn't mean it was disturbed, uncomfortable or in danger. Your baby moves a lot, no matter what you're doing.

Desire for Sex

Stronger sex drive. Researchers have reported that pregnancy enhances the sex drive for some women. Some women may experience orgasms or multiple orgasms for the first time during pregnancy. This is due to heightened hormonal activity and increased blood flow to the pelvic area.

Less desire. During the first trimester, you may experience fatigue and nausea. During the third trimester, weight gain, an enlarging abdomen, tender breasts and other problems may make you feel less desirous of sex. Any of these may cause you to feel a decreased desire to have sex. This is normal. Tell your partner how you're feeling, and try to work out a solution that is good for both of you.

> *Sex is individual; you won't fit any pattern perfectly.*

Feel "less sexy." You may feel less attractive during pregnancy, but many men find a pregnant woman very attractive. If you experience these feelings, discuss them with your partner.

Sex is individual; you won't fit any pattern perfectly. Tenderness and understanding can help you both.

Physical Discomfort during Lovemaking

You may find new positions for lovemaking are necessary. Your larger abdomen may make some positions uncomfortable. In addition, physicians advise a woman not to lie flat on her back from the beginning of the third trimester until the birth. The weight of the uterus restricts circulation. Lie on your side or with you on top.

As I've mentioned, discuss any complications and concerns with your doctor throughout your pregnancy. If you have unusual symptoms during or following sexual activity, discuss them before resuming sex.

Miscarriage and Early Labor

If you have a history of miscarriage, your doctor may caution you against sex and orgasm. However, no data actually links sexual intercourse and miscarriage.

My friend told me that having sex can cause me to go into labor early. Is that true?
Orgasm causes mild uterine contractions, so if you have a history of early labor your doctor may warn against intercourse and orgasm. Chemicals in semen may also stimulate contractions, so it may not be advisable for the woman's partner to ejaculate inside her. However, in a normal pregnancy, even one near delivery, this is usually not a problem.

What to Avoid

Don't insert any object into the vagina that could cause injury or infection. Blowing air into the vagina is also dangerous because it can force a potentially fatal air bubble into the woman's bloodstream. Nipple stimulation releases oxytocin, which causes uterine contractions. You might want to discuss this with your doctor.

Are there times we should avoid sex during pregnancy?
Avoid sexual activity if you have any of the following problems or conditions:

- placenta previa or a low-lying placenta
- incompetent cervix
- premature labor
- multiple fetuses
- ruptured bag of waters
- pain
- unexplained vaginal bleeding or discharge
- you can't find a comfortable position
- either partner has an unhealed herpes lesion
- you believe labor has begun

Sexually Transmitted Diseases

11

It used to be uncommon for a pregnant woman to see her doctor and be worried about having a sexually transmitted disease (STD). Today, I see more women who have this concern. You may be unsure what an STD is. It is a disease that is contracted during sexual activity, whether it is sexual intercourse, oral intercourse or anal intercourse.

Women can be exposed to many different types of STDs, and we know they can harm a growing baby. This chapter covers the most common sexually transmitted diseases and presents information so you will know what to look for if you think you have been exposed. If you have a sexually transmitted disease, see a doctor for treatment as soon as possible!

Yeast Infections

Monilial vulvovaginitis is an infection caused by yeast, or monilia, and usually affects the vagina and vulva. Yeast infections are more common in pregnant women than in nonpregnant women. This STD has no major negative effects on pregnancy, but it can cause discomfort for you during pregnancy.

Yeast infections may be harder to control when you are pregnant. They may require frequent retreatment or longer treatment (10 to 14 days instead of 3 to 7 days). Creams or suppositories used for treatment are safe during pregnancy, although most physicians recommend avoiding treatment during the first trimester. Your partner does not have to be treated unless he has symptoms.

161

The antifungal drug Diflucan® (fluconazole) is a pill you take just once to clear up a yeast infection. Unfortunately, we do not recommend it during pregnancy or breastfeeding because it has not yet proved safe for use in either situation.

What kind of problems can a yeast infection cause the baby?
A newborn infant can get *thrush* (a mouth infection) after passing through a birth canal infected with a yeast infection. Treatment of the newborn infant with nystatin is effective.

Trichomonal Vaginitis

Trichomonal vaginitis is a venereal infection caused by parasites called *trichomonas*. Symptoms include persistent burning and itching of the vulva area accompanied by a frothy white or yellow discharge. This infection has no major effects on a pregnancy.

Treatment of trichomonal vaginitis is a concern during pregnancy. Metronidazole, the drug used to treat trichomonal vaginitis, should not be taken during the first trimester of pregnancy. It is prescribed after the first trimester.

Venereal Warts

Venereal warts are caused by the human papilloma virus (HPV), which is passed during intercourse. Venereal warts are skin tags or warts that are transmitted by sexual contact. They are called *condylomata acuminatum*.

Venereal warts may cause a problem during pregnancy, but usually don't. These warty skin tags can become enlarged during pregnancy. If a woman has extensive veneral warts, a Cesarean delivery may be necessary to avoid heavy bleeding and other complications. Infants delivered through a birth canal infected with venereal warts have been known to get small benign tumors on the vocal cords (*laryngeal papillomas*) after delivery.

Venereal warts usually aren't treated during pregnancy. If warts become large enough to interfere with delivery, your physician may recommend removing them. If the warts must be removed, excision is the only treatment used during pregnancy.

Genital Herpes Simplex

Genital herpes simplex infection is herpes infection that involves the genital area. It can be significant during pregnancy because the newborn is at some risk of infection with the disease at the time of delivery.

The symptoms of genital herpes are painful clusters of small blisters in the genital area in and around the vaginal opening. At first the blisters tingle and itch. Then they become sore and break, leaving painful ulcers. Symptoms can also include aches and pains, fatigue and fever. The usual time duration of symptoms is 1 to 3 weeks. Subsequent outbreaks can occur at any time but are usually shorter and milder than the first outbreak.

A herpes infection early in pregnancy may be associated with an increase in miscarriage or premature delivery, but this is unusual. Infection in the mother is associated with low birthweight in the baby. We believe an infant can contract the infection when traveling through an infected birth canal. When membranes rupture, the infection may also travel upward to the uterus and infect the baby.

There is no effective cure for herpes. Acyclovir may decrease the intensity and duration of symptoms. The safety of acyclovir in pregnancy has been established. When a woman has an active herpes infection late in pregnancy, a Cesarean section may be performed to prevent the infant from traveling through the infected birth canal.

To avoid getting a herpes infection, you must know your partner is free from infection. If your partner suspects he has herpes, he should see a doctor for treatment. If your partner has herpes or could have been exposed to it, the best way to avoid the disease is through abstinence from sex during outbreaks and having him wear a condom during intercourse at other times.

Chlamydia

Chlamydia is a common sexually transmitted disease. It is estimated that between 3 and 5 million people are infected each year. Symptoms include vaginal discharge and pelvic pain. However, it can be symptomless—you may not know you have been exposed. Between 20 and 40% of all sexually active women have been exposed at some time.

One of the most important complications of chlamydia is pelvic inflammatory disease (PID). This is a severe infection of the female organs that can make it more difficult for you to get pregnant. If you have had PID, your chance of having an ectopic pregnancy is greater.

During pregnancy, a mother-to-be can pass a chlamydial infection to her baby as it travels through the birth canal. The baby will have a 20 to 50% chance of getting chlamydia. A baby exposed to chlamydia may be born with an eye infection or pneumonia.

Tests for chlamydia include a pelvic exam and a cervical swab. Treatment usually involves tetracycline, which should *not* be given to a pregnant woman. During pregnancy, erythromycin is the drug of choice.

Gonorrhea

Gonorrhea is a venereal infection transmitted primarily by sexual intercourse. In a woman, the urethra, vulva, vagina and Fallopian tubes may be involved. However, there may be no symptoms of the disease.

The baby may be infected as it passes through the birth canal, resulting in eye inflammation. Eyedrops are routinely used in newborns to prevent this problem. The baby may get other infections also.

Gonorrheal infections are treated with penicillin and other medications that are safe to use during pregnancy.

Syphilis

Syphilis is a sexually transmitted disease characterized by lesions that may involve any organ or tissue. The disease may be present for years without symptoms.

Syphilis can affect a pregnancy in several ways. It increases the chance of stillbirth. It can also cause various infections in the newborn. Any stage of syphilis during pregnancy can result in an infected infant.

Syphilis can be treated effectively during pregnancy with penicillin and other safe medications.

AIDS

AIDS (acquired immune deficiency syndrome) affects more women today than in the past. Pregnancy may hide some AIDS symptoms, which can make the disease harder to discover. Some treatments for AIDS may not be used during pregnancy.

It is possible for a woman to pass HIV, the virus that causes AIDS, to the baby before birth, during birth and, if she breastfeeds, after birth. The survival rate for children diagnosed with AIDS in the first 6 months of life is low.

Two blood tests are used to determine if a person has AIDS or is positive for HIV (human immunodeficiency virus)—the ELISA test and the Western Blot test. If the ELISA test is positive, it is confirmed by the Western Blot test. Both tests measure antibodies to the human immunodeficiency virus that causes AIDS, not the virus itself. The Western Blot test is believed to be 99% sensitive and specific.

Research has shown that AZT treatment can decrease the likelihood that an infected mother will pass the infection to her baby. The health risk to a baby infected with HIV is serious and significant, but advances continue to be made in AIDS research. If you are concerned about HIV and AIDS, discuss it with your physician. Combinations of medications are being tested with some success.

Substance Use and Abuse 12

I am surprised when a pregnant woman ignores what she eats, drinks, smokes or ingests, in hopes they won't pass to her developing baby. In previous chapters, I've addressed medications and other substances and their effect on a pregnancy. In this chapter, I want to pay special attention to some of the substances most harmful to a pregnancy. I believe *every* pregnant woman, and those around her, should know the dangers of these substances. Many people are unaware of how destructive even the occasional use of some of these can be.

In this chapter, you will learn what harm smoking, alcohol use and various types of drug use can cause you and your baby. Information about the effects of specific substances on a human pregnancy often comes from cases of exposure before the pregnancy is discovered. These cases help researchers understand possible harmful effects, but they don't help us understand the complete picture. For this reason, we cannot make exact statements about particular substances and their effects on the mother or developing baby.

I don't mean to frighten you with this information. However, it is important for every pregnant woman to know about the effects smoking, alcohol and drug use can have on herself and her baby.

Your baby cannot protect itself. It's up to you to give your baby the protection he or she deserves.

What activities affect my developing baby?
Just about anything you do can affect your baby.
Cigarette smoke, alcohol, drugs, tranquilizers—even
caffeine—can affect a fetus.
Some substances that you can use safely may have
adverse effects on a developing fetus. Other
substances are bad for both you and your baby.
It's never too early to start thinking about how your
actions affect the baby growing inside you.

Cigarette Smoking

Cigarette smoking is harmful because tobacco smoke the mother inhales contains many toxic substances, including nicotine, carbon monoxide, hydrogen cyanide, tars, resins and some cancer-causing agents. When a pregnant woman inhales cigarette smoke, these chemicals pass through the placenta to the developing baby.

A pregnant woman who smokes one pack of cigarettes a day (20 cigarettes) inhales tobacco smoke more than 11,000 times during an average pregnancy! Tobacco smoke inhaled by the mother affects a growing baby.

Pregnant women face increased risk of pregnancy complications if they smoke cigarettes. The risk of developing placental abruption increases almost 25% in moderate smokers and 65% in heavy smokers. Placenta previa occurs 25% more often in moderate smokers and 90% more often in heavy smokers. For further information on these problems, see chapter 14.

Infants born to mothers who smoke weigh less than other babies.

In addition, cigarette smoking during pregnancy increases the risk of miscarriage, death of the fetus or death of a baby soon after birth. This risk is directly related to the number of cigarettes a woman smokes each day. It can increase as much as 35% for a woman who smokes more than a pack of cigarettes a day.

What effects can my cigarette smoking have on the baby?

Infants born to mothers who smoke weigh less than other babies. This can cause problems for the baby. Lower IQ scores and increased incidence of reading disorders have been noted in children born to mothers who smoked during pregnancy. Hyperactivity is also higher among babies born to women who smoked. Research has shown that smoking during pregnancy interferes with the body's absorption of vitamins B and C and folic acid. One recent study linked cigarette smoking by a mother-to-be with mental retardation in her baby. In addition, newborns of mothers who smoke may experience nicotine deprivation. Adults who suffer from nicotine deprivation exhibit symptoms such as cravings, nervousness and irritability.

Stop-Smoking Systems

The stop-smoking patches and gum contain many of the same substances cigarettes do. The specific effects of the Nicoderm® patch and Nicorette® gum on fetal development are unknown. If you are pregnant, researchers advise *not* using either of these "stop-smoking" systems because you and your baby might be exposed to the harmful substances you are trying to avoid.

What can I do if I smoke?

The best way to help yourself is to quit smoking completely before and during your pregnancy. If you can't do this—it's hard to quit cold turkey—reduce the number of cigarettes you smoke. It may help reduce your risks.

Can Partner's Smoking Affect Mother and Baby?

Some research indicates a nonsmoker and her unborn baby are exposed to carboxyhemoglobin and nicotine through secondary smoke. These substances may harm you and your baby. Ask your partner to stop smoking while you are pregnant. You might suggest he quit smoking altogether. At the very least, ask him not to smoke around you or in the home. It's also a good idea to avoid smoky environments such as bars.

Alcohol Use

A pregnant woman's alcohol use carries considerable risk. Even moderate use of alcohol has been linked to an increase in the chance of miscarriage. Excessive alcohol consumption during pregnancy can result in abnormalities in the baby. Chronic use of alcohol during pregnancy can lead to fetal alcohol syndrome, which is abnormal fetal development.

Is it all right to drink alcohol while I'm pregnant?
Alcohol use by a pregnant woman carries considerable risk. Even moderate use of alcohol has been linked to an increase in the chance of miscarriage. Excessive alcohol consumption during pregnancy can result in abnormalities in the baby. Chronic use of alcohol during pregnancy can lead to fetal alcohol syndrome, which is abnormal fetal development.

Fetal Alcohol Syndrome (FAS)

Fetal alcohol syndrome is a collection of problems that affect children born to women who drink excessive amounts of alcohol during pregnancy. It is characterized by growth retardation before and after birth. Defects in the heart and limbs, and unusual facial characteristics, such as a short, upturned nose, a flat upper jawbone and "different" eyes, have also been seen in FAS children. These children may also have behavioral problems, impaired speech and impaired use of joints and muscles.

For a definite diagnosis of fetal alcohol syndrome, specific criteria must be met. The mother-to-be must have a history of alcohol consumption during pregnancy. The baby must exhibit three medical criteria—abnormalities of the face or skull, growth retardation and damage to the central nervous system, usually a mental deficiency.

Fetal Alcohol Exposure (FAE)

If the mother's consumption of alcohol cannot be proved as described above, we generally refer to the condition as *FAE* or *fetal alcohol exposure*. A baby with a mild birth defect may be diagnosed with FAE if the mother had anything to drink during pregnancy.

How much alcohol is "too much"?

At this time, we believe *any* amount of alcohol is too much. Most studies indicate four to five, or more, drinks a day are required to cause FAS, but mild abnormalities have been associated with as little as two drinks a day (1 ounce of alcohol). It's best to avoid alcohol completely while you're pregnant.

There is a lot of disagreement about whether it is OK for women to have a "social" or occasional glass of alcohol during pregnancy because we don't know what is a "safe" level of alcohol consumption during pregnancy. I recommend not drinking any alcohol during pregnancy. Why take the risk?

The possibility of birth defects is the reason alcoholic beverages carry warning labels. The warning advises women to avoid alcohol during pregnancy because of the possibility of causing problems in the fetus, including FAS and FAE.

Occasional Drink before Pregnancy

I am frequently asked if it's OK for women to have an occasional alcoholic beverage during the time they are trying to conceive a baby. If you're trying to get pregnant, you probably won't know exactly when you do conceive. Why take chances? It's a good idea to stop drinking while you're trying to conceive—that way you'll know you've avoided any problems of this type.

Some researchers believe heavy alcohol consumption by the baby's father close to the time of conception may result in FAS in the baby. Alcohol intake by the father has also been linked to intrauterine-growth retardation.

Drugs and Alcohol Together

If drugs are taken with alcohol, it increases the chance of damaging the fetus. Drugs that cause the greatest concern include analgesics, antidepressants and anticonvulsants.

Other Precautions

Be very careful about substances you use that may contain alcohol. Over-the-counter cough medicines and cold remedies often contain alcohol—as much as 25%!

Drug Use and Drug Abuse

Drug abuse usually refers to drugs prohibited by law, but it can also include use of legal substances, such as alcohol, caffeine, tobacco and prescription medications. "Abuse" of these substances means not using them as they were prescribed or using them to excess.

Dependence on Drugs

Physical dependence implies the drug must be taken to avoid unpleasant withdrawal symptoms—it does not always mean addiction or drug abuse. For example, many caffeine users develop withdrawal symptoms if they stop drinking coffee, but they are not considered drug abusers or drug addicts.

Psychological dependence means the user has developed an emotional need for a drug or medication. This need may be more compelling than a physical need and can provide the stimulus for continued drug use.

Can drug use affect my pregnancy?
Yes! Certain drugs damage the developing fetus. In addition, a woman who abuses drugs may have more complications of pregnancy.

Pregnancy Problems Are More Frequent

Nutritional deficiencies may be more common in pregnant women who abuse drugs. Anemia and fetal-growth retardation can also occur. A pregnant woman may face an increased chance of pre-eclampsia.

Marijuana

Marijuana contains tetrahydrocannabinol (THC). Research has shown the use of marijuana by a mother-to-be can cause problems to the child later in life, including attention deficits, memory problems and impaired decision making. These problems appear between ages 3 and 12 years. Hashish also contains tetrahydrocannabinol (THC). Avoid using it during pregnancy.

Amphetamines

Researchers have shown that use of central-nervous-system stimulants, such as amphetamines, during pregnancy is associated with an increase in cardiovascular (heart) defects in babies.

Barbituates

Barbiturate use may be associated with birth defects, although this has not yet been proved definitely. However, we have seen withdrawal, poor feeding, seizures and other problems in babies born to mothers who abused barbiturates during pregnancy.

Other Tranquilizers

Tranquilizing agents include benzodiazepines (Valium® and Librium®) and other, newer agents. Several studies have related the use of these drugs to an increase in birth defects.

Opioids

Opioids are derived from opium and synthetic compounds with similar actions. They produce euphoria, drowsiness or sleepiness, and decreased sensitivity to pain. Habitual use can lead to physical dependence. Opioids include morphine, Demerol®, heroin and codeine.

These drugs are associated with a variety of congenital abnormalities and complications of pregnancy. Women who use opioids during pregnancy are often at high risk for premature labor, intrauterine-growth retardation and pre-eclampsia. The baby may experience withdrawal symptoms after birth.

If the mother uses the drugs intravenously, other problems may occur, such as AIDS, hepatitis and endocarditis (inflammation of the lining of the heart). Any of these is considered very serious during pregnancy.

Hallucinogens

The use of some hallucinogens, such as LSD, mescaline and peyote, is not as common as it was several years ago. However, use of phencyclidine (PCP), a powerful hallucinogen, is growing.

PCP, also called *angel dust*, can cause severe mental illness and loss of contact with reality in the mother. Research has shown it causes abnormal development in some humans, so we believe it can cause abnormal development in human babies, although it has not been definitely proved.

Cocaine and Crack

Today, cocaine use is a more common complication of pregnancy. Often a user consumes the drug over a long period of time, such as several days. During this time, the user may eat or drink very little, which in itself can have serious consequences for a developing fetus.

Cocaine use has been associated with convulsions, arrhythmia, hypertension and hyperthermia in a pregnant woman. Continual use of cocaine can affect maternal nutrition and temperature control, which can harm the fetus. Cocaine use has been linked with miscarriage, placental abruption and congenital defects. Crack is an even more potent form of cocaine; the effects and warnings regarding cocaine apply to crack as well.

I've heard that cocaine use during early pregnancy can cause serious problems. Is this true?

A woman who uses cocaine during the first 12 weeks of pregnancy has an increased risk of miscarriage. Damage to the developing baby can occur as early as 3 days after conception!

Infants born to mothers who use cocaine or crack often have lower IQs and long-term mental deficiencies. Sudden infant death syndrome (SIDS) is also more common in these babies. Many babies are stillborn.

A Final Thought

You may know someone who used drugs a few times while pregnant, but gave birth to a baby who seemed healthy. You might wonder if the dangers of drug abuse in pregnancy are exaggerated. These dangers are *not* exaggerated! Anyone who abuses drugs but happens to have a healthy baby anyway is lucky. A fetus is totally dependent on the mother-to-be for all of its needs, so *everything* a woman does can affect her baby. What may seem like a small amount of a certain substance to a grown woman can have a major effect on the fetus whose organs are still being formed. Your baby's health is up to you. Do all you can to help your baby have the best possible start in life.

Special Concerns of the Single Mother-to-Be

13

Many women today are having their babies alone, by choice or because the baby's father is unable or unwilling to be with them. Others have the support of the expectant father but have decided not to marry. My goal in providing the information in this chapter is to give you a foundation for seeking answers to questions about your particular situation. I feel comfortable discussing some of the medical and emotional aspects of such a pregnancy because I have been asked many questions about them before.

I do not answer the questions in the second half of this chapter because they concern legal matters I am not qualified to address. However, I include them because this situation has legal ramifications. I hope you will use this set of questions to formulate discussion points about your personal situation to talk over with your attorney, a patient advocate, a hospital social worker, your healthcare provider or family members.

I'm a single woman who has chosen to have my baby alone. What should I tell people who ask me why I am doing this?

It doesn't matter what people ask you—really it's none of their business. What is important is how you feel about the pregnancy. It's up to you to decide what you want to tell people and how much explanation you want to provide.

Dealing with Others

Family

Dealing with your family can be difficult if they are against your decision to have a baby alone. If you're comfortable with your decision, deal with their discomfort by asking them to talk about the reasons they are against your pregnancy. You will never change some people's minds, so you will have to learn to live with their disapproval or ignore it.

Acquaintances

Don't encourage others to ask you questions about your pregnancy unless you are comfortable with their questions. Some people are genuinely concerned about you; others are just nosy. Before you answer, decide if they are truly interested in you. Then share with them as much or as little as you are comfortable discussing.

I'm having a lot of trouble emotionally with this pregnancy. Whom should I talk to about it?
Begin by talking with your healthcare provider. Office personnel can direct you to a counselor or a support group, depending on what you need.

Preparing for the Birth

Like any pregnant woman, you must decide who will be with you when you labor and deliver, and who will be on hand to help afterward. The only special plan I can think of is to decide how you will get to the hospital. One woman decided to have a friend drive her, but couldn't reach her in time. Her next option (all planned in advance) was to call a taxi, which got her to the hospital with time to spare.

Ask a good friend, a relative or someone else who is close to you to be with you during labor. Not all women have their partner as their labor coach. I've found that often a woman who has already given birth using the same method is an excellent labor coach. She will understand your discomfort and be able to identify with your experience.

Reactions in the Hospital

I've been asked if nurses in the hospital will treat a single woman differently than a married woman giving birth. In all my experiences in medical school, during my residency and in my practice, the nurses I have dealt with have been complete professionals. Their job is to provide the best care they possibly can. They pride themselves in taking care of their patients. I have never known any of them to treat any person differently for any reason.

Some people think I'm crazy to have a baby alone. What should I say to them?
Your *friends* won't treat you this way. Once they understand your situation, they will support you. If others give you a hard time, don't talk with them about your pregnancy or your reasons for having your baby alone.

Taking Baby Home

A new baby is an incredible challenge in any situation. You will probably need more support from family and friends when you come home from the hospital because you won't have someone with whom to share the responsibilities. Don't hesitate to ask for help. If you have no one you can ask to give of their time, consider hiring someone to stay with you at night for the first week or two, so you can get back on your feet.

Single mothers who are my patients sometimes wonder if they or their baby will be treated differently by others in the community. Today, being a single mother isn't that unusual, so I doubt you will be treated differently. Many women of all ages have made this decision. A few people may treat you differently; others won't care. Good friends and family members should draw closer to you.

Common Concerns

Small Family

Some single mothers worry their child may miss out on having an extended family, or a second set of grandparents, aunts, uncles and cousins. Families today are different than they were in the past. *Many* children don't have a complete set of parents or grandparents, even in the closest family units. I've found in these situations that an older family friend can be just as loving and giving to a child as a grandparent. Encourage older friends to take an active part in your child's life.

Are there support groups for single parents?
Yes. Ask your healthcare provider for the names of groups in your area. The organizations below can provide local referrals.

Parents without Partners
401 N. Michigan Ave.
Chicago, IL 60011
Tel: (800) 637-7974 or (312) 644-6610
Local chapters in the United States and Canada.

National Organization of Single Mothers
P.O. Box 68
Midland, NC 28107-0068
Tel: (704) 888-KIDS

One-Parent Family Association of Canada
6979 Yonge St., Suite 203
Toronto, Ont. M2M 3X9
Tel: (416) 226-0062

Single Parent Association of Montreal
CP 114
Succe Champlain
LaSalle, Quebec H8P 3H9
Tel: (514) 366-8600

Who Else Can Care for the Child?

It isn't morbid to consider what would happen to your baby if you were to become seriously ill or disabled. Plan ahead for this situation. Find a family member or close friend who can be called upon to help in case this happens. Knowing you have provided for such an event should give you peace of mind.

Together, Not Married

If you are pregnant and you are together with your partner as a couple, most people will assume you are married. You may wonder how important it is to let other people know your actual situation. If it's a sales clerk or a waitress, it probably isn't important to clarify your situation. If it's your doctor, let him or her know the status of your relationship.

I feel as if I have no one close to share my pregnancy problems and concerns with. What can I do?

Share your problems and concerns with your family and friends. Mothers of young children can identify with your experiences—they have had the same or similar experiences recently. If you have friends or family members who have young children, talk with them. Even if you were married, you would probably share your concerns with all of these people. Try not to let your situation alter this.

Legal Questions

The following questions are included without answers because they are legal questions that should be reviewed with an attorney who specializes in family law. Use them as a guide to developing the questions you need to ask about your particular situation.

A friend who's had a baby alone told me I'd better consider the legal ramifications of this situation. What was she talking about?

I've heard that in some states, if I'm unmarried I have to get a special birth certificate. Is this true?

I'm having my baby alone, and I'm concerned about who can make medical decisions for my expected baby and me. Is there anything I can do about this concern?

I'm not married, but I am deeply involved with my baby's father. Can my partner make medical decisions for me if I have problems during or after the birth?

If anything happens to me, can my partner make medical decisions for our baby after it is born?

What are the legal rights of my baby's father if we are not married?

Do my partner's parents also have legal rights in regard to my child (their grandchild)?

My baby's father and I went our separate ways before I knew I was pregnant. Do I have to tell him about the baby?

I chose to have donor (artificial) insemination. If anything happens to me during my labor or delivery, who can make medical decisions for me?

Who can make medical decisions for my baby?

I got pregnant by donor insemination. What do I put on the birth certificate under "father's name"?

Is there a way I can find out more about my sperm donor's family medical history?

Will the sperm bank send me updates if medical problems appear in my sperm donor's family?

I had donor insemination. Does the baby's father have any legal right to be part of my child's life in the future?

Someone was joking with me that my child could marry its sister or brother some day (because I had donor insemination) and wouldn't know it. Is this possible?

As my child grows up, he or she may need some sort of medical help (like a donor kidney) from a sibling. Will the sperm bank release this kind of information?

Problems and Warning Signs 14

I assure my patients who are pregnant that it's completely normal to be somewhat concerned about problems during pregnancy. I'd wonder if they didn't have *any* concerns, so don't feel self-conscious if you're a little afraid of this unknown experience. You're definitely not alone!

By being aware of what problems might occur, and knowing what signs or symptoms to look for, you can help your healthcare team, and we can more easily treat you. I try to impress upon my patients that they are part of their medical care, and you should think the same way. You know your body better than any doctor ever will, so you know when things are "right."

By expressing a concern at one of your prenatal appointments or calling the office if you have a question about something, you and your healthcare professionals will be working together to make this a great pregnancy. And hopefully you'll be able to deal with any situation that arises before it becomes serious.

Express your concerns at your prenatal appointments or call the office if you have a question. By working together, you and your healthcare professionals can make this a great pregnancy experience!

Warning Signs

If you think you have something to worry about in your pregnancy, don't hesitate to ask for help. General warning signs include:

- vaginal bleeding
- painful urination
- severe abdominal pain
- loss of fluid from the vagina, usually a gushing of fluid but sometimes a trickle or continual wetness
- a big change in the movement of the baby or a lack of fetal movement
- high fever (more than 101.6F; 38.7C)
- chills
- severe vomiting or inability to keep food or liquids down
- blurring of vision
- severe swelling of the face or fingers
- a severe headache or a headache that won't go away
- an injury or accident serious enough to concern you about the well-being of your pregnancy, such as a fall or an automobile accident

Bleeding during Pregnancy

Be assured that bleeding during pregnancy is not unusual and doesn't always mean a problem. About one woman in five bleeds sometime in early pregnancy. Tell your doctor about any vaginal bleeding you experience; he or she may want you to have an ultrasound. If it is early in the pregnancy, you may be worried about having a miscarriage. Usually we cannot give a definite answer as to what causes the bleeding, but we do know that it is not usually a problem.

Can Bed Rest Help Stop Bleeding?

Going to bed and resting may help stop vaginal bleeding. My suggestion is to contact your physician before you do anything. Follow his or her instructions. Your doctor knows your medical and pregnancy history, so follow his or her advice.

I called my doctor and told him I had some bleeding. He told me to rest and not to have intercourse. Can't I take some medicine or do something to stop the bleeding and make sure everything is going to be OK?
Your doctor gave you good advice—there isn't a surgical procedure or medicine that will stop the bleeding. If you or your doctor are very concerned, he may schedule you for an ultrasound. An ultrasound won't stop anything from happening; it may give some reassurance, but you may still bleed. Decisions about a course of treatment or actions to take are individual and must be discussed with your doctor, who knows your past history and personal situation.

Falling while Pregnant

A fall is the most frequent cause of minor injury during pregnancy. Fortunately, a fall is usually without serious injury to the fetus or to the mother. If you fall, call your doctor; you may require attention. If it's a bad fall, your doctor may advise monitoring the baby's heartbeat or having an ultrasound.

If I fall, what signs indicate a problem for my pregnancy?
Some signs and symptoms that alert you to a possible problem include:
• bleeding
• a gush of fluid from the vagina, indicating rupture of membranes
• severe abdominal pain
Movement of the baby after a fall is reassuring.

Miscarriage

A *miscarriage* is a loss of a pregnancy before 20 weeks of gestation. An embryo or a fetus is delivered before it can survive outside the womb. This may also be called a *spontaneous abortion*.

Do miscarriages occur very often?
Miscarriages occur in one out of every four pregnancies.

The Warning Signs of Miscarriage

The first warning sign is bleeding from the vagina, followed by cramping. Call your doctor if you experience these problems! The longer you bleed and cramp, the more likely you are to have a miscarriage.

Most of the time we don't know why miscarriages occur—they can happen for many different reasons. The most common finding in early miscarriages is abnormal development of the early embryo. Research indicates that more than half of these miscarriages have chromosomal abnormalities. Outside factors, called *teratogens*, can also cause miscarriage. Examples are radiation and some chemicals (drugs or medications), which research has shown may cause a miscarriage.

Maternal factors are also believed to be relevant in some miscarriages. The list below describes some of the maternal factors that have been identified by researchers.

- Unusual infections in the mother-to-be, such as listeriosis, toxoplasmosis and syphilis, may cause miscarriage.
- A deficiency of progesterone is believed by some to be a cause of early miscarriage; if detected early enough, it may be treatable, but not everyone agrees with this.
- Genital infections have been shown to trigger miscarriage. When an infection is found, the woman and her partner are treated.
- Sometimes a woman's body makes antibodies that attack the fetus or disrupt the function of the placenta.
- Women who smoke have a higher rate of miscarriage.
- Alcohol also been blamed for an increased rate of miscarriage.

Higher Rate of Miscarriage

We have found that some couples are more likely to suffer miscarriages than others. The reason for this has to do with the couple's unique genetic profile. When genes unite upon fertilization of the egg by the sperm, the union can produce genetic abnormalities that cause a miscarriage. Genetic screening can sometimes reveal this problem.

Five Types of Miscarriage

There are five types of miscarriage, which tends to confuse people. The definitions below describe different medical situations.

Threatened miscarriage. A threatened miscarriage occurs when there is a bloody discharge from the vagina during the first half of pregnancy. Bleeding may last for days or weeks. There may be cramping and pain—pain may feel like a menstrual cramp or mild backache. Bed rest is about all a woman can do to try to prevent the miscarriage from happening, although being active does not cause miscarriage.

Inevitable miscarriage. An inevitable miscarriage occurs with the rupture of membranes, dilation of the cervix and passage of blood clots and even tissue. Loss of the pregnancy is almost certain under these circumstances. Contraction of the uterus usually occurs, expelling the embryo or products of conception.

Incomplete miscarriage. In an incomplete miscarriage, the entire pregnancy is not immediately expelled. Part of the pregnancy may be passed while the rest remains in the uterus. Bleeding may be heavy and continues until the uterus is empty or is emptied by a doctor by D&C (see page 186).

Missed miscarriage. A missed miscarriage occurs when an embryo that has died earlier is retained in the uterus. A woman may not bleed or have any other symptoms. The time period between the failure of the pregnancy and the discovery of the miscarriage is usually weeks.

Habitual miscarriage. A habitual miscarriage usually refers to three or more consecutive miscarriages.

Does Nutrition Affect Miscarriage?

We have no concrete evidence that deficiency of any particular nutrient or even moderate deficiency of all nutrients can cause a miscarriage.

Can I Cause a Miscarriage?

Not usually, so don't blame yourself if you have a miscarriage. It's a normal reaction to look for a reason for losing a pregnancy and to think you might have done something wrong. Many women try to blame stress, emotional upset or physical activity for causing a miscarriage. These things do not usually cause miscarriages.

Usually no reason can be found for a miscarriage.

A woman shouldn't blame herself, her partner or anyone else for a miscarriage. It is usually impossible to look back at everything a woman did, ate or was exposed to and find a cause. Remember, usually no reason can be found for a miscarriage.

If Miscarriage Occurs

If you are having a miscarriage and you expel all of the products of the pregnancy, bleeding stops and cramping goes away, you may be done with it. If everything is not expelled, it will be necessary to perform a D&C (dilatation and curettage), which is minor surgery to empty the uterus. It is preferable to do this surgery so you won't bleed for a long time, risking anemia and infection.

What can I do if I think I'm having a miscarriage?
Talk to your doctor. In nearly all instances, you can do nothing to stop a miscarriage from happening. No surgical procedure or medicine can stop a miscarriage. Most physicians recommend bed rest and decreased activity. Some recommend use of the hormone progesterone, but not all agree with its use. Ultrasound and blood tests may be used to help your doctor determine whether you are going to miscarry, but you may have to wait and see.

Rh-Sensitivity after Miscarriage

If you're Rh-negative and have a miscarriage, you will need to receive RhoGAM. This applies only if your blood is Rh-negative.

What Does a Miscarriage Look Like?

You won't see a fetus usually. What you pass looks like white, gray or red tissue. It will not be possible to tell if it was a boy or girl. Some doctors want you to bring the tissue to the lab to verify it was really the pregnancy that was passed and not just a blood clot.

If I am having a miscarriage, will my pregnancy test be positive?
Yes. Hormones will make your pregnancy test positive.

Difference between Miscarriage and Stillbirth

In medical terms, loss of the fetus before 20 weeks is a *miscarriage*. Loss of the fetus after 20 weeks is a *stillbirth*.

Ectopic Pregnancy

Ectopic pregnancy, sometimes called *tubal pregnancy*, occurs about once in every 100 pregnancies. Ectopic pregnancy happens when implantation of the embryo occurs outside the uterine cavity, usually in the Fallopian tube. It can also occur on the ovary, in the entrance to the tube, at the point the tube joins the uterus and at the mouth of the uterus. An ectopic pregnancy is serious because heavy bleeding may result when the ectopic pregnancy ruptures.

It isn't unusual to have mild pain early in pregnancy from a cyst on the ovary or stretching of the uterus or ligaments. Sometimes women are afraid this signals an ectopic pregnancy. It probably doesn't, but if the pain is bad enough to cause you concern, call your doctor.

Symptoms associated with ectopic pregnancy include abdominal pain and bleeding from the vagina. It may be confused with appendicitis, the flu or a bladder infection. Factors that can increase your risk for an ectopic pregnancy include:

- pelvic infections (PID or pelvic inflammatory disease)
- previous ruptured appendix
- previous ectopic pregnancy
- surgery on your Fallopian tubes (such as reversal of a tubal ligation)
- use of an IUD

Diagnosis

Diagnosis can be difficult and may require a couple of tests and some waiting. Tests used include ultrasound, quantitative HCGs and laparoscopy (a visual examination inside the abdomen). Even with these tests, it may be a few days or weeks before a definitive diagnosis can be made.

A quantitative HCG (human chorionic gonadotropin) is a special pregnancy test done with your blood. HCG is a hormone produced during pregnancy; it increases very rapidly early in pregnancy. A regular pregnancy test, using blood or urine, gives you a positive or negative ("yes" or "no") answer. A quantitative HCG assigns a number

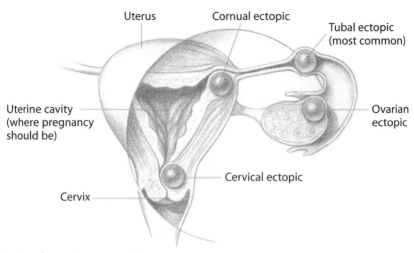

Uterus   Cornual ectopic

Tubal ectopic
(most common)

Uterine cavity
(where pregnancy
should be)

Ovarian
ectopic

Cervical ectopic

Cervix

Sites of ectopic pregnancies.

to tell how pregnant you are. The numbers aren't exact, but they
increase in a way that can help your doctor decide if it is a normal
pregnancy. This test is not used in normal pregnancies but can be very
helpful when you are concerned about a miscarriage or ectopic
pregnancy. The hormones produced with an ectopic pregnancy still
make your pregnancy test positive.

Treatment

Many ectopic pregnancies result in reabsorption of the embryo
before the tube ruptures. The woman may never know she was
pregnant. If you are diagnosed with an ectopic pregnancy, you may be
treated with methotrexate (a medication), but often surgery is
necessary to correct the problem, which results in loss of the
pregnancy. An ectopic pregnancy cannot be carried to full term. It is
either terminated by the woman's body or terminated surgically.

Blood Clots during Pregnancy

Blood clots in the leg are occasionally diagnosed during pregnancy.
This condition, called *thrombophlebitis*, is more likely to occur during
pregnancy because of changes in blood circulation. Blood flow in the
legs slows down (a condition called *stasis*) because of pressure from the
uterus on blood vessels and because of changes in the blood and its

clotting mechanisms. Blood clots occur in less than 1% of all pregnancies.

Blood clot problems may also be called venous thrombosis, thromboembolic disease, thrombophlebitis *and* lower deep-vein thrombosis.

The condition is serious because the blood clot may break loose and travel to another part of the body, such as the lungs (called a *pulmonary embolism*). Fortunately, that happens only rarely.

If you have had any kind of blood clot in the past, don't ignore it. Tell your doctor. This is important information!

Blood clots may also occasionally appear in veins near the surface of the leg. This condition is not serious. This type of thrombosis does not require hospitalization and is treated with mild pain relievers, elevation of the leg, heat and support of the leg with an Ace™ bandage or maternity support stockings.

Signs and symptoms of deep-vein thrombosis can vary widely and include:

- paleness of the leg
- leg is cool to the touch
- a portion of the leg may be tender, hot and swollen
- skin of the leg may have red streaks over the veins
- squeezing the calf or walking may be very painful
- rapid, abrupt onset of the above symptoms

To diagnose deep-vein thrombosis in a pregnant woman, an ultrasound of the legs is done. In a nonpregnant woman, either X-ray or ultrasound is used.

Treatment

Treatment of this condition during pregnancy usually consists of hospitalization and administration of heparin to thin the blood and to allow the clot to dissolve. While heparin is being given, the woman is required to stay in bed with heat applied to her elevated leg.

If you had a blood clot in a previous pregnancy, tell your doctor. You will probably need heparin during this pregnancy. It should be started right away. Heparin is administered by injections that you give yourself two or three times a day, by a long-dwelling I.V. (intravenous drip) or by a heparin pump.

Another blood thinner, called *warfarin* (Coumadin®), is available in pill form, but it is not usually given during pregnancy because it is not safe for the baby. Heparin is safe for use during pregnancy. After you deliver, you may have to take warfarin for a few weeks, depending on the severity of the blood clot.

Breast Lumps in Pregnancy

If you are pregnant and find a lump in your breast, tell your doctor immediately. It's normal for your breasts to change and get larger during pregnancy, but lumps need to be checked out.

The first test is to examine yourself; have your doctor check you if you find a lump. After your examination, your doctor may schedule you for a mammogram or an ultrasound. If a mammogram is done, be sure to tell the technicians you are pregnant. They will cover your abdomen with a lead shield.

Often a lump in the breast can be drained or aspirated during pregnancy. If it cannot be drained, biopsy or removal of the lump may be necessary. Depending on how serious it is, surgery or other treatment may be needed. A breast lump doesn't always mean cancer, but it's important to check breast lumps.

Some patients ask me if pregnancy can make a breast cancer grow faster. Not everyone agrees on the answer to this question. Most medical experts don't believe pregnancy accelerates the course or growth of a breast cancer.

Pre-eclampsia

Pre-eclampsia, once called *toxemia of pregnancy,* is development of the following symptoms:
- hypertension (high blood pressure)
- protein in the urine
- swelling, usually in the legs, or elsewhere in the body
- changes in muscle reflexes

Pre-eclampsia occurs only during pregnancy. It develops in about 5% of all pregnancies. The condition is serious because it can lead to eclampsia. *Eclampsia* refers to seizures or convulsions in a woman with pre-eclampsia.

A seizure is a loss of body control. Seizures often include twitching, shaking or convulsions of the body. If you think you've had a seizure, contact your doctor immediately!

How can I know if my pre-eclampsia is getting worse and I am beginning to develop eclampsia?
Warning signs include:
• pain under the ribs on the right side
• headache
• seeing spots or other changes in your vision

Having swollen legs is a sign of pre-eclampsia *and* often part of a normal pregnancy. Most pregnant women experience swelling of their legs and other parts of the body. Development of pre-eclampsia includes evidence of the other symptoms in addition to swelling.

An elevated blood pressure is also a sign of pre-eclampsia, but other symptoms are necessary to make a diagnosis. You may experience some of the symptoms without having pre-eclampsia.

Causes and Treatment

Researchers have not been able to isolate a definite cause for pre-eclampsia, but it occurs most often during a woman's first pregnancy.

The goal in treating pre-eclampsia is to avoid seizures, which occur if the woman develops eclampsia. The first step in treatment is bed rest. The woman is advised to drink lots of water and to avoid salt and foods containing large amounts of sodium.

If these measures don't control the condition, medication is prescribed in some cases to prevent seizures. These medications include magnesium sulfate, antiseizure medicines, such as phenobarbital, and medications that reduce blood pressure.

Prevention

According to a recent study, if you consume between 1500 and 2000mg of calcium a day during pregnancy, you can lower your risk of developing the problem by at least 60%. You can't get this much calcium from a prenatal vitamin alone, which contains only 200 to 300mg of calcium. Eat calcium-rich foods also. See page 84 for ways to increase your calcium consumption. Be aware that this is a new finding and will require more study. It may not be appropriate for everyone.

When Your Water Breaks

When your water breaks, the amniotic sac that surrounds the baby and placenta ruptures. (The amniotic sac is also called *the bag of waters.)* Amniotic fluid inside the sac may gush at first, then leak more slowly. This occurrence often signals the beginning of labor. If you think your water has broken, call your doctor.

Amniotic fluid is clear, but if it is bloody, yellow or green, tell your doctor right away.

It's important to distinguish between occasional vaginal leakages and your water breaking. As your pregnancy grows, your uterus grows larger and gets heavier. Because the uterus sits on top of the bladder, it can put a lot of pressure on your bladder as its size increases. The increasingly large uterus prevents your bladder from holding as much urine. Leakages can occur, especially when you lift something or bounce up and down. You may notice your underwear or clothing is damp.

What to Do

Call your doctor when your water breaks. Don't have sexual intercourse; it increases the possibility of an infection inside your uterus.

Certain tests can identify if your water has broken or not. One is a **nitrazine test**. Fluid is placed on a piece of nitrazine paper; if membranes have ruptured, the paper changes color. Another test is a **ferning test**. When viewed under a microscope, dried amniotic fluid looks like a fern or the branches of a pine tree.

Problems with the Placenta

The placenta is a flat, spongy structure that grows inside the mother's uterus. It is attached to the fetus by the umbilical cord and carries nourishment and oxygen from the mother to the baby. It also carries waste products from the baby to the mother for excretion. Problems with the placenta sometimes occur, and they are discussed below.

Placenta Previa

With placenta previa, the placenta covers part or all of the cervix. When the cervix begins to open (dilate), the placenta tears away from the cervix as it opens, causing heavy bleeding. An emergency C-section is likely to follow. Heavy bleeding can be dangerous for the mother-to-be and the baby.

Symptoms. The most characteristic symptom of placenta previa is painless bleeding. Your doctor will order an ultrasound exam if you have not already had one to determine the location of the placenta. He or she will not do a pelvic exam because it may cause heavier bleeding. If you see a different doctor or when you go to the hospital, tell whoever examines you that you have placenta previa and should not have a pelvic exam.

Most physicians recommend avoiding intercourse, not traveling and not having a pelvic exam if you have placenta previa.

Birth. The baby is more likely to be in a breech position. For this reason, and also to avoid bleeding, a C-section is almost always performed.

How common? Placenta previa occurs in about 1 birth in 200.

Placental Abruption

Placental abruption is separation of the placenta from the wall of the uterus during pregnancy. Normally the placenta does not separate until *after* delivery of the baby. When the placenta separates before birth, it can be very serious for the baby.

The cause of placental abruption is unknown; however, certain conditions may make it more likely to occur. These include:

- trauma to the mother, such as from a fall or a car accident
- an umbilical cord that is too short
- very sudden change in the size of the uterus, as in the case of the rupture of membranes
- hypertension
- dietary deficiency
- an abnormality of the uterus, such as a band of tissue in the uterus called a *uterine septum*

Symptoms. Signs and symptoms include:

- heavy bleeding from the vagina
- uterine tenderness
- uterine contractions
- premature labor
- lower-back pain

Placental abruption may occur without the presence of any or all these symptoms. Ultrasound may be helpful to diagnose placental abruption, but it does not always provide an exact diagnosis.

Risks to the mother-to-be include shock, severe blood loss and the inability of the blood to clot.

Treatment. The most common treatment is delivery of the baby. However, the decision of when to deliver the baby varies, depending on the severity of the problem.

Birth. In some situations, if the baby needs to be delivered rapidly, you will need a Cesarean section. That decision is made on an individual basis.

How common? The frequency of placental abruption is estimated to be about 1 in every 80 deliveries.

Prevention. We now believe folic-acid deficiency may play a role in causing placental abruption. Extra folic acid may be prescribed during pregnancy. Maternal smoking and alcohol use may make it more likely for a woman to have placental abruption. If you smoke or drink alcohol, you may be advised to stop both activities.

Retained Placenta

A retained placenta is a placenta or placental tissue that does not deliver following the birth. Usually the placenta separates on its own from the uterus a few minutes after delivery. In some cases, it doesn't separate because it is attached to the wall of the uterus. This can be very serious and can cause extreme blood loss.

Reasons for a retained placenta include a placenta attaching
  • over a previous C-section scar or other incision scar on the uterus
  • in a place that has been curetted (scraped), such as for a D&C
  • over an area of the uterus that was infected

Treatment. The most significant problem caused by a retained placenta is heavy bleeding after delivery. If the placenta is not delivered, it must be removed some other way. One solution is to perform a D&C. However, if the placenta has grown into the wall of the uterus, it may be necessary to remove the uterus by performing a hysterectomy.

How common? A retained placenta occurs in about 1% of all deliveries.

Part 3

Your Baby's Birth

Labor and Delivery 15

Your pregnancy is almost over! By this time, you're probably very happy about that, but you may also be a little nervous about what happens next. That's natural. You're going to go through an experience you may have heard described in different ways from friends and family. Some experiences you heard described may have sounded a little scary.

The best advice I can give you—the same advice I give my patients—is to relax. No one knows what's going to happen during labor and delivery; even medical professionals are sometimes surprised by what occurs. But if you open yourself up to the experience, it may be wonderful.

The end result of your pregnancy, and labor and delivery, is the birth of your baby. You are also important in this event—we want *you* to be happy and healthy, too. Work with your healthcare team to make labor and delivery a positive experience. Learn what you need to know to be prepared, the medications you might be offered and any other concerns you may have. Before you know it, you'll be holding the baby you've been waiting for.

Before you know it, you'll be holding the baby you've been waiting for.

I've already felt some contractions, and I'm only 6 months pregnant. Am I going into labor?
Probably not. You are probably experiencing Braxton-Hicks contractions, which are painless and nonrhythmical. They can begin early in pregnancy and continue off and on until your baby is born. They are felt at irregular intervals and may increase in number and strength when your uterus is massaged.

I heard a woman describe her baby as "dropping." Does this mean the baby was falling out?
No, it doesn't. The feeling of having your baby drop, also called *lightening*, means the baby's head has moved down deep into your pelvis. It is a natural part of the birthing process and can happen a few weeks to a few hours before labor begins. You may feel that you have more room to breathe when the baby descends into your pelvis, but there may also be more pelvic pressure or discomfort.

Water Breaking

Bag of waters is another name for the amniotic sac, which is full of fluid that protects the baby. When the amniotic sac ruptures (your "water breaks"), the amniotic fluid flows out (see also page 192). Many times the water breaks shortly before labor begins. However, in most cases membranes are ruptured after the woman goes to the hospital and she is in labor.

When your water breaks, you may feel a gush of fluid, followed by slow leaking, or you may just feel a slow leaking, without the gush of fluid. A sanitary pad helps absorb the slow leaking so you are not embarrassed by it.

Despite what you may hear about a woman's water breaking when she is in public, it doesn't happen very often.

Contact your doctor as soon as your water breaks. You may be told to go to the hospital if labor is beginning. If you are not near term, you may be asked to go to your doctor's office for an examination. You may not be ready to deliver your baby yet, and your doctor wants to prevent you from getting an infection. The risk of infection increases when your water breaks.

Despite what you may hear about a woman's water breaking when she is in public, it doesn't happen very often. If it happens to you, people will be very understanding and helpful. At that stage your pregnancy is very obvious!

What should I do when my water breaks?
Contact your doctor immediately; some precautions must be taken.
If you are not near term, your doctor may ask you to come to his or her office to be examined. If labor and delivery are imminent, you may be advised to go to the hospital.

Inducing Labor

Your doctor may decide to induce labor if the situation calls for it. There are many medical reasons for inducing labor. Inducing labor is a decision that must be carefully considered by your doctor.

You may be tempted to ask your doctor to induce your labor for convenience or because you are tired of being pregnant. Listen to your doctor's advice.

My doctor said she might have to induce me. How is this done?
If labor is induced, your bag of waters will be broken or you will receive oxytocin (Pitocin) intravenously. The medication is given in gradually increasing doses until contractions begin.

The length of your labor is extremely individual. It varies from pregnancy to pregnancy and depends on how many pregnancies you have had.

With a first pregnancy, the first and second stages of labor can last 14 to 15 hours, or more. A woman who has already had one or two children will probably have a shorter labor, but that's not always the case.

Is there any way for my doctor to know when I will go into labor?
No one knows when labor will begin.

Childbirth-Education Classes

Plan ahead for childbirth-education classes. When you are around 20 weeks pregnant, begin looking into classes that are offered in your area. You should be signed up or just beginning classes by the beginning of the third trimester or about 27 weeks. It's a good idea to plan on finishing the classes at least a few weeks before you are due.

Why Take Classes?

Childbirth-education classes are a good way to prepare for this very important and exciting time of your life! You will find other people have the same concerns you have. The classes provide a lot of good information. They are a very helpful way to learn about the birth process or to refresh your memory if you have had a baby before.

Classes aren't for first-time moms only. They are recommended for women with a new partner, if it has been a few years since you've had a baby, if you have questions or if you would like a review of labor and delivery.

Classes are offered in various settings. Most hospitals that deliver babies offer classes. They are often taught by labor-and-delivery nurses or by a midwife.

To find a class, ask your healthcare provider to recommend classes in your area. He or she is familiar with what is offered. Check local hospitals. Friends can be good sources. Or look in the yellow pages under "Childbirth Education."

Studies have shown that women who have taken classes need less medication, have fewer forceps deliveries and feel more positive about the birth than women who do not take classes.

What You'll Learn

Classes cover aspects of labor and delivery including breathing techniques, vaginal birth, Cesarean delivery, hospital procedures, ways to deal with the discomfort and pain of labor and delivery, various pain-relief

Couples often take childbirth-education classes together. Nearly 90% of all first-time expectant parents take some type of childbirth-education class.

methods and the postpartum or recovery period.

Some insurance companies and a few HMOs offer at least partial reimbursement for class fees. Classes are usually reasonably priced.

Lamaze classes. Lamaze is the oldest technique of childbirth preparation. It emphasizes relaxation and breathing as ways to handle labor and delivery.

Bradley classes. The Bradley method teaches relaxation and inward focus, using many types of relaxation. Bradley class members are typically people who have decided they do not want to use any type of medication for labor-pain relief.

Grantly Dick-Read classes. The Grantly Dick-Read method attempts to break the fear-tension-pain cycle of labor and delivery. These classes were the first to include fathers in the birth experience.

How will I know a childbirth-education class is right for me?

There are quite a few ways to evaluate a class.

- Find out what is available in your area.
- Talk to friends and relatives who have taken various classes.
- Decide whether you want a drug-free birth or whether you are willing to consider pain relief if it is necessary.
- Learn about the qualifications of the instructors in various programs.
- Visit classes or talk to the teachers of a class in your area to choose the best one for you.

Premature Labor

Preterm birth refers to a baby born more than 4 weeks early. It is also called *premature birth*. About 10% of all babies are born more than 4 weeks early. Preterm delivery of a baby can be dangerous because the baby's lungs and other organ systems may not be ready to function on their own.

In most cases, the cause of premature labor is unknown. Causes we do understand include:

- a uterus with an abnormal shape
- a large uterus (such as with multiple fetuses)
- hydramnios (excessive amniotic fluid)
- an abnormal placenta
- premature rupture of the membranes
- incompetent cervix (a weak cervix that dilates very early)
- abnormalities of the fetus
- fetal death
- retained IUD
- maternal illness, such as high blood pressure, or some maternal infections
- incorrect estimate of gestational age, which means the baby is really not premature

It is important to try to halt the contractions if you go into labor too early. Your doctor may have special advice for you. Most doctors start by recommending bed rest and increased fluids to stop labor.

Bed rest means lying in bed on your side.

Bed rest means lying in bed on your side. Either side is OK, but the left side is best.

You may have to lie in bed for a simple reason: It works. Bed rest may mean you have to modify or to stop your activities, but we have found that it helps end premature labor. Before we had medications, bed rest was the only treatment for premature labor.

Medication

Medications that relax the uterus and decrease contractions include:

- • magnesium sulfate, which is usually given through an I.V.; sometimes it is given orally
- • beta-adrenergics, including ritodrine and terbutaline, which are given orally, through an I.V. or by injection
- • sedatives or narcotics, which may be used in early attempts to stop premature labor

Even if you take medication, you will probably be advised to rest in bed. Bed rest is an essential part of the treatment plan for premature labor.

It is better for both mother and baby if premature labor is stopped. Premature delivery increases the possibility of fetal problems and maternal problems, such as an increased risk of C-section.

You may have to lie in bed for a simple reason: Bed rest works.

Going to the Hospital

I'm nervous about preparing to go to the hospital. What should I be concerned about?

Going to the hospital to have a baby can make anyone a little nervous, even an experienced mom! If you make some plans before you go, you'll have less to worry about.

- • Tour the labor and delivery area of your hospital.
- • Ask about preregistering at the hospital (see page 206).
- • Plan the trip; know who will take you, and have a backup person available.
- • Pack your bag (see pages 204 and 205).

What Should I Bring to the Hospital?

There are a lot of details to remember, but the lists below should cover most of what you might need.

Pre-register

Consider pre-registering at the hospital several weeks before your due date (see page 206). It will save time when you arrive at the hospital in labor.

For You

Have these items ready to go about 5 or 6 weeks before your due date.

- 1 cotton nightgown or T-shirt for labor
- extra pillows to use during labor
- lip balm and lollipops or fruit drops to use during labor
- light diversion, such as books or magazines
- 1 nightgown for after labor (bring a nursing gown if you are going to breastfeed)
- slippers with rubber soles
- 1 long robe for walking in the halls
- 2 bras (nursing bras and pads if you breastfeed)
- toiletries you use, including brush, comb, toothbrush, toothpaste, soap, shampoo, conditioner
- hairband or ponytail holder, if you have long hair
- eyeglasses (you can't wear contact lenses)
- underwear and loose-fitting clothes for going home
- sanitary pads, if the hospital doesn't supply them

For Your Partner

It's a good idea to include some things in your hospital kit for your partner to help him get through the experience. You might consider the following items:

- completed insurance or pre-registration information
- talc or cornstarch for massaging you during labor
- a paint roller or tennis ball for giving you a low-back massage during labor
- tapes or CDs and a player, or a radio to play during labor
- labor handbook
- camera and film
- list of telephone numbers and a long-distance calling card
- change for telephones and vending machines

For the New Baby

The hospital will probably supply most of what you will need for your baby. However, here are a few things you should have ready:

- clothes for the trip home, including an undershirt, sleeper, outer clothes (a hat if it's cold)
- a couple of blankets
- diapers, if your hospital doesn't supply them

Be sure you have an approved infant car seat in which to take your baby home. It's important to put your baby in a car seat the very first time he or she rides in a car!

Personal Items to Bring with Us to the Hospital:

List any other personal items you want to take with you to the hospital here.

Hospital Pre-registration

It will save time if you register at the hospital a few weeks before your due date. It is wise to do this before you go to the hospital in labor because then you may be in a hurry or concerned with other things.

You will be able to pre-register with forms that you receive from your doctor's office or from the hospital. Take your insurance card or insurance information with you. Know your doctor's name, your pediatrician's name and your due date. It is also helpful to know your blood type and Rh-factor.

At the Hospital

After you are admitted, you will probably be settled into a labor room, and you will be checked to see how much you have dilated. A brief history of your pregnancy will be taken. Vital signs, including blood pressure, pulse and temperature, are noted. You may receive an enema, or an I.V. may be started. Blood will probably be drawn. You may have an epidural put in place, if you have requested it.

It may be necessary through questions or tests to determine if your membranes have ruptured. There are several ways to confirm it:

- By your description of what happened, such as a large gush of fluid from your vagina.
- With nitrazine paper. Fluid is placed on the paper; if membranes have ruptured, the paper changes color.
- With a ferning test. Fluid is placed on a glass slide, allowed to dry and examined under a microscope. If it has a "fern" appearance, it is amniotic fluid.

Birth Preparation

Shaving pubic hair. This is not done routinely; it is not always necessary for a woman to have her pubic hair shaved before delivery. Many women are not shaved these days. However, some patients who chose not to have their pubic hair shaved later told me they experienced discomfort when their pubic hair became entangled in their underwear due to the normal vaginal discharge after the birth of their baby.

I.V. An I.V. is necessary with an epidural. If you have chosen not to have an epidural, an I.V. is not always required. Most physicians agree an I.V. is helpful if the woman needs medications or fluids during labor or delivery or after delivery.

If you think you might *refuse* an I.V. when you go into the hospital to deliver your baby, discuss this with your doctor at one of your prenatal appointments. In many situations, an I.V. can be an important safeguard.

Labor

Labor is defined as the dilation (stretching and expanding) of your cervix. This occurs when your uterus, which is a muscle, tightens (contracts) to squeeze out its contents (your baby). Tightening of the uterus can cause pain.

Labor is different for every woman; that's the reason we can't predict what your labor will be like before it begins. You may also find your labor is different from one delivery to the next.

There are differences between true labor and false labor. Look at the chart on page 208 so you'll be better able to tell the difference.

Will my doctor be available when I go into labor?
Talk to your doctor about this possibility. If your doctor believes he or she might be out of town when your baby is born, ask to meet the doctors who "cover" when your doctor is unavailable. Although your physician would like to be there for the birth of your baby, sometimes it is not possible.

The Stages of Labor

Labor is divided into three stages—each stage is distinctly different and serves a specific purpose. Review the chart on pages 209 to 211 to see what you might expect during the various stages of labor and delivery.

Stage 1. Stage 1 of labor is the longest and consists of three phases—early, active and transition. This first stage of labor usually lasts 6 to 8 hours but can be longer for a first birth.

In the early phase, labor is just getting started and dilation of the cervix has just begun. In the active phase, the cervix dilates at a fairly constant rate. Transition includes complete dilation. Contractions help the cervix dilate and thin out. They also help move the baby down the birth canal for delivery.

At the transition phase, the pace and intensity of labor increases, signaling that labor is moving into the second stage.

True Labor or False Labor?

Considerations	True Labor	False Labor
Contractions	Regular	Irregular
Time between contractions	Come closer together	Do not get closer together
Contraction intensity	Increases	Doesn't change
Location of contractions	Entire abdomen	Various locations
Effect of anesthetic or pain relievers	Will not stop labor	Sedation may alter or stop frequency
Cervical change	Progressive cervical change	None

Stage 2. In stage 2 of labor, you are fully dilated and begin to push. Contractions change and become much harder, longer and more frequent. Along with your pushing, these contractions help deliver the baby. This stage can take 2 hours or longer. Anesthesia at this point, especially an epidural block, may prolong this stage of labor because your urge to push is decreased. At the end of the second stage, your baby is born.

Stage 3. Stage 3 of labor doesn't usually take too long. During stage 3, the uterus contracts and expels the placenta (afterbirth). You will be given oxytocin to help contract the uterus.

Some doctors describe a fourth stage of labor, referring to the time period after delivery of the placenta, while the uterus continues to contract. Uterine contractions are important in controlling bleeding after the birth of your baby.

It's a good idea to ask your doctor certain questions about preparing to go to the hospital. He or she may have specific instructions for you. You might want to ask the following questions:

- When should I go to the hospital once I am in labor?
- Should I call you before I leave for the hospital?
- How can I reach you after regular office hours?
- Are there any particular instructions to follow during early labor?

The Three Stages of Labor

Stage of Labor	Stage 1—Early Phase
What's happening	• Cervix opens and thins out due to uterine contractions • Cervix dilates to about 2cm • This phase can last 1 to 10 hours
Mother is experiencing	• Membranes may rupture, accompanied by gush or trickle of amniotic fluid from vagina • Pinkish discharge may appear (*bloody show*) • Mild contractions begin at 15- to 20-minute intervals and last about 1 minute; contractions become closer together and more regular
Mother and/or partner can do	• Mother should not eat or drink once labor begins • Mother may be able to stay at home, if she is at term • Begin using relaxation and breathing techniques learned in childbirth class • If water has broken, if labor is preterm, if there is intense pain, if pain is constant or there is bright red blood, contact doctor immediately!

Stage of Labor	Stage 1—Active Phase
What's happening	• Cervix dilates from about 2cm to 10cm • Cervix continues to thin out • This phase can last 20 minutes to 2 hours
Mother is experiencing	• Contractions become more intense • Contractions come closer together • Contractions are about 3 minutes apart and last about 45 seconds to 1 minute
Mother and/or partner can do	• Keep practicing relaxation and breathing techniques • An epidural can be administered during this phase

More ...

The Three Stages of Labor, *continued*

Stage of Labor	Stage 1—Transition Phase
What's happening	• Stage 1 begins to change to Stage 2 • Cervix is dilated to 10cm • Cervix continues to thin out • This phase can last a few minutes to 2 hours
Mother is experiencing	• Contractions are 2 to 3 minutes apart and last about 1 minute • Mother may feel strong urge to push; she shouldn't push until cervix is completely dilated • Mother may be moved to delivery room, if she is not in a birthing room
Mother and/or partner can do	• Relaxation and breathing techniques help counteract mother's urge to push

Stage of Labor	Stage 2
What's happening	• Cervix is completely dilated • Baby continues to descend into the birth canal • As mother pushes, baby is delivered • Doctor or nurse suctions baby's nose and mouth and clamps umbilical cord • This stage can last a few minutes to a few hours (pushing the baby can last a long time)
Mother is experiencing	• Contractions occur at 2- to 5-minute intervals and last from 60 to 90 seconds • With an epidural, the mother may find it hard to push • An episiotomy may be done to prevent tearing vaginal tissues as baby is born
Mother and/or partner can do	• Mother will begin to push with each contraction after cervix dilates completely • Mother may be given analgesic or local anesthetic • Mother listens to doctor or nurse when baby is being delivered; doctor or nurse will tell mother when to push • As mother pushes, she may be able to watch baby being born, if mirror is available

More ...

The Three Stages of Labor, *continued*

Stage of Labor	Stage 3
What's happening	• Placenta is delivered • Doctor examines placenta to make sure all of it has been delivered • This stage can last a few minutes to an hour
Mother is experiencing	• Contractions may occur closer together but be less painful • Doctor repairs episiotomy
Mother and/or partner can do	• You'll meet and hold your baby • You may need to push to expel the placenta • You may be able to hold your baby while the doctor repairs your episiotomy • Nurse will rub or massage the uterus through the abdomen to help it contract to control bleeding

Stage of Labor	Stage 4
What's happening	• Placenta has been delivered • Uterus continues to contract, which is important to control bleeding • This stage usually lasts a couple of days

The Bloody Show

You may bleed a small amount following a vaginal exam or at the beginning of labor. This "bloody show" occurs as the cervix stretches and dilates. If it causes you concern or appears to be a large amount of blood, contact your healthcare provider immediately.

Along with a bloody show, you may pass some mucus, sometimes called a *mucus plug*. Passing this mucus doesn't always mean you'll have your baby soon or that you are beginning labor.

Timing Contractions

It helps to time contractions correctly once they begin. There are two goals in timing contractions:

- to find out how long a contraction lasts
- to find out how often contractions occur

It helps for your doctor or the nurses to have this information so they can decide if it's time for you to go to the hospital.

Be sure to ask your doctor which method he or she prefers, because there are two ways to time contractions.

- Start timing when the contraction starts and time it until the next contraction starts. *This is the most common method.*
- Start timing when the contraction ends and note how long it is until the next contraction starts.

Labor and Your Partner

Well before your delivery date, sit down and talk with your partner about how you will stay in touch as your due date approaches. Some of my patients' partners rent personal pagers for the last month or so. (Some hospitals or HMOs supply pagers for expectant couples the last few weeks.) Line up a backup support person, in case your partner cannot be with you or if you need someone to take you to the hospital.

Your partner may be your labor coach, or you may have chosen another person for this important job. A labor coach can do a lot to help you through labor. He or she can:

- time your contractions so you are aware of the progress of your labor
- encourage and reassure you during labor
- help you deal with your physical discomfort
- help create a mood in the labor room
- report symptoms or pain to the nurse and/or doctor
- keep a watch on the door and protect your privacy
- control traffic into your room

Eating and Drinking during Labor

Women often get nauseated as they labor, which may cause vomiting. For that reason your stomach should be empty during labor. You are not allowed to eat or drink anything during labor for your own safety.

You will not be allowed to drink anything, even if your labor is long. You may be allowed sips of water or ice chips to suck on. If labor is long, you may be given fluids through an I.V.

I'm nervous about whether my baby is too big for me to deliver. Can my doctor tell if I'll have problems before labor begins?
Even with an estimation of how much your baby weighs, your doctor cannot really know if the baby is too big for you until after you deliver. Usually labor must begin so your doctor can see how the baby fits into your pelvis and if there is enough room for the baby to pass through the birth canal.

Enemas

You may not be required to have an enema—it is usually a choice. Discuss this with your healthcare provider at one of your prenatal appointments. There are benefits to having an enema early in labor. It decreases the amount of contamination by bowel movement or feces during labor and at the time of delivery. It may also help you after delivery if you have an episiotomy because having a bowel movement very soon after delivery can be painful.

Bowel Movement

Your first bowel movement usually occurs a day or two after delivery. If you had an enema, it could take a few days longer. It could be painful, especially if you have an episiotomy.

Most doctors prescribe stool softeners after delivery to help with your bowel movements. They are safe to take, even if you are nursing.

Back Labor

Back labor occurs when the baby comes out through the birth canal looking straight up. This type of presentation often causes lower-back pain.

Back labor may make delivery last longer. It may require rotation of the baby's head so it comes out looking down at the ground rather than looking up at the sky.

Who Will Be Present at the Birth?

You may want lots of family or no one except your partner present when you have your baby. Whomever you want present at the birth should be OK with your partner. As long as it's acceptable to your doctor, you may make some of the decisions like this about the birth. My advice is to keep it small; don't let friends or family make you feel they have a "right" to be there.

> *Whomever you want present at the birth should be OK with your partner.*

Too many people in the delivery room can be a problem. Delivery is a very personal experience for you and your partner; it is not a spectator sport. Don't feel pressured to invite others to be with you at this time if you'd rather have privacy. For every additional person in the room, there is an increased risk of infection for you and the baby.

Tests during Labor

Fetal Monitoring

In many hospitals, a baby's heartbeat is monitored throughout labor, making it possible to detect any problems early so they can be resolved. There are two types of fetal monitoring during labor—external fetal monitoring and internal fetal monitoring.

External fetal monitoring can be done before your membranes rupture. A belt with a receiver is strapped to your abdomen, and it records the baby's heartbeat. See the illustrations on this page and page 68.

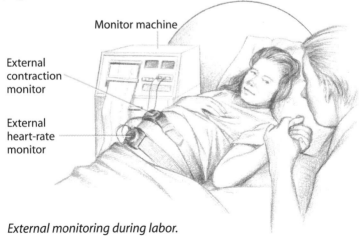

Monitor machine

External contraction monitor

External heart-rate monitor

External monitoring during labor.

Internal fetal monitoring is the more precise method of monitoring the baby. An electrode is placed on the fetal scalp to record the fetal heart rate. See the illustration on page 69.

Fetal Blood Sampling

This is another way of evaluating how well a baby is tolerating the stress of labor. Membranes must be ruptured, and the cervix must be dilated at least 2cm. An instrument is applied to the scalp of the baby to make a small nick in the skin. The baby's blood is collected in a small tube, and its pH (acidity) is checked.

The pH level can help determine whether the baby is having trouble during labor. Results help the physician decide whether labor can continue or if a Cesarean section needs to be done.

Dealing with Pain in Childbirth

Childbirth is accompanied by pain; expectation of this pain can evoke fear and anxiety in you. This is normal. If you're concerned about pain and how you'll handle it, the best way to deal with it is to become informed about it.

Many women believe they'll feel guilty after their baby is born if they ask for pain relief during labor. Sometimes they believe the baby will be harmed by the medication. Some believe they'll deprive themselves of the complete birth experience. I tell my patients the main goal of any labor and delivery is a healthy baby and healthy mom. If a woman wants pain relief to help her, it doesn't mean she's failed in any way!

How can I find out more about the different pain-relief methods available during labor and delivery?

Learn more about the different pain-relief methods available during labor and delivery by discussing it with your doctor. Childbirth class is another good place to ask about these medications. You may also want to talk to friends to see what they did.

Analgesia and Anesthesia

These two methods of pain relief have effects that are quite different. *Analgesia* is pain relief without total loss of sensation. *Anesthesia* is pain relief with total loss of sensation.

Analgesia. An analgesic is injected into a muscle or vein to decrease the pain of labor, but it allows you to remain conscious. It provides pain relief but can make you drowsy, restless and nauseous. You may experience difficulty concentrating. It may slow the baby's reflexes and breathing, so it is usually given during the early and middle parts of labor.

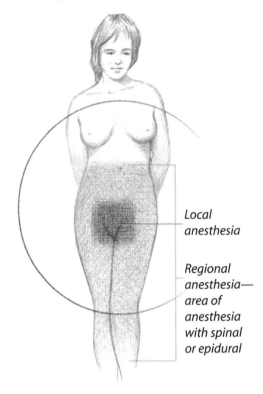

Local anesthesia

Regional anesthesia— area of anesthesia with spinal or epidural

Anesthesia. There are three types of anesthesia— general, local and regional anesthesia. With general anesthesia, you are completely unconscious, so it is used only for some Cesarean deliveries and emergency vaginal deliveries. Local anesthesia affects a small area and is particularly useful for an episiotomy repair. Regional anesthesia affects a larger body area than local anesthesia.

General anesthesia is not used as much today as in the past. The advantage of general anesthesia is that it can be administered quickly in an emergency. Disadvantages include causing the mother to vomit or to aspirate vomited food or stomach acid into her lungs. With general anesthesia, the baby may be "asleep" when delivered. By contrast, local anesthesia rarely affects the baby and usually has few lingering effects.

There are several types of local and regional anesthesia. The three most common types are pudendal block, spinal block and epidural block.

Pudendal block. A pudendal block is medication injected into the vaginal area to relieve pain in the vagina, the perineum and the rectum. Side effects are rare. It is considered one of the safest forms of pain relief; however, it does not relieve uterine pain.

Spinal block. With a spinal block, medication is injected into spinal fluid in the lower back, which numbs the lower part of the body. This type of block is administered only once during labor, so it is often used just before delivery. It works quickly and is an effective pain inhibitor. It is also used for a Cesarean delivery.

Epidural block. In an epidural block, a tube is inserted into a space outside the mother's spinal column in the lower back. Medication is administered through the tube for pain relief. The tube remains in place until after delivery so additional medication can be administered when necessary, or it can be given continuously with a pump.

An epidural causes some loss of sensation in the lower part of the body. It helps relieve painful uterine contractions, pain in the vagina and rectum as the baby passes through the birth canal and the pain of an episiotomy. A woman can still feel pressure, so she can push adequately during vaginal delivery.

An epidural block is not effective in some women. Because an epidural may make it harder to push, vacuum extraction or forceps may be necessary during delivery.

Side effects of spinal block or epidural block. Either block can cause a woman's blood pressure to drop suddenly, which in turn can cause a decrease in the baby's heart rate. These blocks are not used if the woman is bleeding heavily or if the baby has an abnormal heartbeat. A woman may experience a severe headache if the covering of the spinal cord is punctured during needle insertion with either type of anesthesia. This happens rarely.

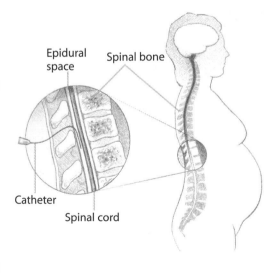

Epidural anesthesia

Walking spinal. A walking spinal, also called *intrathecal anesthesia,* can be given to women who suffer extreme pain in the early stages of labor (dilated less than 5cm). A small amount of narcotic, such as Demerol, is injected through a thin needle into the spinal fluid, which eases the pain and causes few side effects.

Because the dose is small, neither the mother nor baby becomes overly drowsy. Sensory and motor functions remain intact, so the mother can still walk around with help or sit in a chair.

A walking epidural numbs you only in the pelvic area; it doesn't interfere with your ability to move your legs. Another advantage is that fewer women who have had a walking epidural have a "spinal headache" after the epidural wears off.

As with a regular epidural, you must have an I.V. in place during most of your labor. This is because the walking epidural, like a regular epidural, requires I.V. fluids to keep your blood pressure from falling.

At present, its use is limited, but the number of hospitals using walking epidurals is growing. Further testing is necessary before the procedure becomes widely available.

Cesarean Delivery

When a woman has a Cesarean delivery (also called a *C-section*), her baby is delivered through an incision made in the mother's abdominal wall and uterus. The amniotic sac containing the baby and placenta is cut, and the baby is removed through the incisions. After the baby is delivered, the placenta is removed. The uterus is closed in layers with sutures that are absorbed (they don't have to be removed). The abdomen is then sewn together.

In 1965, only 4% of all deliveries were Cesarean. Today, about 20% of all deliveries are Cesarean deliveries. We believe the increase is related to better monitoring during labor and safer procedures for C-sections. Women are also having bigger babies. Another factor in this increase may be rising malpractice rates and the fear of litigation.

Can't my doctor tell if I'll need a C-section before I go into labor?

It would be nice to know this so you wouldn't have to go through labor, but it isn't that easy. We often have to wait for labor to see how your baby handles it. And we have to wait to see if the baby fits through the birth canal.

With most C-sections, the anesthesiologist will give you an epidural or a spinal anesthetic. You are awake with these.

Why is a Cesarean operation performed?
There are many reasons for doing a C-section, but the main purpose is to deliver a healthy baby. Specific reasons include:
- a previous Cesarean delivery
- to avoid rupture of the uterus
- the baby is too big to fit through the birth canal
- fetal distress
- compression of the umbilical cord
- baby is in the breech position
- placental abruption
- placenta previa
- multiple fetuses (in some cases)

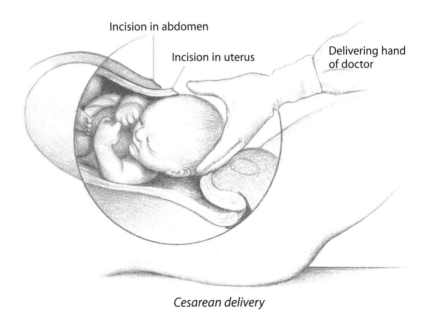

Incision in abdomen

Incision in uterus

Delivering hand of doctor

Cesarean delivery

Advantages and Disadvantages

The most important advantage of a Cesarean delivery is delivery of a healthy baby. On the other hand, this is major surgery and carries with it those risks. You will probably have to stay in the hospital 2 or 3 days.

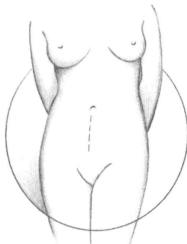
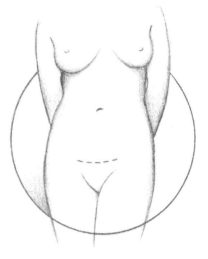

Midline Cesarean-section incision.   *Bikini or pfanensteil
                                              Cesarean-section incision.*

Recovery time. Recovery at home takes longer with a Cesarean than it does with a vaginal delivery. The normal time for full recovery is 4 to 6 weeks.

How many C-sections? Many doctors recommend no more than two or three, but this is evaluated at the time of each delivery. There is no exact, "safe" number of C-sections a woman may have. I have one patient on whom I recently performed her eighth C-section. This is unusual however.

Usually the doctor will use the same incision site. If you have a large scar, your doctor may cut out the old scar.

Some women at my childbirth-preparation class said if you have a Cesarean, you've failed as a woman. Is this true?

No, if you have a Cesarean, you have not failed in any way! The goal in pregnancy, labor and delivery is a healthy baby and a healthy mother. In many situations, the only way to achieve that is with a Cesarean delivery.

Vaginal Birth after Cesarean (VBAC)

In the past it was believed that once a woman had a C-section, all later deliveries would have to be Cesarean also. Today it is becoming more common for women who have had a C-section to deliver vaginally with later pregnancies. This is called *vaginal birth after Cesarean (VBAC)*.

Various factors must be considered in the decision to have a VBAC. The type of incision done with the Cesarean delivery is important. If the incision on the uterus (not the woman's abdomen) is high, labor is not permitted in subsequent pregnancies. If the woman is small and the baby is large, it may cause problems. Multiple fetuses and medical complications, such as diabetes or high blood pressure, may require a repeat C-section.

The American College of Obstetricians and Gynecologists states a woman may have two Cesarean deliveries and still be a candidate for VBAC, other factors permitting. This is a very individual decision. Discuss it with your doctor.

Women who have the best chance of having a successful vaginal delivery after a C-section include women:

- whose original cause for a Cesarean delivery is not repeated with this pregnancy
- who have no major medical problems
- who had a low incision on the uterus with their previous C-section
- who have a normal-size baby
- whose babies are in the normal, head-down position

If you want to try a vaginal delivery after a C-section, the most important thing to do is to discuss it with your doctor well in advance of labor so plans can be made. It may be helpful to get the records from your other delivery. Discuss the benefits and risks, and ask your doctor for his or her opinion as to your chances of a successful vaginal delivery. He or she knows your health and pregnancy history. Include your partner in this decision-making process.

Will I Need an Episiotomy?

An episiotomy is a surgical incision in the area behind the vagina, above the rectum. It is made during delivery to avoid tearing the vaginal opening or rectum.

Most women

having their first

or second baby

will have an

episiotomy.

Discuss with your physician at your prenatal visits whether you will need an episiotomy. Most women having their first or second baby will have an episiotomy. The more children a woman has had, the less likely it is she will need an episiotomy. It also depends on the size of the baby. Some situations do not require an episiotomy, such as a small baby or a premature baby. Often the decision cannot be made until the time of delivery.

Why Have One?

An episiotomy is done to allow room for the baby to fit through the birth canal and to avoid tearing into the mother's other organs. If a woman has had a few pregnancies and deliveries, she may not need an episiotomy with her later children.

Some factors leading to an episiotomy include:
- the size of the mother's vaginal opening
- the size of the baby's head and shoulders
- the number of babies previously delivered
- a forceps or vacuum delivery

Episiotomies vary by degree according to the depth of the incision. There are four degrees that describe incision depth:
- 1st degree—cuts only the skin
- 2nd degree—cuts the skin and underlying tissue, called *fascia*
- 3rd degree—cuts the skin, underlying tissue and rectal sphincter, the muscle around the anus
- 4th degree—goes through the three layers described above and the rectal mucosa, which is the lining of the rectum

Episiotomy Pain

After delivery of your baby, the most painful part of the birth process might be your episiotomy. Don't be afraid to ask for help with this pain. Pain medication, ice, sitz baths and laxatives can help relieve the discomfort.

Baby's Birth Position

At one time or another, you may have heard an unborn baby described as being in a "breech position." A breech presentation means the baby is not in a head-down position, and the legs or buttocks come into the birth canal first.

One of the main causes of breech presentation is prematurity of the baby. Near the end of the second trimester, it's more common for the baby to be in a breech position. As you progress through the third trimester, the baby usually turns into the head-down position for birth.

In the third trimester, the baby usually turns into the head-down position for birth.

By the last 4 to 6 weeks, your baby should be in a head-down position. If your baby is breech when it is time to deliver, your doctor may try to turn the baby, or you may need a Cesarean delivery.

There are different breech presentations and other abnormal positions. They include:

- Frank breech—lower legs are flexed at the hips and extended at the knees. Feet are up by the face or head.
- Complete breech—one or both knees are flexed, not extended.
- Incomplete breech—a foot or knee enters the birth canal ahead of the rest of the baby.
- Face presentation—the baby's head is hyperextended so the face enters the birth canal first.
- Transverse-lie presentation—the baby is lying almost as if in a cradle in the pelvis. The head is on one side of the mother's abdomen, and the bottom is on the other side.
- Shoulder presentation—shoulder enters the birth canal first.

There is some controversy about how to deliver a baby in the breech position. For a long time, breech deliveries were performed vaginally; then it was believed the safest method was by C-section. Many doctors still believe a Cesarean delivery is the safest way to deliver a baby in the breech position. However, some doctors believe a woman can deliver a breech baby without difficulty if the situation is right.

Sometimes the doctor will try to turn a baby in the breech position. Your physician may attempt to change its position by using external cephalic version (ECV). The doctor places his or her hands on your abdomen. Using gentle movements, he or she attempts to shift the baby manually into the head-down position. An ultrasound is usually done first so the doctor can see the position of the baby. It is used during the procedure to guide the doctor in changing the baby's position.

Most physicians who use this method do so before labor begins or in the early stages of labor. ECV is successful in about 50% of the cases in which it is used.

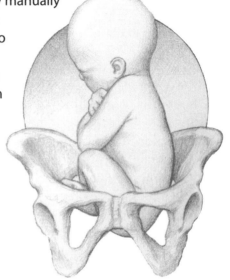

Complete-breech presentation of baby.

Delivery of Your Baby

For a vaginal delivery, the actual delivery of the baby and placenta (not including the laboring process) takes anywhere from a few minutes to an hour. A Cesarean delivery usually takes between 30 and 60 minutes. The part that takes the longest in a Cesarean delivery is *not* the birth of the baby—that is performed rather quickly. Stitching closed the skin and muscle layers after the baby is born takes the most time.

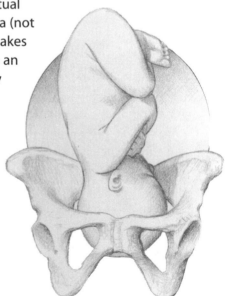

Preferable alignment for birth.

Will I deliver in the same room I labor in?
The setup in some hospitals enables women to deliver in the same room they labor in. It is called LDRP, which means "labor, delivery, recovery and postpartum." With LDRP, you labor and deliver in the same room, then remain there during recovery and your stay at the hospital. Not all hospitals or birthing centers are equipped this way. In many places you will labor in a labor room and move to a delivery room to deliver. Then you will recover in a wardlike setting, where you remain until you go home.

Different Birthing Positions

Other birth positions are acceptable besides lying on your back with your feet in stirrups. You may not have to use stirrups, or you may deliver lying on your side or squatting, if you make arrangements to do this.

Forceps Use

Whether your doctor uses forceps to aid in the delivery of your baby depends on the situation at the time. Factors involved include the size of the baby, the size of your pelvis, how well you are able to push and whether your baby needs to be delivered immediately.

Forceps look like two metal hands and are used to protect the baby's head during delivery. They are not used as much today as they were in the past. Instead, physicians more often use a vacuum extractor or perform a Cesarean section.

Vacuum Extractor

A vacuum extractor is a plastic cup that fits on the baby's head by suction. When you push during labor, your doctor is able to pull and help to deliver the baby more easily.

About Lamaze

This is perhaps the most popular childbirth method. Classes are widely available.

What is the Lamaze method of childbirth?
The Lamaze method provides education and practice for the mother and labor coach in the weeks before birth. The woman learns breathing exercises to help her through her labor and learns ways to concentrate on objects to block out pain or to help reduce pain.

Can every woman use the Lamaze method?
The Lamaze method works very well for many women in labor. However, this approach requires a very serious commitment from the woman and her labor coach. It takes a great deal of practice and a lot of hard work during labor, but it can be rewarding.

Are there other methods of childbirth preparation I could use besides Lamaze?
There are two other methods of prepared childbirth. *The Bradley method* teaches relaxation and inward focus; many types of relaxation are used. Preparation emphasizes relaxation and deep abdominal breathing to make labor more comfortable. *The Grantly Dick-Read method* attempts to break the fear-tension-pain cycle of labor and delivery.

Videotaping the Birth

I often hear from a patient that her partner wants to videotape the birth, but she doesn't want him to. You may be in the same situation and wonder if you are being unreasonable. No, you're not. The birth process is very private for many women, and they don't want to be videotaped or photographed or forced to share it with others. If this is your wish, explain it to your partner. He should respect your wishes. If he won't listen, discuss it with your doctor. Ask him or her to explain your objections to your partner. It would also be a wise idea to check on the hospital's policy regarding videotaping.

After Your Baby Is Born

Several things will happen soon after your baby is born. First, the baby's mouth and throat are suctioned to clear out any mucus. Then the doctor clamps and cuts the umbilical cord. The baby is wrapped in clean blankets and may be placed on your abdomen. At 1 minute and 5 minutes after birth, Apgar scores are recorded to evaluate the baby's response to birth and to life on its own. An ID band is placed on the baby's wrist. Usually a brief physical or an assessment is done right after delivery. The baby receives eye drops to prevent infection and is given a vitamin-K shot to prevent bleeding.

You will be asked if you want your baby to receive the hepatitis vaccine. You may want to discuss this with your doctor or your pediatrician. The vaccine is given to protect the baby against hepatitis in the future.

Once the initial evaluation is complete, the baby is returned to you. See the chart on page 246 for a description of tests commonly performed on newborns.

Umbilical Cord

Your husband may have told you he wants to cut the umbilical cord after the baby is delivered. Talk to your doctor about your husband's participation in the delivery. What he is allowed to do varies from place to place and from doctor to doctor.

Bleeding after Birth

Following the birth, the uterus shrinks from the size of a watermelon to the size of a volleyball. The uterus contracts and becomes smaller so it won't bleed.

You can expect to bleed after you deliver, but heavy bleeding is not very common. Bleeding is controlled by massaging the uterus (called *Credé*) and medications; it lessens gradually over time, then stops.

Heavy bleeding after the baby is born can be serious. A loss of more than 17 ounces (500ml) in the first 24 hours after your baby's birth is called *postpartum hemorrhage*.

The most common causes of heavy bleeding include:

•a uterus that won't contract

•tearing of the vagina or cervix during birth

•a large or bleeding episiotomy

•a tear, rupture or hole in the uterus

•failure of blood vessels inside the uterus to compress

•retained placental tissue

•clotting or coagulation problems

If bleeding becomes heavy after a few days or weeks, contact your doctor. Sometimes the bleeding is normal, but it is best to talk to your doctor about it. He or she may want to see you to determine if the amount of bleeding is normal and, if necessary, to prescribe medication.

Cord-Blood Banking

Cord blood—blood saved from the umbilical cord—may be "banked" and saved for future use. Umbilical-cord blood can be used to treat cancer and genetic diseases that are now treated by bone-marrow transplants. Cord blood has been used successfully to treat childhood leukemia, some immune diseases and other blood diseases.

Blood is collected directly from the umbilical cord immediately after delivery. It is transported to a bank facility to be frozen and stored. This procedure poses no risk to the mother or baby.

Whether to bank your baby's cord blood is a decision for you and your partner to make. It is expensive and may not be for everyone. If you are interested, your doctor can tell you more. Or you may ask (or you may be asked) to donate the umbilical-cord blood for others to use.

If Your Baby Is Late

About 10% of all babies are born more than 2 weeks past their due date.

Babies born 2 weeks or more past their due date are considered *postdate* or *post-term births*. About 10% of all babies are born more than 2 weeks past their due date.

Carrying a baby longer than 42 weeks can cause some problems for the fetus and the mother. Most pregnancies do well. Doctors conduct tests on these babies and induce labor, if necessary.

A doctor can determine if the baby is moving around in the womb and if the amount of amniotic fluid is healthy and normal. If it is determined the baby is healthy and active, the mother-to-be is usually monitored until labor begins on its own. Tests are done as reassurance that an overdue baby is OK and can remain in the womb. These tests include a nonstress test, a contraction stress test and a biophysical profile. If problems are found, labor is often induced. Read about these tests in chapter 3.

Emergency Childbirth

Occasionally a woman goes into labor and can't make it to the hospital. Emergency childbirth can happen to anyone, so it's best to be prepared. Read and study the information on these two pages. Have the names and telephone numbers of your doctor or healthcare provider and those of friends or family written down near the phone. And if it happens to you, try to relax and follow these instructions.

Emergency Delivery If You Are Alone

1. Call 911 for help.
2. Call a neighbor, close family member or friend (have phone numbers available).
3. Try not to push or bear down.
4. Find a comfortable place, and spread out towels or blankets.
5. If the baby comes before help arrives, try to use your hands to ease the baby out while you gently push.
6. Wrap the baby in a clean blanket or clean towels; hold it close to your body to keep it warm.
7. Use a clean cloth or tissue to remove mucus from the baby's mouth.
8. Do not pull on the umbilical cord to deliver the placenta—it is not necessary.
9. If the placenta delivers on its own, save it.
10. Tie string or a shoelace around a section of the cord. You don't need to cut the cord.
11. Try to keep yourself and your baby warm until medical help arrives.

Emergency Delivery at Home

1. Call 911 for help.
2. Call a neighbor, family member or friend (have phone numbers available).
3. Encourage the woman not to push or to bear down.
4. Use blankets and towels to make the woman as comfortable as possible.
5. If there is time, wash the woman's vaginal and rectal areas with soap and water.
6. When the baby's head delivers, encourage the woman not to push or bear down. Instead, have her pant or blow, and concentrate on not pushing.
7. Try to ease out the baby's head with gentle pressure. Do not pull on the head.
8. After the head is delivered, gently push down on the head and push a little to deliver the shoulders.
9. As one shoulder delivers, lift the head, delivering the other shoulder. The rest of the baby will follow quickly.
10. Wrap the baby in a clean blanket or clean towels.
11. Use a clean cloth or tissue to remove mucus from the baby's mouth.
12. Do not pull on the umbilical cord to deliver the placenta—it is not necessary.
13. If the placenta delivers on its own, wrap it in a towel or clean newspapers, and save it.
14. Tie string or a shoelace around a section of the cord. You don't need to cut the cord.
15. Keep the placenta at the level of the baby or above the baby.
16. Keep mother and baby warm with towels or blankets until medical help arrives.

Emergency Delivery on the Way to the Hospital

1. Pull over and stop the car.
2. Try to get help, if you have a cellular phone or a CB radio.
3. Put on your flashing warning lights.
4. Place the woman in the back seat, with a towel or blanket under her.
5. Encourage the woman not to push or bear down.
6. When the baby's head delivers, encourage the woman not to push or bear down. Instead, have her pant or blow, and concentrate on not pushing.
7. Try to ease out the baby's head with gentle pressure. Do not pull on the head.
8. After the head is delivered, gently push down on the head and push a little to deliver the shoulders.
9. As one shoulder delivers, lift the head, delivering the other shoulder. The rest of the baby will follow quickly.
10. Wrap the baby in a clean blanket or clean towels. Clean newspapers can be used if nothing else is available.
11. Use a clean cloth or tissue to remove mucus from the baby's mouth.
12. Do not pull on the umbilical cord to deliver the placenta—it is not necessary.
13. If the placenta delivers on its own, wrap it in a towel or clean newspapers and save it.
14. Tie string or a shoelace around a section of the cord. You don't need to cut the cord.
15. Keep the placenta at the level of the baby or above the baby.
16. Keep mother and baby warm until you can get them to the hospital or medical help arrives.

After Your Part 4
Baby is Born

After Your Baby's Birth

16

When your baby arrives, your new life as a parent begins. Before you jump into this new responsibility, take care of yourself so you're in the best shape possible.

Your doctor and the nurses at the hospital will have good advice and suggestions to help you recover and begin the task of taking care of your baby. Ask questions about anything you are curious about. If you decide to breastfeed, you may not know exactly how to start. Ask for the nurses' help; they've had lots of experience helping new moms get started.

If you have questions about the care of your newborn, don't hold back—ask before you leave the hospital. Take advantage of all the people there who can help you.

When you get home, take it easy! You need time to recover and to get back on your feet. Your partner can be a great help in this. It may take a little time to work out a schedule or divide up duties, but by working together, you will be surprised how quickly things will fall into place.

After Your Baby Is Born

If you have had a vaginal delivery, a nurse will check your blood pressure and bleeding closely for the first few hours after the birth. You will be offered medication for pain relief, and you will be encouraged to nurse your baby. If you have had a Cesarean delivery, you will be in a recovery area where a nurse will monitor you. You will be offered pain medication. After about an hour, you will be moved to your room. A nurse will measure your urine output after delivery to make sure your kidneys and bladder are working.

How long will I have to stay in the hospital?
Most women are discharged within a day or two, if labor and delivery are normal and the baby is doing well. If you have a Cesarean delivery, you may need to stay a few days longer.

Episiotomy

After childbirth, you may experience two main areas of pain—your abdomen and your episiotomy (if you have one). You can ask for pain medication for both.

It is unusual for an episiotomy to become infected. Usually an infection doesn't appear for a few days. Antibiotic treatment will take care of an infection.

How can I tell if my episiotomy is OK?
It will be hard for you to tell. The nurses will check it for you.

Tubal Ligation

Some women choose to have a tubal ligation done while they are in the hospital after the birth of their baby. However, this is not the time to make a decision about a tubal ligation if you haven't thought seriously about it before.

There are advantages to having a tubal ligation after delivery. You are already in the hospital; if you have an epidural, you already have the anesthesia necessary for a tubal ligation. If you didn't have an epidural for delivery, this procedure requires general anesthesia.

There are also disadvantages. Consider tubal ligation permanent and irreversible. If you have your tubes tied within a few hours or a day after having your baby, then change your mind, you will regret it.

Should I avoid any activities after my baby is born?
Avoid lifting any objects heavier than the baby the first few weeks. If possible, avoid climbing stairs whenever you can.

Not Breastfeeding

Women who decide not to breastfeed sometimes ask if they can take a pill or have a shot to dry up their milk. We do not give medication to stop your milk from coming in at this time. (It was done in the past, but those medications are no longer available.) Bind or wrap your breasts to stop the milk flow. Keep in mind this decision should be considered final. If you stop your milk from coming in, you won't be able to start it later.

Getting Enough Rest

Many women are surprised by how tired they are emotionally and physically for the first few months after the birth of the baby. Be sure to take time for yourself—you'll have a period of adjustment.

Sleep and rest are essential after the baby is born to help you get back in shape. To get the rest you need, go to bed early when possible. Take a nap or rest when the baby naps.

You may feel exhausted having to deal with your baby. Parenthood is easier and more enjoyable when both partners share the responsibilities and chores. Couples should form a parenthood partnership. It will take a cooperative effort from both of you, but it can be done.

To form this partnership, sit down together before the baby is born and discuss what changes you will face. You may be able to avoid problems before they occur. Sharing tasks, such as bathing and diaper changing, seems to work out the best.

Problems to Watch For

You should not feel ill after birth. Call your doctor immediately if you have any of the following problems:

- unusually heavy or sudden increase in vaginal bleeding (more than your normal menstrual flow or soaking more than two sanitary pads in 30 minutes)
- vaginal discharge with strong, unpleasant odor
- a temperature of 101F (38.3C) or more, except in the first 24 hours after birth
- breasts that are painful or red
- loss of appetite for an extended period of time
- pain, tenderness, redness or swelling in your legs
- pain in the lower abdomen or in the back

Baby Blues

After your baby is born, you may feel sad and cranky. This feeling is called *postpartum distress*; up to 80% of all women have the "baby blues." It usually appears between 2 days and 2 weeks after the baby is born. The situation is temporary and tends to leave as quickly as it comes.

Symptoms of the baby blues include:
• anxiety
• crying for no reason
• exhaustion
• impatience
• irritability
• lack of confidence
• lack of feeling for the baby
• low self-esteem
• oversensitivity
• restlessness

Postpartum reactions, whether mild or severe, are temporary and treatable. One of the most important ways you can help yourself is to set up support before the birth. Ask family members and friends to help. Have your mother or mother-in-law stay for a while. Ask your husband to take some leave from his job, or hire someone to come in and help each day. Do some form of moderate exercise every day. Eat nutritiously, and drink plenty of fluids. Go out every day.

Postpartum depression. Postpartum depression is a more severe problem than baby blues. Medication may be necessary. Medications of choice include antidepressants and tranquilizers; often they are used together. In most cases, a course of antidepressants that lasts from 6 months to 1 year successfully treats the problem.

Postpartum reactions, whether mild or severe, are temporary and treatable.

Your partner can be affected if you suffer from the baby blues or postpartum depression. It's important to prepare him for this situation. Explain to him that if it happens to you, it is only temporary.

Physical Changes

Abdominal skin. For some women, skin returns to normal naturally. For others, it never returns to its prepregnancy state.

Abdominal skin is not muscle, so it can't be strengthened by exercise. One of the main factors that affects your skin's ability to return to its prepregnancy tightness is connective tissue, which provides suppleness and elasticity. As you get older, your skin loses connective tissue and elasticity. Other factors include your state of fitness before pregnancy, heredity and how greatly your skin was stretched during pregnancy.

Breasts. Most women find their breasts return to their prepregnancy size or decrease a little in size. This is a result of the change in the connective tissue that forms the support system in a woman's breasts. Exercise will not make breasts firmer, but it can improve the underlying muscle so breasts have better support.

Weight. It's normal to lose 10 to 15 pounds (4.5 to 6.75kg) immediately after your baby is born. Extra weight may be harder to lose. Your body stored about 7 to 10 pounds (3.15 to 4.5kg) of fat to provide you with energy for the first few months after birth. If you eat properly and get enough exercise, these pounds will slowly come off.

Shouldn't I go on a strict diet to lose weight after the birth?
No, don't go on a strict diet right away. Even if you don't breastfeed your baby, your body requires a well-balanced, nutritious diet for you to stay healthy and to keep up your energy level.

I've heard I shouldn't diet if I'm breastfeeding. Why?
All the nutrients your baby receives while breastfeeding depend on the quality of food you eat. Breastfeeding places more demands on your body than pregnancy. Your body burns up to 1,000 calories a day just to produce milk. When breastfeeding, you need to eat an extra 500 calories a day. Be sure to keep up fluid levels also.

Exercise. It's generally OK to exercise after you have a baby, but be careful about beginning an exercise program too soon. Before you start any postpartum exercise program, be sure to check with your doctor. He or she may have some particular advice for you. Don't overtire yourself. Get adequate rest.

Do something you enjoy, and do it on a regular basis. Walking and swimming are excellent exercises to help you get back in shape. Take it slowly. Ask your doctor when and how you can increase your exercise program.

Choosing Your Baby's Pediatrician

Your doctor can help you arrange for a pediatrician before your baby's delivery. He or she may be glad to give you a referral. When your baby is born, the pediatrician will be notified so he or she can come to the hospital and check the baby.

Although it isn't necessary, you may wish to choose and visit a pediatrician for your baby 3 or 4 weeks before your due date. If the baby comes early, you will have already made these arrangements.

Friends, co-workers and family members may be able to provide you with references to pediatricians they know and trust. Or contact your local medical society and ask for a reference.

Questions to Ask

Below is a list of questions to help you create a dialogue with your new pediatrician about your child's care.

• What are your qualifications and training?
• What is your availability?
• Are your office hours compatible with our schedules?
• Can an acutely ill child be seen the same day?
• How can we reach you in case of an emergency or after office hours?
• Who responds if you are not available?
• Is the office staff cordial, open and easy to talk to?
• Do you return phone calls the same day?
• Are you interested in preventive, developmental and behavioral issues?
• How does your practice operate?
• Does it comply with our insurance?
• What is the nearest (to our home) emergency room or urgent-care center you would send us to?

What to Consider When Selecting a Pediatrician

Some issues can be resolved only by analyzing your feelings after you've visited this doctor— examining your "gut reactions" to certain issues. Below is a list of questions you and your partner might want to discuss after an initial visit.

- Are the doctor's philosophies and attitudes acceptable to us, such as use of antibiotics and other medications, childrearing practices or medically related religious beliefs?
- Did the doctor listen to us?
- Was he or she genuinely interested in our concerns?
- Did the physician appear interested in developing a rapport with our expected child?
- Is this a person I feel comfortable with and with whom our child will be comfortable?

- *Did the doctor listen to us?*

- *Is this a person I feel comfortable with and with whom our child will be comfortable?*

If conflicts develop over time or you don't see eye to eye on important matters, you may be able to choose another pediatrician within the practice or elsewhere, depending on your insurance coverage.

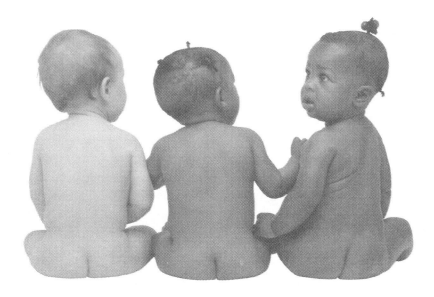

Your Postpartum Checkup

A postpartum checkup is scheduled between 2 and 6 weeks after delivery, depending on the circumstances of the birth. Don't skip this appointment! It's the last part of a complete prenatal-care program. It is just as important as seeing your healthcare provider during pregnancy.

You will have a physical exam, similar to the one at your first prenatal exam. Your doctor will also do an internal (pelvic) exam. It's done to determine if your uterus is returning to its prepregnant size and position, which normally takes about 6 weeks. If there are any problems, they can be taken care of at this time.

Don't skip this appointment!

If you had any birth tears or incisions, you will be examined to see how they are healing. This is a good time to discuss birth control, if you haven't already made plans.

Birth Control after Pregnancy

You usually can resume sexual relations with your partner 6 weeks after delivery. Wait until after your postpartum checkup, ask your doctor and make sure you are ready.

If you're not planning another pregnancy immediately, discuss contraception methods with your doctor. Your postpartum checkup is the perfect time to bring up the subject. You may decide on oral contraceptives, Norplant® or an IUD. You will need a prescription for an oral contraceptive. If you decide on Norplant or an IUD, you will have to make arrangements for the procedure.

Breastfeeding and Birth Control

Breastfeeding decreases your chances of getting pregnant, but you *cannot* rely on breastfeeding or the lack of menstruation to protect you against getting pregnant again. You need to use some type of protection when you resume intercourse.

You have a number of contraception choices while breastfeeding—condoms, "minipill" birth-control pills, birth-control foam or jelly, diaphragms, IUDs, Norplant or Depo-provera® injections. Talk about your options with your healthcare provider.

Making Your Home Safe for Baby

You cannot completely baby-proof a house. Accidents can and do happen. But there is much you *can* do to safeguard your baby's environment and make it baby-safe. Keep these points in mind:

- Crib slats should be no farther apart than 2-3/8 inches (6cm).
- Be sure the mattress fits the crib securely.
- Keep the crib away from windows, wall decorations, heating units, climbable furniture, blind and drapery cords and other possible dangers.
- Never use a pillow in the crib.
- Keep the dropside up and locked when baby is in the crib.
- Keep mobiles and other crib toys out of baby's reach. You may have to remove them as baby grows older.
- Never hang a pacifier or anything else around your baby's neck.
- Never leave baby unattended on a sofa, chair, changing table or any other surface above the floor.
- Never put your baby in an infant seat on the counter or a table.
- Use safety straps with all baby equipment.
- Never leave a baby unattended in any water. A baby can drown in 1 inch of water.
- Never hold your baby while you're cooking or while drinking a hot beverage of any kind.
- If you warm formula or baby food in the microwave, it can heat unevenly, causing hot spots. Be sure to shake the bottle or stir the food well before serving.
- Don't hang anything on stroller handles, such as a purse or bag. The extra weight could tip over the stroller.

Your New Baby 17

The long wait is over! You have your baby home and are ready to begin life as a family. You may be a little nervous about handling this tiny little person. It may help to know that babies are very resilient—you don't have to handle them as though they're made of china. Be careful to support their heads, keep them comfortably dressed (not too hot, not too cold), feed and change them—as you get the hang of things, these tasks will become much easier.

The most important thing you can give your baby is your love. As a father of five children, I know this won't be a difficult task. Babies are lovable; it's hard not to devote all of your time to them! Enjoy this wonderful, magical time with your child.

Baby at Birth

After your baby is born, he or she will have some routine tests. The tests performed depend on your medical history, findings obtained during examination of the newborn and other factors. Tests performed on the baby include:

- Apgar test
- Brazelton neonatal behavioral assessment scale
- Coombs test
- assessment of neonatal maturity
- reflex assessment
- screening for hyperphenylketonuria, anemia and hypothyroidism
- additional blood tests

See the chart on page 246 for an explanation of these tests.

Tests on the Newborn

Test	How Test Is Performed	What Test Indicates
Apgar test	At 1 and 5 minutes after birth, baby is assessed for color, heart rate, muscle tone, reflex response, breathing.	Gives an indication of general condition at baby's birth. Helps hospital staff decide if newborn needs extra care. Each category receives a score from 0 to 2 points, for a maximum of 10 points. Does not indicate what future may hold.
Blood screen	Blood is taken from baby's heel.	Detects hyper-phenylketonuria, anemia and hypothyroidism.
Coombs test	Blood is taken from umbilical cord if mother's blood is Rh-negative, type O or has not been tested for antibodies.	Detects whether Rh-antibodies have been formed.
Reflex assessment	Tests several specific reflexes, including the rooting and grasp reflexes.	If a particular reflex is not present, further evaluation is necessary.
Assessment of neonatal maturity	Many characteristics of baby are assessed to evaluate neuromuscular and physical maturity.	Each characteristic is assigned a score; sum indicates infant's maturity.
Brazelton neonatal behavioral assessment scale	Tests broad range of behaviors in babies where a problem is suspected. Some hospitals test all babies.	Provides information to doctors and parents about how a newborn responds to the environment.
Other blood tests	Blood is taken from baby's heel.	Tests for sickle-cell anemia, blood-glucose levels or other problems. Results indicate whether baby needs further evaluation.

Birthweight. We've found three distinct differences in the birthweight of babies. However, these are general statements and do not apply in all cases.

- Boys weigh more than girls.
- Birthweight of an infant increases with the number of babies you deliver.
- White babies at term weigh more than black babies at term.

Your Newborn's Appearance

What does the baby look like at birth?
The baby is wet and usually has some blood on his skin. Vernix, a white or yellow waxy substance, may cover part or much of his body.

A baby's head is large in proportion to the rest of her body. At birth, it measures one-quarter of her entire length. As she grows, this will change until her head is one-eighth of her adult height.

Nose

The shape of your baby's nose at birth may look funny to you—flat or lumpy, as though the baby has been in a fight. This shape has little to do with what it will look like when she is an adult. A newborn's nose may look too flat to breathe through, but babies do manage to breathe through them.

Hair

A baby may be born with lots of hair or none at all. If he has lots of hair, this first hair may fall out during the first 6 months and may be replaced by hair that may be entirely different in color and texture. If he doesn't have any hair, that's not a permanent condition, either. He will eventually grow hair.

My little boy's head is misshapen. Will it always be like this?
If your baby made his appearance into this world through the birth canal, he may have an elongated head. The shape is only temporary and will become more "normal" in the next few days.

Eyes

A newborn's eyes are often swollen or puffy immediately after birth. This is caused by pressure in the birth canal and subsides in a few days.

Your baby's eyes may look greasy and a little red when the nurse brings him to you. His eyes may have been slightly irritated and reddened by the antibiotic ointment applied to them shortly after birth. This is used to prevent eye infections. Redness usually disappears within 48 hours after birth.

One of your baby's eyes may wander when she looks at you, or she may look cross-eyed. Don't worry. Her eye muscles aren't strong enough yet to control her eye movements. A wandering eye usually corrects itself by the time the baby is 6 months old. If she has a problem after that, discuss it with your pediatrician.

Skin folds at the inner corners of his eyes may make it look as if your baby is squinting at you. As time passes, these folds become less prominent, and he won't look as if he's squinting anymore.

Skin

Within hours after birth, a baby's skin begins to dry out and may become flaky and scaly. This can last for a few weeks after birth. Dry skin can worry parents who have heard a baby's skin is always soft and beautiful. You don't need to treat it, but you may want to rub a little lotion on your baby's delicate skin.

Your baby may get a lot of different rashes. Don't be alarmed. Contact your healthcare provider if any rash lasts longer than a few days or if your baby seems to be extremely uncomfortable.

Diaper rash. This is the most common rash. It appears as bumps in the diaper area. Keep the area dry and clean, and apply a protective ointment that contains zinc oxide.

Dress baby in a hat and protective clothing for even a brief outing in the sun.

Prickly heat. A red, blistery rash may be prickly heat. Apply cornstarch to the affected area, and don't overdress the baby.

Milia. Tiny yellow bumps on the face, called *milia*, affect about half of all newborns. Large yellow pimples on splotchy skin is called *newborn rash*. This affects about 70% of all newborns. Swollen pink pimples are called *newborn acne*. Treatment for milia, newborn rash and newborn acne is time—you don't need to do anything. They disappear without treatment in a little while.

Sunlight. It's best to avoid exposing your baby to direct sunlight. A newborn's skin has little or no ability to protect itself from sun damage. Sunscreens are not recommended for babies under 6 months, so keep your little one in the shade for the best protection. Dress baby in a hat and protective clothing for even a brief outing in the sun, especially in very hot, sunny areas like the Southwest.

Pets and a New Baby

When a baby is born to a couple with a dog or cat that has been the center of attention for a long while, problems may arise. A dog in particular may act up. Sometimes the dog resents the attention the baby gets and growls at the infant, barks or demands attention. The animal may even revert to unacceptable behavior, such as wetting or tearing things up.

Helping the dog accept the baby. If your dog has never been around children, begin introducing her to the sights, sounds and smells of a new baby before your baby is born. When you bring the baby home, give your dog positive attention while introducing her to the new baby. Be firm when your dog misbehaves—don't let her get away with bad behavior. Be sure your dog is neutered; unneutered dogs are more apt to growl, snap and bite. Don't isolate your dog when you bring the baby home. Make her a part of the interactions with the baby. Don't leave the dog alone with the baby. Use common sense, and take things slowly.

Helping the cat accept the baby. Cats are affected in many of the same ways as dogs, and much of the advice on dogs applies to cats. Expect a cat to take longer to adjust to a new baby than a dog does. You may have to train your cat to stay out of the baby's crib.

Your Baby's Health

It's easy to worry about your newborn's health when everything is so unfamiliar at first. In this section I review a few of the more common ailments you may encounter with your baby. Be sure to read the box below. It lists some of the symptoms of illness you should be able to recognize in your baby. If you notice any of them, call your doctor.

I've never had a baby before. I'm concerned I won't know when he's ill or when I should call the doctor. What do you recommend?
If your baby shows any of the following symptoms, call your doctor:
- fever higher than 101F (38.3C)
- inconsolable crying for long periods of time
- problems with urination
- projectile vomiting, in which stomach contents come out with great force
- baby appears lethargic or floppy when held
- severe diarrhea
- unusual behavior
- poor appetite
Any of these could be an indication your baby is ill.

Ear Infection

It may be difficult for you to tell that your baby has an ear infection. Symptoms that may indicate an ear infection in babies under 6 months old include:
- irritability that lasts all day
- sleeplessness
- lethargy
- feeding difficulties

Besides being hard to discern, these symptoms may not be accompanied by fever. For babies between 6 and 12 months of age, symptoms are similar, except that fever is more common. The onset of ear pain may be sudden, acute and more noticeable.

Dehydration

If dehydration occurs, call your doctor immediately. Below are some warning signs to watch for.

- Baby wets fewer than six diapers a day.
- Baby's urine is dark yellow or orange. It should be pale yellow.
- Baby has fewer than two loose stools a day.
- Baby seems to be having trouble sucking.
- The soft spot on baby's head is sunken in.
- Baby is listless or otherwise appears unhealthy.

Diarrhea

If you're concerned about diarrhea, call your doctor. A change in the number of diapers used or a change in the consistency of the bowel movement is the first clue.

If your baby has diarrhea, he or she will need extra water and minerals to prevent dehydration. Your healthcare provider may recommend an oral electrolyte solution to help replenish your baby's lost fluids and minerals.

Jaundice

I've heard about newborns having jaundice. What is jaundice?
Jaundice is the yellow staining of the skin, sclera (eyes) and deeper tissues of the body. It is caused by the newborn's inability to handle bilirubin, a chemical produced in the liver.

Jaundice is common. It is caused by too much bilirubin in the baby's blood and can be dangerous if left untreated. It is usually not difficult to treat.

To diagnose jaundice, the baby's color is observed by the pediatrician and the nurses in the baby nursery. The baby looks yellow because of the excess amounts of bilirubin in the blood. Bilirubin is measured by a blood test.

Phototherapy is the treatment of choice. The baby is placed under special lights; the light penetrates the baby's skin and destroys the bilirubin. In some parts of the country, such as the Southwest, special lights may not be necessary. The baby is merely placed in the sunshine for short periods of time, and the sunlight destroys the excess bilirubin. In more severe cases, blood-exchange transfusions may be necessary.

Colic

Colic is a condition marked by episodes of loud, sudden crying and fussiness, which can often last for hours, in a baby that is otherwise healthy. About 20% of all babies experience the pain and crying caused by colic. In full-blown colic, the abdomen becomes distended and the infant passes gas often.

The only way to know if your baby has colic is to see your pediatrician or family physician. He or she can determine if it is colic or if your baby is having some other problem.

Colic usually appears gradually in the infant about 2 weeks after birth. As days pass, the condition worsens, then often disappears around the age of 3 months. Occasionally colic lasts until 4 months. Colic attacks usually occur at night beginning in the late afternoon and early evening and last 3 to 4 hours. The attacks cease as quickly as they begin.

Researchers have been studying colic and its causes for a long time, but we still have little understanding of why it occurs. Theories about its causes include:

- immaturity of the digestive system
- intolerance to cow's-milk protein in formula or breast milk
- fatigue in the infant

If our baby suffers from colic, what can we do?
Most doctors recommend using a variety of methods to try to ease the baby's discomfort.
- Offer the baby the breast or a bottle of formula.
- Try noncow's-milk formula, if you bottlefeed.
- Carry your baby in a sling during an attack. Motion and closeness often help somewhat.
- Try a pacifier to soothe the baby.
- Put the baby on its stomach across your knees and rub its back.
- Wrap the baby snugly in a blanket.
- Massage or stroke the baby's tummy.

Your Baby's Sleeping Habits

It can be difficult to get a baby to go to sleep at night. It's best to establish a routine to help your baby develop healthy sleeping habits.

- Wait until your baby is tired to put him to bed.
- Develop a regular, predictable bedtime routine.
- Establish good sleep associations, such as a favorite blanket or toy, or a pacifier. Don't put your baby to bed with a bottle!

Some babies want to sleep all day and stay up all night. A parent can try a couple of strategies to change the day/night situation with her baby.

- Limit daytime naps to a few hours each.
- Don't overstimulate the baby when you get up for nighttime feedings.
- By day, let baby nap in a light area, with some noise. At night, put baby in a very quiet, dark room to sleep.
- Keep baby up during the day by talking and singing or providing other stimulation.

I heard it's better to put a baby down to sleep on its side or back, rather than on its stomach. Is this true?
Yes. We have discovered the back or side positions greatly reduce the incidence of SIDS (sudden infant death syndrome).

There may be a difference in the sleep habits of bottlefed and breastfed babies. Bottlefed babies often sleep longer at night as they mature. Breastfed infants may not shift to longer sleep patterns until around the time they are weaned. See the chart below for a comparison of bottlefed and breastfed babies' sleep patterns.

Length of Nighttime Sleep Patterns

Age	Bottlefed Babies	Breastfed Babies
Newborn	5 hours	4 to 7 hours
4 months	8 to 10 hours	4 to 7 hours
6 months	9 to 10 hours	4 to 7 hours
Total sleep in 24 hours	13 to 15 hours	11 to 14 hours

Taking Care of Baby

Umbilical-Cord Care

It isn't difficult to deal with the stump of the umbilical cord. It will fall off 7 to 10 days after birth. Until it does, clean your baby with sponge baths instead of tub baths. Follow your pediatrician's advice.

Eye Care

To remove sleepers (also called *sleep* or *sand*) from your baby's eyes, use a moistened cotton ball. Place the cotton ball at the inner corner of the eye, and wipe vertically down the nose.

Nose Care

Never put anything inside your baby's nose. If you need to remove dried nasal secretions, gently wipe around the nose. Dried nasal secretions are usually sneezed out.

Ear Care

Never probe your baby's ears with any object! Ear wax is there for a purpose. It's OK to clean around the outside of the ears with a soft washcloth, but don't put anything inside your baby's ears.

Diaper Choices

Take into consideration your routine, your budget and your baby when deciding whether to use disposable diapers or cloth diapers. Disposable diapers are convenient. You don't need pins or plastic pants, and you never have to wash them. Cloth diapers can be used many times. Some styles don't need pins or plastic pants. You will need adequate washing and drying facilities, or you may choose a diaper service. Many of my patients use a combination of disposable and cloth diapers.

Weight Concerns

Some women are concerned that their baby looks "fat." A chubby baby is not really a concern at this early age. Focus on whether your baby is growing and developing appropriately, not how fat he is. Do *not* put your baby on a diet to keep him slim!

Your doctor will be mainly concerned about where your child fits on the growth charts in relation to other children. Usually a child's weight and height are given by using a percentile for each. For example, if you are told your daughter is in the 80th percentile for height, it means 80 out of 100 children are shorter than she is, and 20 children are taller. If your son is in the 60th percentile for weight, it means 60 out of 100 children weigh less than he does, and 40 children weigh more.

Preventing obesity in later life. You can start now to help give your baby the best nutritional start possible.

- Breastfeed your baby.
- Do not introduce solid foods until the age of 4 to 6 months.
- Feed your baby in response to hunger, not to meet other needs or just because it's "time to eat."
- Encourage physical activity and sound eating habits for everyone in your family.

Car Restraints—For Your Baby's Safety

Your baby needs to ride in a special safety-restraint seat whenever he is placed in an automobile. In an accident, an unrestrained child becomes a missilelike object in a car. The force of a crash can literally pull a child out of an adult's arms!

This rule applies even for the shortest trips. It's incredible, but one study showed *more than 30 deaths a year* occur to unrestrained infants going home from the hospital after birth! In nearly all these cases, if the baby had been in an approved infant-restraint system, he or she would have survived the accident. Don't take chances—keep your baby safely restrained.

The safest spot for a baby's car seat is in the middle of the back seat.

Many states now have laws that govern safety-restraint systems. Call your local hospital or police department and ask for information. Some hospitals won't let you take the baby home if he or she is not going to ride in an approved safety-restraint seat. Many hospitals have loaners you can borrow until you get your own.

The safest spot for a baby's car seat is in the middle of the back seat. In this position, it is more protected in the event of a side collision. Manufacturers recommend not putting the car seat in the front seat, especially if you have a passenger-side airbag.

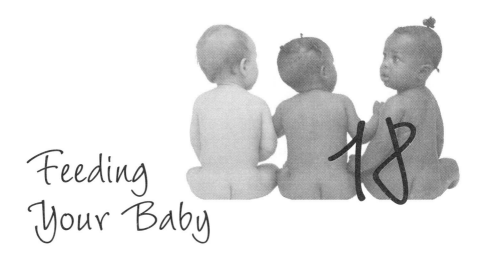

Feeding Your Baby

18

Feeding your baby is one of the most important tasks you will perform as a new mother. The nutrition you give your baby now will have an effect on the rest of his or her life.

You may decide to breastfeed your baby. This is probably the best nutrition you can provide. The baby receives more than just breast milk from you. He or she will also receive important nutrients, antibodies to help prevent infections and other substances important for growth and development. However, if you choose to bottlefeed—as the majority of new mothers still do—you can still provide good nutrition for your baby. You just have to be aware of the various nutrients that different formulas provide.

This chapter provides information to help you give your baby the best start nutritionally you can. If you have questions about a particular topic, discuss them with your obstetrician or your baby's pediatrician. Work together as a team in this important undertaking.

Feeding Basics

Early in life, most babies eat every 3 to 4 hours, although some babies feed as often as every 2 hours. It may help your baby get on a schedule if you feed at regular intervals. Or you can let your baby set the schedule—some babies need to nurse more often than others. Sometimes your baby will need to feed more often than she usually does. See how often your baby wants to feed and whether she is growing properly. These are the best guides to feeding your baby.

Usually as the baby grows older, she waits longer between feedings
and feeds longer at each feeding.

How will I know when my baby is hungry?
A baby exhibits definite signs of hunger, including:
- fussing
- putting his hands in his mouth
- turning his head and opening his mouth when his
  cheek is touched

How Much to Feed?

A baby is usually the best judge of how much he or she should
take at each feeding. Usually a baby will turn away from the nipple
(mother or bottle) when he is full.

OK to Give Water?

Discuss the matter of giving your baby water to drink with your
healthcare provider. Much depends on your baby's weight, how well
he is doing and whether he is hungry or thirsty. Your healthcare
provider will give you answers.

Burping

It's a good idea to burp your baby after each feeding. Some babies
need to be burped during a feeding as well. Hold your baby over your
shoulder or sit your baby in your lap, and gently rub or pat the back.
You will probably want to place a towel over your shoulder or at least
have one handy in case he or she spits up. If your baby doesn't burp,
don't force it.

Spitting Up

Spitting up is common during the early months of life because the
muscle at the top of the stomach is not yet fully developed. When a
baby spits up enough to propel the stomach contents several inches,
it is called *vomiting*. If your baby vomits after a feeding, do not feed
him or her again immediately—the stomach may be upset. It may be
wise to wait until the next feeding time.

Breastfeeding Is Best for Baby

If you can breastfeed, we have found it is best for the baby. Breast
milk contains all the nutrients a baby needs, and it's easy to digest.
Breastfed babies have lower rates of infections, and breastfeeding

provides the baby a sense of security and the mother a sense of self-esteem. However, if there are reasons you cannot or choose not to breastfeed, be assured that your baby will do well on formula.

If you cannot breastfeed, it will not harm your baby. Don't feel guilty if you don't breastfeed. Sometimes you cannot breastfeed because of a physical condition or other problem. Sometimes you choose not to breastfeed because of other demands on your time, such as a job or other children to care for. Your baby can still get all the love and attention and nutrition he or she needs if breastfeeding is not possible for you.

Bottlefeeding

Statistics show that more women choose to bottlefeed than breastfeed their babies. Iron-fortified formula provides good nutrition for your baby if you bottlefeed.

Bottlefeeding has advantages that are sometimes overlooked.
• Some women enjoy the freedom bottlefeeding provides. Someone else can help care for the baby.
• Fathers can be more involved in the care of the baby.
• Bottlefed babies are often able to last longer between feedings because formula is usually digested more slowly than breast milk.
• You can determine exactly how much formula your baby is taking at each feeding.

Formula Temperature

There's no evidence that feeding refrigerated formula without warming it will harm your baby. If you usually warm it, your baby will probably prefer it that way. If your baby is usually breastfed, he or she will probably prefer a warmed bottle. Be careful that formula is not too hot.

Types of Formula

Most babies do very well on milk-based formula, but some babies need specialized formulas. Several types are available on the market today, including:
• **milk-based, lactose-free formula** for babies with feeding problems caused by lactose intolerance, such as fussiness, gas and diarrhea

- **soy-based formula**, milk-free and lactose-free, for babies with milk allergies or sensitivity
- **hypoallergenic protein formula**, easier to digest and lactose-free, for babies with colic or other symptoms of milk-protein allergy

Helpful Hints for Bottlefeeding Your Baby

Here are some special tips to remember as you bottlefeed your baby.
- Snuggle your baby close to you during feeding.
- Heat the formula to body temperature by running it under warm water.
- Hold the baby in a semi-upright position, with his head higher than his body.
- Place the bottle's nipple right side up, ready to feed.
- Don't touch the tip of the nipple.
- Brush the nipple lightly over the baby's lips, and guide it into the baby's mouth. Don't force it.
- Tilt the bottle so the neck is always filled, keeping the baby from sucking in too much air.
- Remove the bottle during feeding to let the baby rest. It usually takes 10 to 15 minutes to finish feeding.
- Don't leave the baby alone with the bottle. Never prop up a bottle and leave the baby alone to suck on it.
- Never put a baby to bed with a bottle.

Slanted Bottle

Research has shown that feeding a baby with a slanted bottle is better. This design keeps the nipple full of milk, which means baby takes in less air. A slanted bottle also helps ensure baby sits up to drink. When a baby drinks lying down, milk can pool in the Eustachian tube, where it can cause ear infections.

How Long to Feed with Formula?

The American Academy of Pediatrics recommends that a baby be fed iron-fortified formula for the first year of life. Feeding formula to your baby for this length of time helps maintain adequate iron intake.

Breastfeeding

You can usually begin breastfeeding your baby within an hour after birth. This provides your baby with *colostrum*, the first milk your breasts produce. Colostrum contains important factors that help boost the baby's resistance to infection. Breastfeeding also causes your pituitary gland to release oxytocin, a hormone that contracts the uterus and decreases bleeding.

How to Start

Don't be discouraged if it doesn't feel natural to breastfeed at first. It takes some time to find out what will work best for you and your baby. Hold your baby so she can reach the breast easily while nursing. Hold her across your chest, or lie in bed. Your baby should take your nipple fully into her mouth, so her gums cover the areola. She can't suck effectively if your nipple is only slightly drawn into her mouth.

Most babies breastfeed every 2 to 3 hours for 5 to 15 minutes per breast.

Breastfeeding and Bonding

Breastfeeding is an excellent way to bond with your baby because of the closeness between mother and child established during the feeding process. However, you can bond with your baby in other ways. Studies have shown that carrying your baby close to your body in a slinglike carrier helps the bonding process. It's great because dads can bond this way with baby, too!

Breastfeeding and Allergy Prevention

It's nearly impossible for a baby to become allergic to his mother's breast milk. This is important if there is a history of allergies in your family or your partner's family. The longer a baby breastfeeds, the less likely she is to be exposed to substances that could cause allergic problems.

Someone told me I had to drink lots of water while I'm breastfeeding. Is this true?
Yes. Keep up your fluid intake if you breastfeed. Drink at least ten 8-ounce glasses of water a day.

Disadvantages

The greatest disadvantage for many mothers is the fact they are tied to the baby so completely. They must be available when their baby is hungry. Breastfeeding can make other family members feel left out. Mothers who breastfeed must also pay careful attention to their diet, both to get proper nourishment and to avoid foods that pass into their breast milk and cause problems for the baby. Caffeine, alcohol and some medications can pass into breast milk.

How Breastfeeding Affects You

Dieting

It's best not to diet while breastfeeding. All the nutrients your baby receives from breastfeeding depend on the quality of the food you eat. Breastfeeding places more demands on your body than pregnancy. Your body burns up to 1000 calories a day just to produce milk. When breastfeeding, you need to eat an extra 500 calories a day.

Breastfeeding and Pregnancy Prevention

Hormonal changes that go along with breastfeeding make it less likely that you'll get pregnant, but *don't* rely on breastfeeding to protect you against pregnancy. You need to use some type of protection when you resume intercourse.

Don't use a regular oral contraceptive pill while you are breastfeeding. The hormones in regular oral contraceptives get into your milk and are passed along to your baby, possibly causing problems with the baby's development. The minipill is a good choice, or choose some other form of birth control until you are finished breastfeeding.

Spicy Foods and Caffeine

Most substances you eat or drink (or take orally, as medication) can pass to your baby in your breast milk. Spicy foods, chocolate and caffeine are just a few things your baby can react to when you ingest them. Caffeine in breast milk can cause irritability and sleeplessness in a breastfed baby. Be careful about what you eat and drink while breastfeeding.

Insufficient Milk Syndrome

Insufficient milk syndrome is rare. The baby becomes dehydrated because of breastfeeding problems, such as the mother's low milk supply or the baby's failure to drink enough milk.

This situation can happen when a mother has the idea that breastfeeding is the only "right" method of feeding and takes it to extremes. She views using a bottle, even when breastfeeding complications occur, as a personal failure. It can also happen when a mother is unable to produce enough breast milk, due to genetic defect, injury or breast surgery. Again, this problem is rare.

Milk Production, Expressing and Storage

With some practice and patience, just about every woman can breastfeed her baby. The experience is different for everyone. Ask the nurses at the hospital for help. Many hospital nurses welcome you to come back for help after you have gone home.

Expressing Breast Milk

You can express breast milk so your baby can drink it when you are away from home. Use a breast pump that is hand-, battery- or electrically operated. Expressed milk can be refrigerated or frozen and saved.

You'll need 10 to 30 minutes to express your milk, depending on the type of pump you have. You'll need to express a few times a day (around the time you would normally nurse). You also need a refrigerated place to store the milk and a comfortable, private place where you can relax enough for milk letdown to occur.

Storage

You must take several steps to store breast milk safely.
- Pump or express milk into a clean container.
- Label the container with the date and amount of milk collected.
- Freshly pumped breast milk can be kept at room temperature for up to 2 hours, but it's best to refrigerate milk as soon as possible.
- You may store breast milk safely in the refrigerator for up to 72 hours.

Freezing breast milk. For longer storage, freeze breast milk. You can keep it in a refrigerator freezer for 6 months or in a deep freezer (-20F; -29C) for up to 12 months. Fill container only 3/4 full to allow for expansion during freezing. Freeze milk in small portions, such as 2 to 4 ounces (57 to 114ml), because these amounts thaw more quickly.

Thawing frozen breast milk. Take some care when you thaw frozen breast milk. Here are some useful suggestions.

- Put the container of frozen milk in a bowl of warm water for 30 minutes, or hold the container under warm running water.
- Never microwave breast milk; it can alter its composition.
- Swirl the container to blend any fat that might have separated during thawing.
- Feed thawed milk immediately, or store in the refrigerator for up to 24 hours.

Combining fresh breast milk with frozen breast milk. Yes, this is possible. First, cool breast milk before combining it with previously frozen milk. The amount of thawed breast milk must be more than the amount of fresh breast milk. Never refreeze breast milk!

Switch Breasts during a Feed

Switch breasts during a feeding, but wait until your baby finishes with one breast before switching to the other one. The consistency of breast milk changes from thinner to richer as the baby nurses. At the next feeding, start your baby on the breast you nursed last. Doing so maintains milk production in both breasts. If your baby only wants to nurse from one breast each feeding, simply switch to the other breast at the next feeding.

Bottlefeeding and Breastfeeding

Your milk supply may be reduced if you try to combine bottlefeeding with breastfeeding. Your milk supply is driven by the baby's demand. If you bottlefeed with formula part of the time, your baby will not be demanding the breast milk from you, and your body will slow production of it.

Common Breastfeeding Problems

Pain when Breast Milk Comes In

Breast milk becomes more plentiful between 2 and 6 days after birth, when it changes from colostrum to more nourishing, mature milk. Your breasts may become engorged and cause you some pain for 24 to 36 hours. Continue breastfeeding during this time. Wear a support bra, and apply cold compresses to your breasts for short periods. Take acetaminophen (Tylenol) for pain, or ask your doctor for something stronger.

Tingling Sensation while Breastfeeding

Soon after a baby begins to nurse, the mother experiences tingling or cramping in her breasts called *milk letdown*, which means milk is flowing into the breast ducts. It occurs several times during feeding. Occasionally a baby will sputter a bit when the rush of milk comes too quickly.

Sore Nipples

If your baby doesn't take your nipple into his mouth fully during breastfeeding, the jaws can compress the nipple and make it sore. But take heart—sore nipples rarely last longer than a couple of days. Continue breastfeeding while your breasts are sore.

Nipple shields, worn inside your bra between the nipple and fabric, provide some relief. (They keep tender skin from rubbing on the bra fabric.) A mild cream can also be applied to sore nipples to provide some relief. Ask your pharmacist or doctor for the names of products that are OK to use during nursing.

Breast Infection

Large red streaks that extend up the breast toward the armpit usually indicate a breast infection. If you develop red streaks, call your doctor. An infection can cause a fever to develop within 4 to 8 hours after the streaks appear.

If you have a plugged duct, apply a warm compress to the affected area or soak the breast in warm water. Then express milk or breastfeed while massaging the tender area. (For more information about plugged ducts, see page 266.) If you develop flulike symptoms with a sore breast, call your doctor. You will be put on antibiotics. You may also need to rest in bed and empty the infected breast by pumping or breastfeeding every hour or two.

A breast infection that isn't treated can turn into an abscess. This is a painful condition. The abscess may need to be opened and drained.

Prevention. You can do several things to help prevent a breast infection.

- Eat right, drink lots of fluid and get enough rest. Doing these things helps reduce stress and keeps your immune system in top fighting form.
- Don't wear tight-fitting bras—especially underwire bras—because they can block milk flow. This can cause an infection.
- Empty your breasts on a regular schedule to avoid engorgement.
- After each feeding or pumping, let nipples air dry for a few minutes.

Should I stop nursing if I get a breast infection?
No. It's important to continue breastfeeding. If you stop, the infection may get worse.

Plugged Ducts

A plugged milk duct in the breast prevents milk from flowing freely. Tender or firm areas of the breast develop that become more painful after breastfeeding. A plugged duct may not be red, and you may not have a fever.

A plugged duct usually takes care of itself if you continue to nurse frequently.

It usually takes care of itself if you continue to nurse frequently. Apply warm compresses to the sore area to help with the pain and to open the duct. You may take acetaminophen if you like.

Breastfeeding while Ill

If you have a cold or other common virus, it is all right to breastfeed. It's OK to breastfeed if you're taking an antibiotic, as long as you know the drug is OK to use during nursing. Ask your healthcare provider or pharmacist if any medication prescribed for you should not be taken while breastfeeding. Be sure to ask *before* you begin taking it.

You Should Also Know

Breast Size

The size of your breasts doesn't influence the amount of milk you have.

Breastfeeding in Public

In many countries, breastfeeding is a natural part of life. In North America, people are now more accepting of breastfeeding than was true in the past. My best advice is to gauge each situation separately. If you're comfortable nursing at a friend's house, go ahead. If you feel uncomfortable nursing in a public place, go into the ladies' room or a lounge, and feed your baby there. Look at each instance by itself—you'll soon learn how comfortable you feel feeding your baby away from home.

Establishing a Feeding Pattern

You may be unprepared at how often your baby will want (and need) to nurse in the first week after birth. You may wonder if it's worth it to continue. Relax and be patient. It takes time for your baby to establish his or her nursing pattern. By the end of the second week, a pattern will probably be established, and your baby will sleep longer between feedings.

Substituting Bottles for Breast

It's best to avoid bottles, if possible, for the first month of breastfeeding. This is for two reasons—your baby may come to prefer feeding from a bottle (it's not as hard to suck) and your breasts may not produce enough milk otherwise.

How Long to Breastfeed?

For various reasons, you may need to stop breastfeeding after a certain period. For example, you may be returning to work or school. You may wonder how long you need to breastfeed to do the most good for your baby.

Nursing the first 4 weeks of your baby's life provides the most protection for your baby and the most beneficial hormone release to help you recover after the birth. Nursing for the first 6 months is very beneficial for your baby—it provides excellent nutrition and protection against illness. After 6 months, the nutrition and protection aspects are not as critical for your baby. Even if you can nurse only a short period of time, stick with it as long as you can.

Breastfeeding after Returning to Work

It is possible to breastfeed after you go back to work or school. If you breastfeed exclusively, you'll need to pump your breasts or arrange to see your baby during the day. Or you can nurse your baby at home and provide formula for when you're away.

If you do not feel support from co-workers for your breastfeeding or pumping at work—either immediately or after some time has passed—you may have to talk to your employer and co-workers about the situation. You may need to work together toward a solution that is fair to everyone.

Business trips. If your job requires you to go on business trips, you probably will need to pump your breast milk while you are away. You may be uncomfortable if you don't because you will continue to produce milk. Take a breast pump with you and discard the breast milk after it is pumped.

Nursing Bras

Nursing bras are special bras worn for breastfeeding. They have cups that open so you can breastfeed without having to undress.

When to buy. Wait until at least the 36th week of your pregnancy to purchase one. If you buy one earlier than that, it probably won't fit later, when you need it.

Fit. Your breasts will become larger when your milk comes in, so buy a bra with at least a finger's width of space between any part of the cup and your breast. Be sure to make allowances for the room taken up by nursing pads. When trying on the bra, fasten the hooks at their loosest setting so you can tighten it as your ribcage shrinks, after your baby is born.

Clothes for Nursing

Nighties, shift dresses and full-cut blouses have been designed with discreet openings so you don't have to undress to breastfeed. You can reach inside your outer clothing, unhook your nursing bra and place your baby at your breast without anyone noticing. Draping a light towel or blanket over your shoulder and the baby's head adds further coverage.

Breast Surgeries

Ask your pediatrician for his or her advice if you want to breastfeed your baby and have had breast-enlargement surgery in the past. Many women who have had breast-enlargement surgery are able to breastfeed successfully. Some doctors have advised women not to breastfeed if they have had silicone implants.

If you have had your breasts reduced surgically, you should still be able to breastfeed. The surgery may result in decreased milk production, but usually there is enough.

Someone told me that if I breastfeed, my nipples will drip milk when my baby cries. This isn't true, is it?

It *is* true. This may occur when your baby, or any other baby you hear, cries. This is the milk letdown response, and it is normal. To protect your clothing, wear breast shields.

How to Include Others in Feeding

Your partner can help by getting up at night and bringing the baby to you or by changing the baby. Your partner can also feed your baby expressed breast milk.

You can include your interested children in feeding the baby by letting them hold or burp the baby after she is fed. If you express your milk, a child could feed the baby a bottle of it at some feedings.

If I have a problem breastfeeding, what can I do?

Many hospitals have breastfeeding specialists you can call for help. Also call your doctor's office—they may be able to refer you to someone knowledgeable. You can look in the telephone book for La Leche League, an organization that promotes breastfeeding. Someone from the local group can give you advice and encouragement, and you may also choose to attend support-group meetings. Incidentally, your baby and other small children are also welcome at these meetings.

When Does Nursing Stop?

You can either taper off gradually or stop "cold turkey." Each way has its advantages. If you want to taper off gradually, start offering a bottle every other feeding or offer bottles during the day and nurse at night. If you stop cold turkey, you may have some sleepless nights with a screaming baby, and you may be quite uncomfortable physically with engorged breasts. However, this method takes less time.

The age for weaning a baby varies from woman to woman and baby to baby. Some women like to nurse until they return to work. Others nurse through the first year. It depends on your situation and your desire, and when your baby gets teeth!

Glossary

A

acquired immune deficiency syndrome (AIDS). Debilitating illness that affects the body's ability to respond to infection. Caused by the human immune deficiency virus (HIV).

aerobic exercise. Exercise that increases your heart rate and causes you to consume oxygen.

afterbirth. See *placenta*.

albuminuria. See *proteinuria*.

alpha-fetoprotein (AFP). Substance produced by the unborn baby as it grows inside the uterus. Large amounts of AFP are found in amniotic fluid. Larger-than-normal amounts are found in the mother's bloodstream if neural-tube defects are present in the fetus; smaller-than-normal amounts may indicate Down syndrome.

amino acids. Substances that act as building blocks in the developing embryo and fetus.

amniocentesis. Removal of amniotic fluid from the amniotic sac. Fluid is tested for some genetic defects.

amnion. Membrane around the fetus. It surrounds the amniotic cavity.

amniotic fluid. Liquid surrounding the baby inside the amniotic sac.

amniotic sac. Sac that surrounds baby inside the uterus. It contains the baby, the placenta and the amniotic fluid.

anemia. Any condition in which the number of red blood cells is less than normal. Term usually applies to the concentration of the oxygen-transporting material in the blood, which are the red blood cells.

anencephaly. Defective development of the brain combined with the absence of the bones normally surrounding the brain.

anti-inflammatory medications. Drugs to relieve pain and inflammation.

271

Apgar score. Measurement of a baby's response to birth and life outside the uterus. Taken 1 minute and 5 minutes after birth.

areola. Pigmented or colored ring surrounding the nipple of the breast.

arrhythmia. Irregular or missed heartbeat.

aspiration. Swallowing or sucking a foreign body or fluid, such as vomit, into an airway.

asthma. Disease marked by recurrent attacks of shortness of breath and difficulty breathing. Often caused by an allergic reaction.

autoantibodies. Antibodies that attack parts of your body or your own tissues.

B

back labor. Pain of labor felt in lower back.

beta-adrenergics. Substances that interfere with transmission of stimuli. They affect the autonomic nervous system. During pregnancy, they can be used to stop labor.

bilirubin. Breakdown product of pigment formed in the liver from hemoglobin during the destruction of red blood cells.

biophysical profile. Method of evaluating a fetus before birth.

biopsy. Removal of a small piece of tissue for microscopic study.

birthing center. Facility in which a woman labors, delivers and recovers in the same room. It may be part of a hospital, or it may be a freestanding unit.

bloody show. Small amount of vaginal bleeding late in pregnancy; often precedes labor.

board certification. Doctor has had additional training and testing in a particular specialty. In the area of obstetrics, the American Board of Obstetricians and Gynecologists offers this training. Certification requires expertise in care of a pregnant woman and gynecological surgery.

Braxton-Hicks contractions. Irregular, painless tightening of uterus during pregnancy.

breech presentation. Baby's buttocks or legs come into the birth canal before the head.

C

carcinogen. Any cancer-producing substance.

cataract, congenital. Cloudiness of the eye lens present at birth.

Cesarean section (delivery). Delivery of a baby through an abdominal incision rather than through the vagina.

Chadwick's sign. Dark-blue or purple discoloration of the mucosa of the vagina and cervix during pregnancy.

chemotherapy. Treatment of disease by chemical substances or drugs.

chlamydia. Sexually transmitted venereal infection.

chloasma. Extensive brown patches of irregular shape and size on the face or other parts of the body.

chorionic villus sampling (CVS). Diagnostic test done early in pregnancy. A biopsy of tissue is taken from inside the uterus through the abdomen or the cervical opening (through the vagina) to determine abnormalities of pregnancy.

colostrum. Thin, yellow fluid that is the first milk to come from the breast. Most often seen toward the end of pregnancy. It is different in content from milk produced later during nursing.

condyloma acuminatum. Skin tags or warts that are sexually transmitted. Caused by the human papilloma virus (HPV). Also called *venereal warts.*

congenital problem. Problem present at birth.

constipation. Bowel movements are infrequent or incomplete.

contraction stress test (CST). Response of fetus to uterine contractions to evaluate fetal well-being.

crown-to-rump length. Measurement from the top of the baby's head (crown) to the buttocks of the baby (rump).

cystitis. Inflammation of the bladder.

cytomegalovirus (CMV) infection. Infection caused by any of a group of viruses from the herpes virus family.

D

D&C (dilatation and curettage). Surgical procedure in which the cervix is dilated, the lining of the uterus is scraped, and the uterine cavity is emptied.

developmental delay. Condition in which the development of the baby or child is slower than normal.

diabetes, pregnancy-induced. See *gestational diabetes.*

diastasis recti. Separation of abdominal muscles.

dilatation. Expansion of an organ or vessel. Also, **dilation.**

dizygotic twins. Twins derived from two different eggs. Often called *fraternal twins.*

Down syndrome. Condition in which baby is born mentally retarded and with a generally dwarfed appearance, including a sloping forehead, short, broad hands, a flat nose and low-set ears.

dysplasia. Abnormal, precancerous changes in the cells of the cervix.

dysuria. Difficulty or pain urinating.

E

eclampsia. Convulsions and coma in a woman with pre-eclampsia. Not related to epilepsy.

ectopic pregnancy. Pregnancy that occurs outside the uterine cavity.

edema. Swelling of the feet or legs due to water retention.

effacement. Thinning of cervix.

electronic fetal monitoring. Use of electronic instruments to record the fetal heartbeat and the mother's contractions.

embryo. Organism in the early stages of development.

embryonic period. First 10 weeks of gestation (8 weeks of fetal development).

endometrium. Mucous membrane that lines the inside of the uterine wall.

enema. Fluid injected into the rectum for the purpose of clearing out the bowel.

engorgement. Congested; filled with fluid.

epidural block. Type of regional anesthesia. Medication is injected into the epidural space during labor or for some types of surgery.

episiotomy. Surgical incision of the area behind the vagina and above the rectum. Used during delivery to avoid tearing of the vaginal opening and rectum.

external cephalic version (ECV). Procedure done late in pregnancy in which doctor manually attempts to move a baby from the breech position into the normal head-down position.

F

face presentation. Situation in which baby comes into the birth canal face-first.

Fallopian tube. Tube that leads from the cavity of the uterus to the area of the ovary. Also called *uterine tube*.

false labor. Tightening of uterus without dilation or thinning of the cervix.

fasting blood sugar. Blood test to evaluate the amount of sugar in the blood following a period of fasting.

ferrous gluconate. Iron supplement.

ferrous sulfate. Iron supplement.

fertilization. Joining of the sperm and egg; conception.

fertilization age. Dating a pregnancy from the time of fertilization; 2 weeks shorter than the gestational age.

fetal alcohol syndrome (FAS). Birth defects in an infant born to a mother whose alcoholic intake persisted during pregnancy. Infant will have physical abnormalities and/or mental deficiencies.

fetal anomaly. Fetal malformation or abnormal development.

fetal arrhythmia. See *arrhythmia*.

fetal distress. Problems with the baby that occur before birth or during labor. These endanger the baby and require immediate delivery.

fetal monitor. Device used before or during labor to listen to and to record the fetal heartbeat. Can be external monitoring (through maternal abdomen) or internal monitoring (through maternal vagina) of the baby inside the uterus.

fetal period. Time period following the embryonic period (first 10 weeks of gestation or 8 weeks of development) until birth.

fetal-growth retardation. See *intrauterine-growth retardation*.

fetus. Refers to the unborn baby from 10 weeks of gestation until birth.

forceps. Special instrument placed around the baby's head, inside the birth canal, to help guide the baby out of the birth canal during delivery.

frank breech. Baby presenting buttocks first. Legs are flexed and knees extended.

fraternal twins. See *dizygotic twins*.

full-term infant. Baby born between 38 and 42 weeks of pregnancy.

G

genetic counseling. Consultation between a couple and a specialist about genetic defects and the possibility of presence or recurrence of genetic problems in a pregnancy.

genital herpes simplex. Herpes simplex infection involving the genital area.

gestation. Pregnancy.

gestational age. Dating a pregnancy from the first day of the last menstrual period; 2 weeks longer than fertilization age. See *fertilization age*.

gestational diabetes. Occurrence or worsening of diabetes during pregnancy.

globulin. Family of proteins from plasma or serum of the blood.

glucose-tolerance test. Blood test done to evaluate the body's response to sugar. Blood is drawn at intervals following ingestion of a sugary substance.

glucosuria. Glucose in the urine.

gonorrhea. Contagious venereal infection, transmitted primarily by intercourse. Caused by the bacteria Neisseria gonorrhea.

group-B streptococcal infection (GBS). Serious infection occurring in the mother's vagina and throat.

H

habitual miscarriage. Occurrence of three or more miscarriages.

heartburn. Discomfort or pain that occurs in the chest. Often occurs after eating.

hematocrit. Measurement of the proportion of blood cells to plasma. Important in diagnosing anemia.

hemoglobin. Pigment in red blood cell that carries oxygen to body tissues.

hemolytic disease. Destruction of red blood cells. See *anemia*.

hemorrhoids. Dilated blood vessels in the rectum or rectal canal.

high-risk pregnancy. Pregnancy with complications that requires special medical attention, often from a specialist. Also see *perinatologist*.

Homans' sign. Pain caused by flexing the ankle when a person has a blood clot in the lower leg.

human chorionic gonadatropin (HCG). Hormone produced in early pregnancy. Measured in a pregnancy test.

hydramnios. Increased amniotic fluid.

hydrocephalus. Excessive accumulation of fluid around the brain of the baby. Sometimes called *water on the brain*.

hyperbilirubinemia. Extremely high level of bilirubin in the blood.

hyperemesis gravidarum. Severe nausea, dehydration and vomiting during pregnancy. Occurs most frequently during the first trimester. May require brief hospitalization.

hyperglycemia. Increased blood sugar.

hypertension, pregnancy-induced. High blood pressure that occurs during pregnancy. Defined by an increase in the diastolic or systolic blood pressure.

hyperthyroidism. Elevation of the thyroid hormone in the bloodstream.

hypoglycemia. Decreased or lowered blood sugar.

hypoplasia. Defective or incomplete development or formation of tissue.

hypotension. Low blood pressure.

hypothyroidism. Low or inadequate levels of thyroid hormone in the bloodstream.

I

identical twins. See *monozygotic twins*.

immune globulin preparation. Substance used to protect against infection with certain diseases, such as hepatitis or measles.

incompetent cervix. Cervix that dilates painlessly, without contractions.

incomplete miscarriage. Miscarriage in which part, but not all, of the uterine contents are expelled.

indigestion. Inability to digest food or difficulty digesting food.

induced labor. Labor started by doctor, usually with oxytocin (Pitocin).

inevitable miscarriage. Pregnancy complicated with bleeding and cramping. Results in miscarriage.

insulin. Peptide hormone made by the pancreas. It promotes the use of glucose.

intrauterine-growth retardation (IUGR). Inadequate growth of the fetus during the third trimester of pregnancy. Also called *fetal-growth retardation*.

in utero. Within the uterus.

in vitro. Outside the body.

iron-deficiency anemia. Anemia produced by lack of iron in the diet. Often seen in pregnancy. Also see *anemia*.

isoimmunization. Development of specific antibody directed at the red blood cells of another individual, such as a baby in utero. Often occurs when an Rh-negative woman carries an Rh-positive baby or when she is given Rh-positive blood.

J-K

jaundice. Yellow staining of the skin, sclera (covering of the eyes) and deeper tissues of the body. Caused by excessive amounts of bilirubin. Treated with phototherapy.

ketones. Breakdown product of metabolism found in the blood, particularly in starvation or uncontrolled diabetes.

kidney stone. Small mass or lesion found in the kidney or urinary tract that can block the flow of urine.

L

labor. Contractions resulting in dilation of the cervix to make possible the delivery of a fetus.

laparoscopy. Surgical procedure performed for tubal ligation, diagnosis of pelvic pain, diagnosis of ectopic pregnancy and other procedures.

leukorrhea. Vaginal discharge characterized by a white or yellowish color. Primarily composed of mucus.

lightening. Dropping or descent of fetus into the pelvis before or during labor.

linea nigra. Line of increased pigmentation running down the abdomen from the bellybutton to the pubic area during pregnancy.

lochia. Vaginal discharge that occurs after delivery of the baby and placenta.

L/S ratio. Measurement of the relationship of two substances, lecithin and spingomyelin, in the amniotic fluid. Results give a doctor an indication of the maturity of the baby's lungs.

lupus. See *systemic lupus erythematosus.*

Lyme disease. Infection transmitted to humans by ticks.

M

mammogram. X-ray study of the breasts to identify normal or abnormal breast tissue.

mask of pregnancy. Increased pigmentation over the area of the face under each eye. Commonly has the appearance of a butterfly.

meconium. First intestinal discharge of the newborn; green or yellow in color. It consists of epithelial or surface cells, mucus and bile. Discharge may occur before or during labor or soon after birth.

melanoma. Pigmented mole or tumor, which may or may not be cancerous.

meningomyelocele. Congenital defect of the central nervous system of the baby in which membranes and the spinal cord protrude through an opening or defect in the vertebral column.

menstrual age. See *gestational age.*

menstruation. Regular or periodic discharge of a bloody fluid from the uterus.

microcephaly. Abnormally small development of the fetal head.

milk letdown. Tingling or cramping in woman's breast, experienced when breast milk flows into the breast ducts.

miscarriage. End of pregnancy. Giving birth to an embryo or fetus before it can live outside the womb, usually defined as before 20 weeks of gestation.

missed miscarriage. Failed pregnancy, without bleeding or cramping. Often diagnosed by ultrasound weeks or months after a pregnancy fails.

monilial vulvovaginitis. Infection caused by yeast or monilia. Usually affects the vagina and vulva.

monozygotic twins. Twins conceived from one egg. Often called *identical twins.*

morning sickness. Nausea and vomiting, primarily during the first trimester of pregnancy. Also see *hyperemesis gravidarum.*

mucus plug. Secretions in cervix; often released just before labor.

N

natural childbirth. Labor and delivery in which no medication is used, and the mother remains awake to help deliver the baby. The woman may or may not have taken classes to prepare her for labor and delivery.

neural-tube defects. Abnormalities in the development of the spinal cord and brain in a fetus. Also see *anencephaly; hydrocephalus; spina bifida.*

nonstress test. Test in which movements of the baby felt by the mother are recorded, along with changes in the fetal heart rate, to assess well-being of fetus after 32 weeks of pregnancy.

nurse-midwife. Nurse who has received extra training in the care of pregnant patients and the delivery of babies.

O

obstetrician. Physician who specializes in the care of pregnant women and the delivery of babies.

oligohydramnios. Lack or deficiency of amniotic fluid.

opioids. Synthetic compounds with effects similar to those of opium.

ovarian cycle. Regular production of hormones from the ovary in response to hormonal messages from the brain. The ovarian cycle governs the endometrial cycle.

ovulation. Cyclic production of an egg from the ovary.

ovulatory age. See *fertilization age.*

oxytocin. Medication that causes uterine contractions; used to induce labor.

P

palmar erythema. Redness of palms of the hands.

Pap smear. Routine screening test that evaluates presence of premalignant or cancerous conditions of the cervix.

paracervical block. Local anesthetic for the relief of pain of cervical dilation.

pediatrician. Physician who specializes in the care of infants and children.

perinatologist. Physician who specializes in the care of high-risk pregnancies.

perineum. Area between the anus and the vagina.

phosphatidyl glycerol. Lipoprotein present in amniotic fluid when fetal lungs are mature.

phospholipids. Fat-containing phosphorous compounds. The most important are lecithins and sphingomyelin, which are important in the maturation of fetal lungs before birth.

phototherapy. Treatment for jaundice in a newborn infant. See *jaundice.*

placenta. Organ inside the uterus that is attached to the baby by the umbilical cord. Essential during pregnancy for growth and development of the embryo and fetus. Also called *afterbirth* when it is expelled following birth of baby.

placenta previa. Low attachment of the placenta, very close to or covering the cervix.

placental abruption. Premature separation of the placenta from the uterus.

pneumonitis. Inflammation of the lungs.

polyhydramnios. See *hydramnios.*

postdate birth. Baby born 2 weeks or more past its due date.

postmature baby. Pregnancy of more than 42 weeks gestation.

postpartum blues. Mild depression after delivery.

postpartum depression. Depression after delivery.

postpartum hemorrhage. Bleeding greater than 17 ounces (500ml) at time of delivery.

post-term baby. See *postdate birth.*

pre-eclampsia. Combination of symptoms significant to pregnancy, including high blood pressure, edema, protein in the urine and changes in reflexes.

pregnancy diabetes. See *gestational diabetes.*

premature delivery. Delivery before 38 weeks gestation.

prenatal care. Program of care for a pregnant woman before the birth of her baby.

prepared childbirth. Term used when woman has taken classes to know what to expect during labor and delivery. She may request pain medication if she feels she needs it.

presentation. Describes which part of the baby comes into the birth canal first.

preterm birth. See *premature delivery.*

propylthiouracil. Medication used to treat thyroid disease.

proteinuria. Protein in urine.

pruritis gravidarum. Itching during pregnancy.

pubis symphysis. Bony prominence in the pelvic bone found in the midline. Landmark from which the doctor often measures during pregnancy to follow growth of the uterus.

pudendal block. Local anesthesia for pain relief during labor.

pulmonary embolism. Blood clot from another part of the body that travels to the lungs. Can cause closed passages in the lungs and a decrease in oxygen exchange.

pyelonephritis. Serious kidney infection.

Q-R

quickening. Feeling the baby move inside the uterus.

radiation therapy. Method of treatment for various cancers.

Rh-negative. Absence of rhesus antibody in the blood.

RhoGAM. Medication given during pregnancy and following delivery to prevent isoimmunization. Also see *isoimmunization*.

Rh-sensitivity. See *isoimmunization*.

round-ligament pain. Pain caused by stretching of the ligaments on either side of the uterus during pregnancy.

rupture of membranes. Loss of fluid from the amniotic sac. Also called *breaking of waters*.

S

seizure. Sudden onset of a convulsion.

sexually transmitted disease (STD). Infection transmitted through sexual intercourse.

sickle-cell anemia. Anemia caused by abnormal red blood cells shaped like a sickle or a cylinder. Occurs most often in people of African or Mediterranean descent.

sickle-cell trait. Presence of the trait for sickle-cell anemia; not sickle-cell disease itself.

sickle crisis. Painful episode caused by sickle-cell disease.

skin tag. Flap or extra buildup of skin.

sodium. Element found in many foods, particularly salt. Ingestion of too much sodium may cause fluid retention.

spina bifida. Congenital abnormality characterized by a defect in the vertebral column. Membranes of the spinal cord and the spinal cord itself protrude outside the protective bony canal of the spine.

spinal anesthesia. Anesthesia given in the spinal canal.

spontaneous miscarriage. Loss of pregnancy during the first 20 weeks of gestation.

stasis. Decreased flow.

station. Estimation of the descent of the baby in the birth canal.

steroids. Medications of hormone origin used to treat various diseases. Include estrogen, testosterone, progesterone and prednisone.

stillbirth. Death of baby before it is born, after 20 weeks of pregnancy.

stress test. Test in which mild contractions of the mother's uterus are induced; fetal heart rate in response to the contractions is noted.

stretch marks. Areas of the skin that are torn or stretched. Often occur on the mother's abdomen, breasts, buttocks and legs.

striae distensa. See *stretch marks.*

surfactant. Substance in the lungs that controls surface tension of lungs. Premature babies often lack sufficient amounts of surfactant to breathe without assistance.

syphilis. Sexually transmitted venereal infection.

systemic lupus erythematosus (SLE). Connective-tissue disorder common in women in the reproductive ages. Antibodies made by the person act against person's own tissues.

T

Tay-Sachs disease. Inherited disease characterized by mental and physical retardation, convulsions, enlargement of the head and eventual death. Trait is usually carried by Ashkenazi Jews.

telangiectasias. Dilation or swelling of a small blood vessel. Sometimes called an *angioma*. During pregnancy, a common name is *spider angioma*.

teratogen. A substance that causes abnormal development.

teratology. Branch of science that deals with teratogens and their effects.

thalassemia. Group of inherited disorders of hemoglobin metabolism, which results in a decrease in the amount of hemoglobin formed. Found most commonly in people of Mediterranean descent.

threatened miscarriage. Bleeding during the first trimester of pregnancy without cramping or contractions.

thrombosis. Formation of a blood clot (thrombus).

thrush. Monilial or yeast infection occurring in the mouth or mucous membranes of a newborn infant.

thyroid disease. Abnormality of the thyroid gland and its production of thyroid hormone. Also see *hyperthyroidism; hypothyroidism.*

thyroid hormone. Chemical made in the thyroid that affects the entire body.

thyroid panel. Series of blood tests done to evaluate the function of the thyroid gland.

thyroid stimulating hormone (TSH). Hormone made in the brain that stimulates the thyroid to produce thyroid hormone.

tocolytic agents. Medications to stop labor.

toxemia. See *pre-eclampsia.*

toxic strep A. Bacterial infection that can cause severe damage; usually starts in a cut on the skin, not as a sore throat, and spreads very quickly. It can involve the entire body.

toxoplasmosis. Infection caused by toxoplasma gondii. Can be contracted from handling raw meat or cat feces.

transverse lie. Situation in which fetus is turned sideways in uterus.

trichomonal vaginitis. Venereal infection caused by trichomonas.

trimester. Method of dividing pregnancy into three equal time periods of about 13 weeks each.

tubal pregnancy. See *ectopic pregnancy.*

U

umbilical cord. Cord containing blood vessels that connects the placenta to the developing baby. It removes waste products and carbon dioxide from the baby and brings oxygenated blood and nutrients from the mother through the placenta to the baby.

umbilicus. Bellybutton.

ureters. Tubes that drain urine from the kidneys to the bladder.

urinary calculi. See *kidney stones.*

uterus. Organ in which an embryo/fetus grows. Also called a *womb.*

V

vaccine. Dose of medication given to a person to cause production of antibodies to protect against subsequent infections.

vacuum extractor. Soft rubber device used to provide traction on fetal head to aid in delivery.

varicose veins. Blood vessels (veins) that are dilated or enlarged, most often found in the legs.

vascular spiders. See *telangiectasias.*

VBAC. Vaginal birth after Cesarean.

vena cava. Major vein in the body that empties into the right atrium of the heart. It returns unoxygenated blood to the heart for transport to the lungs.

venereal warts. See *condyloma acuminatum.*

vernix. Fatty substance made up of epithelial cells that covers fetal skin inside the uterus.

vertex presentation. Head first.

W-Y
womb. See *uterus*.
yeast infection. See *monilial vulvovaginitis; thrush*.

Index

A

abdomen, measurement of 150
abdominal pain 182, 183, 187, 237
    severe 182, 183
abdominal skin changes 238
abnormalities in baby 16, 59, 74, 130, 184
    bone 74
    central-nervous-system 74
    chromosomal 16
    eye 74
    fetal 59
    genetic 184
    hand 74
abortion 24, 40, 183
    spontaneous 183
abscess of tooth 143
abscess in breast 266
abuse of various substances 17
accidents 182, 193
Accutane® 74, 76
acetaminophen 27, 37, 49, 77, 101, 136, 140, 141, 265, 266
acne in pregnant woman 136
ACOG, see *American College of Obstetricians and Gynecologists*
acquired immune deficiency syndrome, see *AIDS*
activity level of fetus 140
acyclovir 163
addictionologists 17
Advil® 77
aerobic exercise 93, 94, 271
    for pregnant women 93, 94
    water 93
after baby is born 227-228
afterbirth 271, 280
age of father 16, 157, 158
age of fetus 120
age of woman, over 35 15
AIDS 4, 16, 165, 173, 271
air embolus 38
albuminuria 271
alcohol use 3, 4, 17, 77, 127, 130, 157, 167, 170-171, 184, 194
    by father 157, 171
    safe amount 171
alcohol and drugs 171
alcoholism 130
Aleve® 77
allergies 37, 40, 260
    milk-protein 260
alpha-fetoprotein test 16, 23, 50, 52, 54, 61, 62, 271
    false-positive results 62
American College of Obstetricians and Gynecologists 10, 94, 221
American Academy of Pediatrics 260
amino acids 271
aminopterin 74, 126
amitriptyline 139
amniocentesis 16, 41, 50, 54, 57, 59-61, 63, 64, 129, 271
amnion 271
amniotic sac 271
amniotic fluid 60, 271
amphetamines 173
Amphojel® 36, 77
analgesics 171, 215, 216
androgens 74
anemia 12, 32, 44, 45, 46, 88, 99, 116, 130, 172, 245, 246, 271, 277, 281
    iron-deficiency 45, 116, 277
    sickle-cell 12, 45, 246, 281
anencephaly 60, 62, 271

Illustration and Photo Credits

Illustrations:

David Fischer: pp. 7, 8, 25, 55, 57, 59, 64, 68, 69, 100, 105, 107, 121, 122, 132, 134, 148, 188, 214, 216, 217, 219, 220, 224

© *1997 Artville, LLC:* 3, 4, 6, 10, 14, 84, 90, 94, 114, 126, 131, 147, 200, 201, 230

Gary Smith, Performance Design: 22, 39, 76, 86, 89, 204, 205, 240, 254, 260

Photographs:

© *ZEFA/Masterfile:* cover

© *Digital Vision:* p. 3

© *1999 PhotoDisc:* pp. 21, 51, 73, 81, 99, 111, 119, 131, 153, 161, 167, 175, 181, 197, 235, 241, 245, 257

Helpful Books

$9.95 paperback
$14.95 Canada
6 x 9, 160 pages, b/w illustrations
ISBN 1-55561-175-3

Baby & Toddler Sleep Program
How to Get Your Child to Sleep through the Night, Every Night
John Pearce, MD, with Jane Bidder

You've survived labor, delivery, feeding and bathing them—now, if you could just get them to sleep at night! Here's an easy-to-follow program to make bedtime stress-free for you and your child. Written for tired parents, these techniques and tips will take you step-by-step toward a full-night's sleep. Learn how routines affect your child's sleep, what sleep patterns are normal, how to help your child cope with nighttime fears and much more.

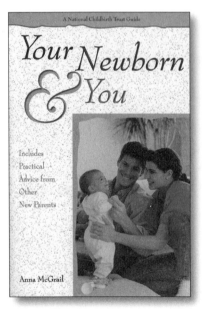

Your Newborn & You
Includes Practical Advice from Other New Parents
Anna McGrail

This guide discusses the development of the newborn and the whole family. It provides essential facts and information such as learning new skills, balancing your budget, handling boredom, planning for the future as a family and planning for another child.

$12.95 paperback
$19.95 Canada
6 x 9, 254 pages, b/w illustrations
ISBN 1-55561-125-7

For New Parents

Breastfeeding Your Baby

Jane Moody, Jane Britten & Karen Hogg

Want first-hand advice on breastfeeding? Written by three breastfeeding counselors and using the experience of over 200 women, this book answers all your questions about breastfeeding. The perfect book to get you and your baby off to a good start.

$12.95 paperback
$19.95 Canada
6 x 9, 234 pages, b/w illustrations
ISBN 1-55561-122-2

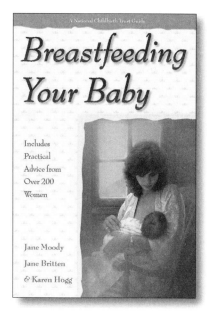

Breastfeeding Naturally
A New Approach for Today's Mother
Hannah Lothrop

Breastfeeding requires physical as well as emotional preparation. Find out the answers to finding the best position for you and your baby, getting your milk to flow, how to use pumps, shields and other breastfeeding aids plus much more. *Breastfeeding Naturally* also covers integrative and natural techniques such as visualization, aromatherapy, Bach Flower Remedies, Middendorf Breathwork and homeopathic remedies.

$12.95 paperback
$19.95 Canada
6 X 9, 288 pages
ISBN 1-55561-131-1

Delightful gifts for first-time parents

Baby Tips™
for New Moms
First 4 Months
Jeanne Murphy

O ver 110 tips in a useful month-by-month format to help you as your baby grows. Written with warm, often hilarious advice from a mother of two. Indexed for quick reference.

$6.95 paperback
$9.95 Canada
6 x 4.5, 144 pages, color illustrations
ISBN 1-55561-166-4

Baby Tips™
for New Dads
Baby's First Year

W hile a new dad might not want to admit it, he will have as much to learn (if not more) than new moms. (First rule—Never, *never* discuss her weight!) This rule and other great tips can help any new dad enjoy this exciting and challenging time. Learn how to bond with your new baby and shape new bonds with your wife. Indexed for quick reference.

$6.95 paperback
$9.95 Canada
6 x 4.5, 144 pages, color illustrations
ISBN 1-55561-169-9

Pregnancy & Childbirth Guides

Your Childbirth Class
A National Childbirth Trust Guide
Mary Nolan

Informative and up-to-date with the facts you will want to help you find the best class and healthcare professional for you. Learn how to work with your healthcare provider to obtain the best outcome for you and your baby. Also includes advice from other parents on coping with prenatal tests, choosing pain relief, having a Cesarean birth, and the first few days as parents.

$12.95 paperback
$19.95 Canada
6 x 9, 240 pages
ISBN 1-55561-127-3

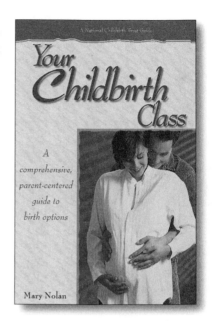

Your Pregnancy After 30
Glade B. Curtis, MD, OB/GYN

Having a child can be an intimidating experience at any age. For the woman over 30, this resource provides sensible, reassuring information that is tailored to your specific needs and interests. *Your Pregnancy After 30* includes topics on specific health concerns, multiple births, workplace safety, the facts on high-risk pregnancy, when to consider genetic counseling, exercise during and after pregnancy, and childcare considerations.

$12.95 paperback
$19.95 Canada
6.125 x 9.25, 384 pages, b/w illustrations
ISBN 1-55561-088-9

One million-copy bestseller

$12.95 paperback
$19.95 Canada
6.125 x 9.25, 384 pages, b/w illustrations
ISBN 1-55561-143-5

Your Pregnancy Week by Week
Third Edition
Glade B. Curtis, MD, OB/GYN

With over a million copies in print and translated into several languages, *Your Pregnancy Week by Week* is essential reading for every pregnant woman. If you are already pregnant, or planning to become pregnant, this unique book will guide you through your pregnancy. Learn how your body changes and how your baby develops each week throughout your entire pregnancy. Completely updated, and in its third edition, this is a must-have book for expectant parents.

Su Embarazo Semana a Semana
Glade B. Curtis, MD, OB/GYN

Your Pregnancy Week by Week is also available in Spanish. Using the same unique format as the English version, *Su Embarazo* shows you how your body changes as your baby grows. The best guide for your pregnancy, this popular book provides helpful and clear advice.

$12.95 paperback
$19.95 Canada
6.125 x 9.25, 436 pages, b/w illustrations
ISBN 1-55561-061-7